Geoffrey Simpson-Scott is a Solicitor and National Head of Clinical Negligence at Simpson Millar LLP. He has worked at the Royal Courts of Justice and practised clinical negligence for 20 years at well-established firms.

A Practical Guide to Clinical Negligence

Third Edition

A Practical Guide to Clinical Negligence

Third Edition

Geoffrey Simpson-Scott,
LLB (Hons), Solicitor,
Partner, Clinical Negligence,
Hodge Jones & Allen

Law Brief Publishing

Published 2023 by Law Brief Publishing, an imprint of Law Brief Publishing Ltd
30 The Parks
Minehead
Somerset
TA24 8BT

www.lawbriefpublishing.com

Paperback: 978-1-914608-51-3

Thank you for purchasing this book. By doing so, you are helping to support the Millie Mittoo Children's Project, a wonderful charity dedicated to helping and educating young ladies in Pakistan. You can find out more by visiting their informative website: www.milliemittoo.com

It is comforting to know that this edition will, in a small way, support those young ladies to get a better start in life. This edition is dedicated to the memories of my father, Christopher Grant Simpson-Scott and Her Majesty Queen Elizabeth II who both sadly passed away in 2022. They lived full lives during which they took the time to provide a light in the darkness to those in need of help.

FOREWORD

As I write this, the NHS faces the worst crisis of its existence. Patients are being failed on a terrifying scale. Thousands are paying with their health; far too many, with their lives. Threadbare provision is measured in GP deserts; overwhelmed ambulance services; massive shortages of beds and clinical staff; rock-bottom morale; desperately ill patients stuck for hours outside A&E; inordinate waiting times for specialist investigations and treatments; and mental health services so inadequate that suicidal children are being refused referral.

Against this grim background, the third edition of Geoff Simpson-Scott's excellent practitioner's handbook could not be more welcome. It deals in depth with key practicalities such as risk assessment, costs budgeting, timetabling, lay and expert evidence, QOCS and the Part 36 regime. It includes sophisticated analyses of liability and limitation issues. Throughout, Geoff deploys his client-centredness, his deep legal knowledge, his professional wisdom and his enthusiasm for good practice.

Clinical negligence lawyers, and their clients, continue to owe him a substantial debt of gratitude.

Joel Donovan KC
Cloisters
February 2023

PREFACE

It is again my genuine pleasure to have been invited to write the 3rd edition of this book to the ever-increasing library of practitioner guides published by Law Brief Publishing Ltd.

My intention remains to cover issues which arise in everyday practice and which have a tendency to cause delay and increased costs. Proportionality (and a possible fixed costs regime) essentially demand efficiency. It still seems incredible that almost 7 years after the 1st edition, we still do not have a fixed costs regime in place. Whilst there are many advantages to one, it is essential that downward costs pressures do not adversely affect access to justice, patient safety or full compensation. The reform proposals we have seen so far do not clearly identify how they achieve these aims which have underpinned successive legal systems since the Code of Hammurabi around 3,700 years ago.

Traditionally, clinical negligence lawyers on both sides of the profession have taken a considerable amount of time and effort to ensure that the complex issues in their clients' cases are explored properly. Anecdotally, downwards costs pressures still seem to be imposed arbitrarily too often. The middle ground remains for us to continue to become more knowledgeable about the underlying medicine and substantive law, good practice and procedure; more skilful and collaborative litigators; and more effective negotiators (as opposed to compromisers). At the heart of this book is still the concept that the complexity of any given clinical negligence case makes at least some aspect of it is inherently ambiguous. With ambiguity comes uncertainty and the natural inclination to explore and fill in the gaps in a case. This book does not pretend to be the definitive guide to clinical negligence but my sincere hope remains that that the issues covered in this book assist in striking a reasonable practical balance between cost effectiveness and effective litigation.

In writing this book, I have drawn on my experience of clinical negligence litigation (now covering 20 years). I have been fortunate to work with a fantastic range of experienced, talented and upcoming lawyers in my time. Especial gratitude goes to Master Turner, Master Ungley and Master Leslie (all now retired); Mr Timothy Briden, Mr Leslie Keegan, Mr Joel Donovan KC; Mr Michael Mylonas KC, Mr Hugh Preston KC, Ms Eva Ferguson, Mr Terry Lee, Mr Colum Smith, Mr John Dyball, Ms Agata Usewicz, Ms Hana Choudhury, Mrs Lara van Zuydam, Ms Ramune Mickeviciute, Ms Agnes Marks, Mrs Elizabeth Reid, Ms Renu Daly, Ms Joanna Ziobro and Ms Aga Prymak for helping me develop these ideas and to put them into practice. You are all a credit to the legal profession and it has been my genuine privilege to have worked with you all. I also wish Mr Paul Whiteing every success as AvMA's new CEO.

The case law referred to in this book shows the relevant underlying legal principles and illustrates how the courts apply them. There is a very interesting mixture of UK and Commonwealth cases included in this 3rd edition. I have endeavoured to correctly state the law as it is at the end of February 2023. However, any errors are mine.

This remains an exciting and continually area of law and I sincerely hope that you enjoy practising it as much as I do.

Geoffrey Simpson-Scott
Solicitor and Partner at Hodge Jones & Allen
London, February 2023

CONTENTS

TABLE OF CASES

Case Name	Page
A	
A v East Kent Hospitals University NHS Foundation Trust [2015] EWHC 1038 (QB)	46
A (Child) v MoD [2004] EWCA Civ 641	55
AB v CD & Others [2011] EWHC 602 (Ch)	302-303, 305
AB v East Lancashire NHS Trust [2019] EWHC 3542 (QB)	268
AB v Mid Cheshire NHS Foundation Trust [2019] EWHC 1889 (QB)	4
ABC v St George's Healthcare NHS Trust & Others [2020] EWHC 455 (QB)	28, 48
AH v Lewisham Hospital NHS Trust [2016] EWHC B3 (Costs)	8
A & M v Royal Mail Group [2015] EW Misc B24 (CC)	7
Adelekun v Ho [2021] UKSC 43	16
Agouman v Leigh Day (A Firm) [2016] EWHC 1324 (QB)	282
Ahuja Investments Ltd v Victorygame Ltd & Another [2021] EWHC 2382 (Ch)	212, 216
Al-Medenni v Mars UK Ltd [2005] EWCA Civ 1041	142, 146

Darnley v Croydon Health Services NHS Trust [2018] UKSC 50	29, 32, 33, 54, 261
Dashwood v Dashwood [1927] WN 276	295
Datec Electronics Holdings Ltd. v UPS Ltd [2007] UKHL 23	71
Davies v Frimley Health NHS Foundation Trust [2021] EWHC 169 (QB)	269-270
De Costa & Another v Sargaco & Another [2016] EWCA Civ 764	286
Delaney v Southmead Health Authority [1995] 6 Med LR 355	39
Diag Human Se & Another v Volterra Fietta (A Firm) [2022] EWHC 2054 (QB)	7
Diamond v Royal Devon & Exeter NHS Foundation Trust [2017] EWHC 1495 (QB)	47
Diamond v Royal Devon & Exeter NHS Foundation Trust [2019] EWCA Civ 565	51, 74
Digicel (St. Lucia) Ltd v Cable & Wireless plc [2008] EWHC 2522 (Ch)	207
Dixon v North Bristol NHS Trust [2022] EWHC 1871 (QB)	137
Donoghue v Stevenson [1932] UKHL 100	28
Doorway Capital Ltd v American International Group UK Ltd [2022] EWHC 182 (Comm)	154
Dowson v Lane [2020] EWHC 642 (QB)	261-262

LEGISLATION & OTHER SOURCES

Civil Procedure Rules 1998, Rule 32.18(1)	158
Civil Procedure Rules 1998, Rule 32.18(2)	158
Civil Procedure Rules 1998, Rule 32.18(3)	158
Civil Procedure Rules 1998, Rule 32.18(4)	158
Civil Procedure Rules 1998, Practice Direction 32, para. 27	279
Civil Procedure Rules 1998, Part 35	112, 158, 177, 235, 236
Civil Procedure Rules 1998, Rule 35.1	237
Civil Procedure Rules 1998, Rule 35.3	237
Civil Procedure Rules 1998, Rule 35.4	237
Civil Procedure Rules 1998, Rule 35.5	113, 238
Civil Procedure Rules 1998, Rule 35.7	239
Civil Procedure Rules 1998, Rule 35.8	239
Civil Procedure Rules 1998, Rule 35.8(5)	240
Civil Procedure Rules 1998, Rule 35.9	240
Civil Procedure Rules 1998, Rule 35.10	113, 240
Civil Procedure Rules 1998, Rule 35.10(4)	240
Civil Procedure Rules 1998, Rule 35.11	241, 244
Civil Procedure Rules 1998, Rule 35.12	178, 242
Civil Procedure Rules 1998, Rule 35.13	243
Civil Procedure Rules 1998, Practice Direction 35	113, 177

Civil Procedure Rules 1998, Pre-Action Protocol for the Resolution of Clinical Disputes, para. 3.25.3	122
Civil Procedure Rules 1998, Pre-Action Protocol for the Resolution of Clinical Disputes, para. 3.29	124
Civil Procedure Rules 1998, Pre-Action Protocol for the Resolution of Clinical Disputes, para. 5.1	124
Civil Procedure Rules 1998, Pre-Action Protocol for the Resolution of Clinical Disputes, para. 5.4	124
Civil Procedure Rules 1998, Pre-Action Protocol for the Resolution of Clinical Disputes, Annex B	102
Civil Procedure Rules 1998, Pre-Action Protocol for the Resolution of Clinical Disputes, Annex C1	117
Civil Procedure Rules 1998, Pre-Action Protocol for the Resolution of Clinical Disputes, Annex C2	117
Civil Procedure Rules 1998, Pre-Action Protocol for the Resolution of Clinical Disputes, Annex C3	122
Co	
Companies Act 2006, s1139(1)	149
Conditional Fee Agreements Order 2013	6
Consumer (Information, Cancellation & Additional Charges) Regulations 2013, The	7
Contempt of Court Act 1981, s14	88
Convention on the Service Abroad of Judicial and Extrajudicial Documents in Civil or Commercial Matters 1969 ('Hague Service Convention')	150

CHAPTER ONE

COSTS & FUNDING

Introduction

Improving results through avoiding ambiguity and adopting a planned approach to managing your caseload remains one of the central themes of this book. This chapter considers why it is essential to get the funding options right at the start of the case in order to avoid fundamental cost recovery problems arising at the end of it. In so doing, it is helpful to consider the costs issues which are likely to arise during the case so that you can have the correct sort of evidence on file to either head off the problem(s) or persuasively deal with them as needed.

Funding

As clinical negligence cases are proportionately more complicated than many other types of civil litigation of comparable value, the incurred costs tend to be higher. This is an attractive lure for claimant firms but not necessarily for claimants themselves. Defendant organisations regularly publish figures purporting to show that claimants' legal costs are excessive and the average claimant cannot take the risk of having to bear legal fees. However, the position post-Jackson is that they are expected to bear at least some of the costs. Clients are consumers of legal services and lawyers are increasingly finding ourselves part of a professional services industry.

This creates fertile ground for conflict on almost every clinical negligence case and so practitioners need a sound plan to deal with it. The winner is entitled to recover their proportionate costs of being required to prosecute or defend the action from the loser. The loser is entitled to seek to minimise these costs and seek assurances that professional obligations (such as the indemnity principal) have been properly complied with. This can leave the clients paying for the shortfall.

Accordingly, it is essential to get the funding and funding advice right from the start. Achieving this will make both your client's and your position much more secure. There is little point in doing an excellent job in winning the case if you then do not get paid for it.

As one case finishes, another starts. You have cases at various stages from initial assessment to costs recovery. The same funding and costs issues are likely to arise again and again on these cases, although not all of them will arise on every case. Using the lessons learned from one case will help you on the others. Developing a professional process which allows you to replicate success again and again will allow you to control your case progression much better.

Client Care Information

A clear explanation of the funding method and potential costs liabilities needs to be given to your client before any substantive work is undertaken. Most firms seek to cover all of the required bases by sending out a detailed client care information pack with the initial explanatory letter. Many clients find the morass of information they receive confusing and so will often not fully understand the minutiae. They tend to appreciate that there is some risk of paying something and will often need to be given a clearer explanation of what their potential liability and obligations are. It is advisable to keep a clear record of what they were told (including any amounts they might need to pay and possible scenarios which might lead to this) in case you need to prove that they were given the correct advice later in the case. Given the day-to-day pressures of running a case, this can be easily overlooked by even the most experienced of practitioners. If the task is delegated to junior colleagues, an effective supervision mechanism needs to be employed and maintained to ensure compliance with these requirements because the act of delegation by itself is rarely sufficient to satisfy a costs judge.

A potential issue which can be encountered at the conclusion of a case is whether the retainer itself was enforceable (e.g. *ST v ZY [2022] EWHC B6 (Costs)* in the context of seeking to deduct a shortfall in recovered costs from the client's damages). There is no requirement that this possibility should be raised during the life of the case by the paying party and so the risk is that too much time has elapsed to correct any problems. Even if a successful relief from sanctions application (under *CPR 1998, Rule 3.9*) is possible, the additional cost, delay and risk this causes is undesirable to your client and your firm. The status of all of the fee-earners who may deal with the case needs to be agreed in advance by your client along with the hourly rates your firm intends to charge for them (see *Pilbrow v Pearless de Rougemont & Co (A Firm) [1999] 3 All E R 355, CA)*. This is particularly so where the hourly rates charged are unusually high (e.g. *Swain v J C & A Ltd [2018] EWHC B3 (Costs), para. 27*). If a fee earner does work on the case but has not been properly described, then those fees are irrecoverable from the losing party.

It is also entirely possible that documents within the client care pack have been updated at different times and so include different rates. If this is not corrected, then the lower rates will usually be applied. Where the rates change during the life of a case, then that must also have been notified to your client with suitable written evidence being kept on your file. Although the client care information is privileged, the losing party will often request sight of it having raised the issue of non-compliance in the points of dispute.

Public Funding

The availability of public funding remains so limited (to high-value birth injury cases) so as to be the exception rather than the rule. If your firm does hold a legal aid Franchise, then the Manual provides detailed guidance on the requirements to be followed.

All claimants' solicitors are under a duty to advise on all of the available funding options. If a prospective client appears to be eligible for public funding, then this means advising them of this and signposting them onto a franchised firm even if this means losing the case. However, one of the issues with public funding is that the hourly rates allowed for experts are still relatively low. This means that your preferred expert may well refuse to act. As the defendant is usually not so constrained, there is a genuine risk of inequality of arms and this can justify advice that public funding is not the best option. If so, then it is usually advisable not to charge the client additional liabilities so that they are in the same position as if public funding had been used.

Although a client who is properly advised is free to choose their funding arrangement (*Campbell v MGN Ltd [2005] UKHL 61),* the courts have shown a willingness to look carefully at whether the client was fully informed of their options in advance. For example, considerable care needs to be taken in the advice given to claimants when switching from legal aid to a CFA (e.g. covering the prospects of success, how this affects the success fee and level of ATE premium, the reasonableness of changing the funding and how the legal aid costs & scope limits have been complied with) following decisions such as *XDE v North Middlesex University Hospital Trust [2020] EWCA Civ 543, Surrey v Barnet and Chase Farm Hospitals NHS Trust [2018] EWCA Civ 451* and *AB v Mid Cheshire NHS Foundation Trust [2019] EWHC 1889 (QB).* As a general guideline, it is advisable to allow the claimant to make a fully informed decision which, perhaps years later, can objectively be seen to have been in their best interests (for both the initial funding arrangement and where a change is required during the case).

<u>Before the Event Legal Expenses Insurance (BTE LEI)</u>

BTE LEI can be included with other insurance policies. The advantage to the claimant is that they obtain a substantial amount of legal cover for little or no additional cost. This is more beneficial to claimants and defendants than After the Event (ATE) insurance policies which have higher premiums and so their availability and suitability needs to be carefully considered at the start of the case.

There may be valid reasons for not using the BTE policy. The indemnity limit may not be sufficient to cover the costs of the entire case to trial. The limit is usually intended to be divided equally between the claimant's and defendants' costs. If you have a multiple defendant case, then this can reduce the amount of cover available for each party's adverse costs and disbursements significantly. The scope of the cover and any exclusions need to be carefully checked to ensure that the particular type of case you are dealing with is covered by the policy. For example, omissions of care or the acceleration of an injury may appear to be excluded and clarification needed.

The claimant ought to be asked for a copy of their *insurance policies* (rather than 'legal expenses' insurance policies which might confuse them) and a clear record kept of these being checked by you.

It is likely that the BTE insurer will require a formal application to be made before it will agree to indemnify your costs. Any costs which you incur before this may well not be covered by the policy. Most BTE insurers have selected a panel of specialist firms of solicitors whom they prefer to instruct and so a freedom of choice application will often be required.

Freedom of choice remains a somewhat vexed question in practice. The European Court of Justice's ruling in *Eschig v UNIQA Sachversicherung AG [2009] EUECJ C-199/08* appears to require insurers to allow freedom of choice in 'proceedings' (which does not necessarily mean just 'issued proceedings') as a result of the relevant EU Directive (now *Directive 2009/138/EC, Article 201(1)(a)).* However, the Financial Ombudsman Service interprets the enabling regulations (the *Insurance Companies (Legal Expenses Insurance) Regulations 1990*) as allowing insurers to refuse granting Freedom of Choice to non-Panel firms pre-proceedings. The FSO's website (www.financial-ombudsman.org.uk/publications/technical_notes/legal-expenses.html) confirms that it will look at each complaint on its merits but will not criticize a refusal unless there are exceptional circumstances.

The panel firm will usually be asked to assess the freedom of choice question and the merits of the case at the same time. It is advisable to send them a helpful breakdown of the proposed case on limitation, breach of duty, causation of damage and quantum issues; the core supporting evidence; and a summary of the proportionate investigative steps you wish to take to minimise the risk of delay. If you can show that you have carefully considered the case, then the chances of agreeing to your request for funding are greatly improved.

In *Orde van Vlaamse Balies & Another v Ministerraad [2020] EUECJ C-667/10,* it was held that this freedom to choose one's own lawyer must also apply to mediation (which comes within the definition of 'proceedings' in *Article 201(1)(a)*)

Conditional Fee Agreements

The *Legal Aid, Sentencing & Punishment of Offenders Act 2012* ('LASPO') allows a success fee of up to 25% of the claimant's damages for past losses and PSLA to be deducted from their damages. Accordingly, a claimant who agrees to this method of funding is likely to receive less compensation than a client who has BTE insurance. This relative disadvantage to clients can only partially justified on the basis that parliament has imposed this change and so the client still needs to be properly advised if problems are to be avoided.

One of the aims of the Jackson reforms was to reduce the amount of satellite costs litigation by making a failure to advise clients properly a regulatory client care issue rather than an *inter partes* issue over whether the success fee had to be paid. Accordingly, the issue should be one between the client and their advisors. If a complaint is raised, it is likely to result in delays to completing the case whilst the complaint (and possibly a solicitor-own client detailed assessment) is resolved. This is likely to reduce cash flow and profitability. However, *XDE (supra)* shows that a challenge to the recoverable part of the ATE premium can also prevent recovery of the entire success fee.

It is often assumed that the success fee cap (under the *Conditional Fee Agreements Order 2013*) means that no detailed risk assessment would be needed. However, because 25% is a *cap* of applicable damages, the success fee can be anywhere between 0-25%. This range creates the scope for clients shopping around and seeking an explanation as to why you set the success fee at a given amount based on the perceived risk of losing.

If it is always set at 0%, then there is probably little need to do a separate risk assessment. However, this does not necessarily make good business sense or reflect the realities of each case. If it is always set at 25%, then a risk assessment helps to show the client why you consider that the risks justify this and may demonstrate that your competitors have missed an important risk issue in the case. Another alternative is to carry out some investigative work before setting the success fee (although this must be funded some other way and this needs to be fully explained to, and agreed by, your client).

It is also important not to forget that the prospects of success remain relevant to setting the success fee. If the risks of losing the case are low, then the amount of the uplift on base costs may be less than 25% of applicable damages. In *Diag Human Se & Another v Volterra Fietta (A Firm) [2022] EWHC 2054 (QB)*, the entire success fee was disallowed where it exceeded the legally permitted 100% of base costs. On the facts of this case, it was not possible to sever the offending parts of the retainer and so, notwithstanding that the firm was also charging a discounted hourly rate, it was ordered to repay the amount of the success fee.

Whatever system is adopted, it must be properly explained to the client so they can make an informed decision. This is essential in children's cases. *CPR 1998 Part 21* requires that the advice given to the litigation friend about how the success fee was set be disclosed to the court before the infant approval hearing along with a witness statement from the litigation friend confirming why they agreed to this. The relevant risks are those relating to the child only not anyone else. Although these rules technically only apply to cases worth under £25,000, it is difficult to see why less protection would be afforded to children with more valuable cases. A bespoke approach to each case is advisable (see *A & M v Royal Mail Group [2015] EW Misc B24 (CC)*).

The relevance of consumer protection legislation should also not be underestimated. *The Consumer (Information, Cancellation & Additional Charges) Regulations 2013* set out specific requirements for advising any consumer of their right to cancel the contract where it is not signed at the place of business. Since most CFAs are sent out to clients for signature and return, that solicitor must ensure that the cancellation rights have been properly explained. *Cox v Woodlands Manor Care Home Ltd [2015] EWCA Civ 415* confirms that failing to do so renders the entire CFA unenforceable and so also prevents the recovery of base costs against the losing party as the indemnity principle has been breached. Although the cancellation point was not in issue in *AH v Lewisham Hospital NHS Trust [2016] EWHC B3 (Costs)*, at *para. 69*, *Deputy Master Campbell* made an observation that *Cox "...is illustrative of the fact that the quality of the advice is capable of having a significant bearing on how much the paying party is required to pay under a costs order even where the client takes no issue with that advice."*

After the Event Legal Expenses Insurance

Qualified One-Way Costs Shifting ('QOCS') operates so as to greatly reduce the risk of paying the defendant's costs if the case is lost. Post-Jackson, the ATE insurance premium is generally unrecoverable from the losing defendant. However, unlike in personal injury actions, part of the ATE premium may be recoverable in clinical negligence actions (see *The Courts & Legal Services Act 1990, s58C* (as amended) and the *Recovery of Costs Insurance Premiums in Clinical Negligence Proceedings (No. 2) Regulations 2013, Regulation 3*). The key word here is 'may' and so it is prudent to notify the defendant that you will be seeking to include the recoverable part of the premium in any monetary settlement as soon as is practicable after taking out the policy. The pre-Jackson practice of giving notice in the letter of claim remains relevant.

At present, the recoverable part of the premium insures against the costs of obtaining expert evidence on liability issues. It may also cover the risk of failing to beat an opponent's *Part 36* offer. The irrecoverable part of the premium tends to cover a wider set of risks and is paid by the claimant out of their damages. The available products vary between providers and new products are always a possibility so the precise terms of the product on offer need to be considered and agreed to by the client (including their cancellation rights). Consideration should be given to reading the terms and conditions of the policy to confirm that they are in your client's best interests. If not, then alternatives ought to be considered with your client even if your firm has a delegated authority agreement with a particular ATE insurer.

Accordingly, the client must decide whether they want to pay for insurance. If they do not, then another means of disbursement funding must be found. There are companies who offer specific disbursement-only funding credit, but a detailed consideration of these (and other) options is outside the scope of this book. Whilst leaving the ATE application until after the letter of response has been received may seem an attractive course of action, if a denial is received, it may lead to cover being justifiably refused or a higher premium being paid by the claimant.

The same considerations as were discussed above for CFA advice apply to the ATE advice. The reasonableness of a fairly typical ATE product was considered in *Nokes v Heart of England Foundation NHS Trust [2015] EWHC B6 (Costs).* Although the premium was found to be reasonable on the facts, it left open the possibility that the issue could be revisited if defendants could find better evidence on another case. In *McNenemy v Peterborough & Stamford Hospitals NHS Trust [2017] EWCA Civ 1941*, it was held that the premium was recoverable even if the expert report had not actually been obtained. In *West & Demouilpied v Stockport NHS Foundation Trust [2019] EWCA Civ 1220*, a comprehensive fact-finding exercise was undertaken and block-rated premiums were effectively found to be reasonable and proportionate. It remains possible that further satellite litigation may focus on further sub-issues surrounding ATE premiums as not every possibility was covered off. However, at present, challenges based on a comparison with another policy should be at an end.

<u>Costs</u>

Although the general rule that costs follow the event remains intact (*CPR 44.2(2)(a)*); the court has a wide discretion in deciding whether to award costs (*CPR 44.2(1) and 44.2(2)(b)*). Relevant factors include the conduct of all parties; the extent to which the winner has succeeded on all of the issues they pursued; and the effect of settlement offers made and refused (*CPR 44.2(4) & (5)*). The court may order that only some of the winner's costs need to be paid (see *CPR 44.2(6)(a-g)*) so recovery may be less than 100% even before the assessment begins. In *Harrap v Brighton & Sussex University Hospitals NHS Trust [2018] EWHC 1063 (QB)*, the claimant discontinued during the trial when lay clinical evidence came to light which had not been contained in the witness statements and failed to do so up to trial. The defendant was bound to reanalyse its case but, likewise, the claimant could have sought clarification of the factual evidence following receipt of the defendant's expert evidence. Rather than ordering the claimant to pay all of the defendant's costs to trial, it was fair and reasonable to order them to pay them up to the service of the expert report with no order as to costs thereafter.

The standard order for '100%' recovery is that the loser pays the winner's costs on the standard basis, to be assessed if not agreed. This does not mean that the winner is likely to recover all of their costs. The twin precepts are that the costs must have been reasonably and proportionately incurred. As this is a question of fact, each case is likely to have significant scope for argument over the amount to be paid. At the start of the case, the client needs to be advised as to who will meet any shortfall and in what circumstances they might become liable. As the costs arguments are largely predictable, your client will expect you to minimise any losses or else expect your firm to bear them.

Proportionality

The Jackson reforms redefined this and 'necessity' is no longer considered relevant. That said, clinical negligence claims are usually complex enough to justifiably include what would have previously been described as 'necessary' within the new definition.

CPR 1.1 requires courts to deal with cases at a proportionate cost. *CPR 44.3* sets out the test for assessing this for costs incurred after 1st April 2013. Specifically, *CPR 44.3(5)* sets out a 5-stage test:

> *"(5) Costs incurred are proportionate if they bear a reasonable relationship to –*
>
> > *(a) The sums in issue in the proceedings;*

> *(b) The value of any non-monetary relief in issue in the proceedings;*
>
> *(c) The complexity of the litigation;*
>
> *(d) Any additional work generated by the conduct of the paying party; and*
>
> *(e) Any wider factors involved in the proceedings such as reputation or public importance."*

There is much scope for interpretation because there is no genuinely authoritative guidance. This rule does not prioritise any one factor. However, it is usually assumed that the emphasis is on *5(a)*. There is no stipulation that costs must be less than the amount recovered although this is the interpretation which should be contended for by the losing party. Costs awards higher than the damages award are well-known, and this can be the position adopted by the winner. Costs which are less than the damages are not automatically or *prima facie* proportionate and so the loser is entitled to seek further reductions. The winner needs to have been planning to address this from the outset not least because the court can make a costs order at any time (*CPR 1.1*) and the case is likely to be costs budgeted.

The value of non-monetary relief is usually the least important of these factors in clinical negligence. However, if receiving an apology (for example) is especially important to a claimant, then this is likely to be relevant. The timing of the apology or the failure to provide one would then also be relevant considerations.

The complexity of the litigation appears to provide much greater support to the winner. However, the point is often made that the case is not, in fact, complex when compared to *other* clinical negligence cases and given the evident expertise of the solicitor who has just won it. Other common arguments are that one-expert cases are obviously not complicated or that suitable admissions render the case a simple one. This is not obviously wrong in the absence of contemporaneous evidence accrued during the life of the case even though the CPR is intended to cover all types of civil litigation. If you want to persuade the court that your position is the more reasonable one, then the winner is well advised to have plenty of evidence showing that they raised specific points regarding the complexity of the matter during the case whilst the loser ought to be able to prove that they sought to keep costs down due to the case's relative simplicity.

'Additional work' or 'conduct' arguments (*5(d)*) are very often useful in this context although they need quite a lot of advanced preparation to be persuasive. The paying party is understandably unlikely to accept that their approach to the case increased costs even when faced with carefully prepared evidence. This means that an assessment hearing is more likely to occur. Conversely, the paying party may raise conduct issues under *CPR 44.2(4) & (5)* even though *CPR 44.3(5)* refers only to the paying party's conduct. It is useful to bear in mind that the loser's costs draftsman is likely to have prepared such points from their client's file so the winner ought to plan ahead for this by raising conduct issues in correspondence. At the very least, the response you will get gives you advanced notice of your opponent's position and may help to resolve the issue more quickly. *Malmstein v Bohinc [2019] EWHC 1386 (Ch)* emphasises the importance of providing directly supportive evidence.

'Wider factors' (*5(e)*) may appear to be less relevant. However, a proportion of cases will be fully defended on the basis that the clinician's professional reputation can only be exonerated by forcing discontinuance or winning at trial. This argument is often persuasive to a judge even where there is no evidence presented that the medic's reputation has actually suffered. However, if the defendant is allowed to use this argument, then the claimant ought also be able to rely on it to show that the costs of the action increased unnecessarily as a result of the refusal to settle.

Reasonableness

Reasonableness is subordinate to proportionality. It is not mentioned in *CPR 44.3(5)*. There is a 2-stage test in assessing costs. Firstly, the court assesses the reasonableness of the costs by analysing the individual items in the Bill, the time reasonably spent on these items and the *CPR 1998, Rule 44.3(5)* factors. Having done so, the judge should then take a step back and decide whether the total figure is proportionate. If it is not, then it should be reduced accordingly (see *Malmstein* (supra)). As the previous test of whether the costs were 'reasonably and necessarily incurred' (under *Lowndes v Home Office [2002] EWCA Civ 365*) is now incorrect, reasonableness depends on proportionality not necessity. If an item of costs looks disproportionate in either being incurred or the amount that was spent on it, then it is probably also unreasonable on the standard basis (where uncertainty is resolved in the paying party's favour). However, the courts still hear arguments that the deduction for unreasonableness is sufficient to also cover proportionality (*Malmstein*, supra). An example of the difficulties some judges are having in separating the two precepts is provided by *Savoye and Savoye Ltd v Spicers Ltd [2015] EWHC 33 (TCC).*

Reasonableness has separate relevance if the assessment is on the indemnity basis as proportionality is irrelevant (*CPR 44.3(3)* does not refer to it) and uncertainty is resolved in favour of the receiving party.

Helpful Case Law

West & Demouilpied v Stockport NHSFT (supra) confirms that a two-stage approach should be used at assessments. A line-by-line assessment considering whether each disputed item is reasonable should be done first. The judge can also consider whether each item is proportionate at the same time. Once that analysis has been done, the judge should consider whether the costs figure produced is itself proportionate. If not, then a further proportionality assessment against costs should be done to arrive at the final figure.

It remains difficult to provide much useful guidance on what level of costs is proportionate and reasonable beyond saying that making it clear in contemporaneous attendance notes and correspondence why you felt that any given costs item was or was not reasonable and proportionate is likely to assist the court in reaching a reasoned decision on this difficult issue. However, many cases do not reach an assessment so you (or your costs draftsman) need to be able to persuasively negotiate the issue.

Such guidance as is available needs to be cited in its proper context. Presently, the general position can perhaps best be illustrated by *Ted Baker plc v Axa Insurance UK plc [2014] EWHC 4178 (Comm).* Lord Neuberger said *obiter* that *"...disproportionate costs, whether necessarily or reasonably incurred, should not be recoverable from the paying party. To put the point quite simply, necessity does not render costs proportionate."*

In *Hobbs v Guy's & St Thomas' NHS Foundation Trust [2015] EWHC B20 (Costs)* the claimant's costs in a fairly straightforward case settling pre-issue were reduced significantly because they had not been reasonably incurred and then because they were still disproportionate. However, *Master O'Hare* also said (at *para. 35*) that *"Even in modest value clinical negligence claims it is necessary to incur costs ... clinical negligence claims have more complexity and involve more work than do other claims of similar value."*

In *May & Another v Wavell Group plc & Another [2016] EWHC B16 (Costs),* the claimant's costs were approximately 9 times the value of the pre-issue settlement (partly because a QC had been instructed via direct access). Reasonable costs were assessed at approximately four times the settlement value and then this was reduced to less than 1½ times on proportionality grounds. At *para. 35, Master Rowley* said *"The amount that can be recovered from the paying party is not the minimum sum necessary to bring or defend the case successfully. It is a sum ... only a contribution to that receiving party's costs in many modest cases."* Similarly, at *para. 42* that proportionality *"will require legal representatives to inform their clients that, even if successful, they will receive no more than a contribution to the costs that will be incurred"* and that this is intended to promote settlement. This creates the risk of the client paying a considerable shortfall, possibly even exceeding the value of their damages. However, at *para. 45*, the Master also said that *"Sir Rupert Jackson refers to the possibility of low value but complex litigation incurring costs above the value of the damages"* so does not preclude recoverable costs exceeding damages.

BNM v MGN Ltd [2016] EWHC B13 (Costs) provided the first indication that judges are prepared to give a ratio to assist in determining proportionality. At *para. 49*, *Master Gordon-Saker* states that base costs of over 3 times the settlement value must be disproportionate and costs of around 1½ times would be proportionate.

In *Murrells v Cambridge University NHS Foundation Trust [2017] EWHC B2 (Costs)*, the 100% success fee was found to be too high because the prospects of success were better than 50/50. An 82% success fee was substituted (*para. 9*). However, the already-reduced base costs were considered to be proportionate and the complexity of a modestly valued clinical negligence claim was recognised (*para. 52*)

In *Rezek-Clarke v Moorfields Eye Hospital NHS Foundation Trust [2017] EWHC B5 (Costs)*, reference was made to the need for the experts' fees to be reasonable and proportionate. At *para. 23*, *Master Simons* reduced some of these fees and noted with some approbation the practice of charging large fees for addendum reports. At *para. 25*, he noted that costs of over £70,000 bore no reasonable relationship to the agreed damages of £3,250.

In *CXS v Maidstone and Tunbridge Wells NHS Trust [2023] EWHC 14 (KB)*, *Master Cook* accepted the Defendant's *"genuine concern"* over the Claimant's incurred profit costs in respect of expert evidence being 9-10 times the amount of incurred disbursements in a catastrophic injury case. This is an area which is likely to continue to see satellite litigation.

Qualified One-Way Costs Shifting (QOCS)

QOCS protects the losing claimant from paying the defendant's proportionate costs. This protection is not guaranteed in every case so caution is needed. The injury element of a clinical negligence claim brings it within the scope of the definition under *CPR 44.13(1)*. However, a pre-action disclosure application is not covered (*CPR 1998, Rule 44.13(1)* and *Sharp v Leeds City Council [2017] EWCA Civ 33*).

A successful claimant may be awarded damages but fail to beat the defendant's *Part 36* offer. In that case, the claimant stands to lose the damages which go towards paying the defendant's costs (e.g. *MRA v The Education Fellowship Ltd [2022] EWHC 1069 (QB)*). *CPR 44.14* allows an order for the full amount of the defendant's costs to be paid (from the date the relevant period of the offer expired) but then limits the payment to the amount of damages recovered. In short, the claimant would get a pyrrhic victory but their solicitor can claim some of the costs (up to the point when the offer should have been accepted). Conversely, QOCS protection puts defendants in substantially the same position as they were when public funding used to be more widely available. In most cases, if they win, they bear their own costs because there is no award of damages. For cases issued before 6th April 2023 (*The Civil Procedure (Amendments) Rules 2023, Rule 1(3)*), *Adelekun v Ho [2021] UKSC 43* confirms this. The court's power under *CPR 1998 Part 44.12(1)* to set off defendants' costs entitlement against claimant' costs does not apply to a QOCS case. If no damages have been awarded, then there is nothing to set the defendant's costs off against.

Furthermore, set-offs against damages do not apply to out-of-court settlements. *Cartwright v Venduct Engineering Ltd [2018] EWCA Civ 1654* confirms that the set-off against damages is unavailable where settlement has occurred by a *Part 36* offer or a Tomlin order. This is because these do not constitute an order for damages within the meaning of *CPR 1998 Rule 44.14*. *Chappell v Mrozek [2022] EWHC 3147 (KB)* confirms that *Adelekun* approves *Cartwright* and that these two decisions prevent set-offs against damages where a *Part 36* offer has been accepted late (see further below in Chapter 8).

For cases issued after 6th April 2023 (*ibid*), *Adelekun* and *Cartwright* have been effectively overruled by *The Civil Procedure (Amendments) Rules 2023, Rule 24*. This amends *CPR 1998 Rule 44.14* such that 'agreements for damages' are 'agreements to pay or settle a claim for damages or costs'; costs orders for or against the claimant will now include deemed costs orders; and the defendant will be able to set off their costs occasioned by the late acceptance of its *Part 36* offer against the claimant's costs. Accordingly, claimants need to be advised of this if a *Part 36* offer has been received on a case pre-issue (including where a limitation amnesty has been agreed or contemplated). It remains to be seen whether and how this affects defendants' pre-issue negotiations (for example, whether they remain willing to consider reasonable counter-offers in order to reach collaborative settlements).

QOCS does not appear to have resulted in defendants making low *Part 36* offers on cases they believe will fail. *CPR 44.15* allows them to recover their costs in full where the case has been struck out but this is a relatively rare occurrence in clinical negligence cases. *CPR 44.16* may provide a more fruitful avenue, however. If the claimant is found to be fundamentally dishonest, then the defendant will be entitled to apply to the court to recover all of its costs. The judge then needs to decide whether it is just to allow this. What amounts to fundamental dishonesty is itself remains fact-sensitive which creates risks for both sides. This is covered further below in Chapter 2.

Wagenaar v Weekend Travel Ltd & Another [2014] EWCA Civ 1105 has held that QOCS is not *ultra vires* and does not apply to *Part 20* proceedings. Accordingly, separately represented defendants in clinical negligence actions appear not to be able to invoke QOCS protection against each other.

Costs Budgeting

The Civil Justice Council's Costs Working Group held a consultation between June and October 2022. This considered costs budgeting, guideline hourly rates, fixed recoverable costs and costs under the Pre-Action Protocols and Portals. Although no recommendations have yet been made, the December meeting indicated that significant changes to Costs Budgeting could be recommended but not abolished. One of the main issues is whether budgeting should be 'default on' or 'default off' for certain damages bands (publicly viewable on YouTube: https://www.youtube.com/watch?reload=9&v=K5N3gVnIM9E).

Subject to knowing these recommendations and what is eventually implemented, QOCS can result in lower and less-controversial costs budgets from defendants for these reasons. Alternatively, it may be that it is in their interests to file budgets at the lower end of the reasonable range in order to improve their chances of reducing their potential exposure to the claimant's costs. Costs budgets which are properly linked to the remaining issues on the case do provide excellent opportunities to prove that the costs being sought are proportionate. However, budgets which are simply too high or low do not achieve this.

The key practical question is knowing how to correctly price the remaining work on the case. If you underestimate it, then you will end up either having to try to get a revised budget approved or face difficulties with your client. Accordingly, it can be safer to over-estimate the work even though the purpose of costs budgets is to assist the court in its duty to prevent disproportionate costs being incurred. However, judges are aware of this. Tactically, it is in the defendant's interests to have lower budgets imposed for both sides because the burden of proof of negligence is on the claimant. As will be seen in later chapters, the claimant generally bears the risk of leaving stones unturned. However, a defendant who has a 'low' budget agreed but then finds the claimant has had a 'high' budget approved has probably only succeeded in hobbling themselves.

The disparity between the parties' budgets is also skewed further because the claimant is likely to have already incurred significant costs in investigating and attempting to settle the case pre-proceedings. Front loading a case remains reasonable; *Jackson LJ* made it clear in his 12th pre-implementation lecture (https://www.judiciary.gov.uk/wp-content/uploads/JCO/Documents/Speeches/lj-jackson-twelfth-lecture-implementation-programme-22032012.pdf) that he expected meritorious cases to settle pre-proceedings.

Incurred costs, however, cannot be budgeted; the best that the court can do is to record an adverse comment as to the amount that has been incurred and to take that amount into account when budgeting the remaining phases. This issue is not helped by the time it takes for Costs CMCs to be listed. A combined hearing (directions and costs) is typically listed for 90 minutes which has resulted in significant listing delays at the RCJ. In the County Court, if the CCMC is listed separately, there are examples of it taking place well into the directions timetable, as late as after expert evidence has been exchanged.

The parties' respective budgets tend to raise the same issues seen at the end of the case. Accordingly, points relating to excessive hourly rates, hours spent, simplicity of the case, etc are frequently raised by defendants to counter what are arguably unreasonably high budgets prepared by claimants. *CPR 1998, Rule PD3E 7.3* provides that the courts approval will relate only to the total for each phase of the budget rather than performing a detailed assessment. It will consider whether the proposed figures are within a reasonable and proportionate range (with reference to the *CPR 1998, Rule 44.3(5)* factors considered above). However, in doing so, the court may take into account the constituent elements of those figures.

As the prescribed budget form (*Precedent H*) requires details of hourly rates, hours spent and disbursements, this creates the opportunity for each side to invite the judge to have regard to those figures because they are used in calculating the phase totals. In *Yeo v Times Newspapers Ltd [2015] EWHC 209 (QB) Warby J* offered this guidance at *para. 65*:

> *"It seems to me that whilst the question of whether the totals are reasonable and proportionate will always be the overall criterion, the courts may need to consider rates and estimated hours. The approach may need to be tailored to the case before the court."*

In cases where the costs run to six or seven figures, *Warby J* felt that this was all the more likely. Where a costs budget has been carefully prepared with reference to the issues still in dispute, it entirely reasonable for the costs to exceed £100,000 even in modestly valued claims. However, a successful challenge to an opponent's budget is a case management decision and therefore very difficult to appeal (see *Havenga v Gateshead NHS Foundation Trust & Another [2014] EWHC B25 (QB)*).

In many cases, however, it is possible to agree most or all of a proposed budget. *Precedent R* requires the parties to file evidence of the negotiations in advance of the CCMC and it is increasingly commonplace for judges to require evidence of the early exchange of costs information and offers being made in respect of the disputed phases. Other courts require a summary of the issues in dispute to be exchanged; and failing to do so can lead to wasted costs orders being made.

The risk of being limited to court fees only for failing to file a correct budget on time is a significant incentive for claimants to adopt an overly cautious approach. Contingencies ought to be included if they appear to be reasonably necessary (but cannot be included in a budget phase) and there is no guarantee that permission will be granted later for the budget to be revised if this is not done.

All-in-all, costs budgeting is only effective if both sides make a determined effort to narrow the issues in dispute to what is genuinely needed to resolve the proceedings. The more that remains in dispute, the higher the costs are likely to be. The judge needs to be presented with clear evidence of this in order to properly understand why these issues remain in dispute and the costs associated with them. They can then make a more reasoned decision also whether the costs of pursing those issues are proportionate and reasonable rather than making 'harsh' decisions on the facts as arguably occurred in *Havenga* (ibid.). The later chapters consider this in further detail.

Effect On Assessments

Once a budgeted case has concluded, the loser is still entitled to seek confirmation that the approved total for each phase has not been exceeded even where the total bill is within the budget's total. *CPR 1998, Rule 3.18(b)* provides that the Court will not depart from the approved costs budget unless there is good reason to do so. This is frequently relied on by the paying party in their Points of Dispute and this needs to be constructively responded to in the Replies or conceded. *ST v ZY (supra)* illustrates that the court is likely to closely analyse the reasons given and cross-reference these with what has been said in the Bill of Costs; the amount charged for the work; and the length or detail of documents produced. Accordingly, you need to have in place an effective system of checking the running total being spent on each phase. If it appears that a phase will be exceeded, then a prospective application for an amended budget will need to be considered. The risk is that your opponent or the court will need to see evidence of why this was not dealt with in the first budget so you need to be prepared to have good evidence on file as to how the problem has arisen since then. The potential challenge then needs to be prompted in the Bill of Costs based on this evidence for any remaining phases exceed the approved budget(s).

As long as the budgeted phases are within the approved totals, then there ought to be little scope for arguing that further reductions should be made. However, it is likely that the budget was approved but the court's position on the hourly rates claimed was reserved. Thus, the traditional arguments over hourly rates remain.

The guideline hourly rates (GHRs) can be found here: https://www.gov.uk/solicitors-guideline-hourly-rates . These were updated on 1st October 2021 and are within the scope of the CJC's Costs Working Group's consultation (*supra*). Subject to that, *Lord Dyson MR* has confirmed that GHRs *" will remain a component in the assessment of costs, along with the application by the judiciary of proportionality and costs management."* (https://www.judiciary.gov.uk/publications/guideline-hourly-rates/ 17th April 2015). It is important to remember that GHRs are for summary assessment not detailed assessment. In *Higgs v Camden & Islington Health Authority [2003] EWHC 15 (QB)*, *Fulford J* held that they were of only limited assistance in that catastrophic injury case and the criteria set out in the *CPR 1998* (i.e. those factors considered above) were relevant. He also stated at *para. 51*:

> *"Further the guideline figures are not supposed to replace the experience and knowledge of those familiar with the local area and the field generally… it is expressly recognised in the Guide that costs and fees exceeding the guidelines may well be justified in an appropriate case as an exercise of discretion."*

In *Choudhury v Kingston Hospital NHS Trust [2006] EWHC 90057 (Costs)*, *Master Rogers* emphasised that relying on past decisions on hourly rates is unhelpful and each case must turn on its own facts. However, he did not feel constrained by the guideline rates where there was evidence of complexity and of how the solicitor's experience contributed to winning the case. At *para. 65*, he commented:

> *"The rates claimed are higher than set out in the SCCO Guide to Hourly Rates, but, as been said many times, that is a document which is intended to govern fast track matters concluding in one day, and other interlocutory matters that conclude in the same period, the rates set out therein are not intended to cover the generality of litigation."*

In *Ohpen Operations UK Ltd v Invesco Fund Managers Ltd [2019] EWHC 2504 (TCC), O'Farrell J (para. 14)* stated that *"[i]t is unhelpful that the guidelines are based on rates fixed in 2010…as they are not helpful in determining reasonable rates in 2019."* This indicates a willingness to consider relevant evidence of changing economic circumstances. At *para. 15* she continued: *"The hourly rates cannot be considered in isolation when assessing the reasonableness of the costs incurred; it is but one factor that forms part of the skill, time and effort allocated to the application. It may be reasonable for a party to pay higher hourly rates to secure the necessary level of expertise, if that ensures appropriate direction in the case, including settlement strategy, with the effect of avoiding wasted costs and providing overall value."*

It is also true that the GHRs are comprised of generalised rates from a basket of local law firms doing a range of work. Accordingly, a specialist area such as clinical negligence is not well represented and a higher rate is justifiable. However, proportionality was not in issue in *Ohpen* (see *para. 16*) whereas it often is in clinical negligence. In *Re RBS Rights Issue Litigation [2017] EWHC 1217 (ChD), Hillyard J* said (at *para. 134*) *"… litigants are free to pay for a Rolls Royce service but not to charge it all to the other side."* It is frequently contended that the GHR will be applied by the costs judge on the facts of the case. Just as inevitably, this means negotiating the best rate you can and carefully picking those cases you allow to go to an assessment hearing. In *Samsung Electronics Co Ltd & Others v LG Display Co Ltd & Another [2022] EWCA Civ 466, Males LJ* said (at *para. 6*): *"If a rate in excess of the guideline rate is to be charged to the paying party, a clear and compelling justification must be provided. It is not enough to say that the case is a commercial case, or a competition case, or that it has an international element, unless there is something about these factors in the case in question which justifies exceeding the guideline rate."* Applying this to the clinical negligence context, planning out the evidence you need from the start of the case and keeping a close eye on developments greatly assists in getting the best result for you, your firm and your client.

The hourly rates claimed in the budget and bill of costs should be accurate and identical. In *MXX v United Lincolnshire NHS Trust [2018] EWHC B23*, *Master Rowley* held that the appropriate sanction where the budget and the final bill of costs contain different hourly rates is to disallow the time claimed in the bill claimed for creating and maintaining the budget as this is where the error occurred (*para. 68*). This followed his reasoning in *Tucker v Hampshire Hospitals NHS Trust & Griffiths (19/5/2017, unreported)*. However, on appeal (*[2019] EWHC 1624 (QB)*), *Slade J* noted that the clear guidance as to what amounted to 'unreasonable and improper conduct' under *CPR 1998, Rule 44.11* in respect of a bill of costs in *Gempride Ltd v Bamrah & Another [2018] EWCA Civ 1367* required this issue to be reconsidered by the Master in the specific context of a costs budget.

Costs Orders

It is also useful to bear in mind the different types of costs orders which the court has permission to make. These are listed in *CPR 1998, PD44 para. 4.2*. Knowing when to use these greatly increases your ability to deal with pre-trial applications and limiting the damage to your client or maximising the prospects of success. They can make the difference between paying your opponent's costs or not.

One area that needs very careful advanced preparation is where you are dealing with multiple opponents. The basic problem is that, because costs follow the event, you may succeed against one party but lose against another, thus reducing or wiping out your client's win. In order to avoid this, it is advisable to plan ahead from the start in any case where you face (or might face) multiple opponents (including *Part 20* claims). The preferable order is a Sanderson Order (*Sanderson v Blyth Theatre Co [1903] 2 KB 53*) which orders the losing party to pay the costs of the other successful parties directly. The next best order is a Bullock Order (*Bullock v London General Omnibus Co. [1907] 1 KB 264*) which requires your client to pay the costs of the other successful parties put allows you to reclaim those costs from the loser.

As NHS Resolution usually does not take issue where you succeed against one Trust but fail against another, this risk tends to be underestimated. It is a very real risk when GPs and hospital Trusts are sued or private treatment is in issue (and the doctor and clinic are separately pursued). It is unclear the extent to which it arises when English and Welsh hospitals are pursued concurrently. The increasing prevalence of private hospitals carrying out NHS treatment also makes this issue relevant.

The need for careful, advanced preparation arises from the fact that you will need to prove that it was reasonable for you to involve the other successful parties so that costs should not follow the event. To do this, there needs to be good evidence that the way in which the unsuccessful party pursued its case meant that your client could not safely release the other parties before they incurred significant costs. You also need evidence to show that you did not delay in trying to release them after it became apparent that they would win. This requires evidence of communication on these issues and of genuine attempts to act reasonably which is why it cannot be left until discontinuance is needed.

Following *Swift v Carpenter [2020] EWCA Civ 165*, it seems unlikely that a protective costs order is available in private litigation, even where the issues are as significant as in this case (*viz.* the effect of the negative discount rate on accommodation claims). However, as the decision was essentially based on public policy reasons, it is possible this may change. Taken in conjunction of the potentially unlimited costs liability of third-party funders following *Chapelgate Credit Opportunity Master Fund Ltd v Money & Others [2020] EWCA Civ 246* the risks associated with making genuinely ground-breaking legal challenges in clinical negligence are very significant.

Recovering Costs Shortfalls

Whilst some practitioners do not seek to recover a costs shortfall from their clients, others do. *ST v ZY (supra)* and *EVX v Smith [2022] EWHC 1607 (SCCO)* both illustrate the difficulties that practitioners face in persuading the courts that the amount is reasonable if the client does not agree to it or if the settlement itself requires approval. A bill of costs setting out the identity, status and litigation experience of the fee earners who acted on the case (*Barking, Havering & Redbridge University Hospitals NHS Trust v AKC [2021] EWHC 2607 (QB)*) is likely to be required. Very clear evidence of the reasonableness and proportionality of the hourly rates charged; time spent; relative complexity of the work done; and of effective costs management are all likely to be required in addition to clear evidence of informed consent of the type referred to above.

If the shortfall cannot be avoided *ab initio*, it is preferable to carefully manage costs during the case and plan ahead with your client if your firm does have a policy of seeking to recover costs shortfalls from them.

Costs Consequences of Discontinuance

Although a claimant usually has the right to discontinue all or part of their case under *CPR 1998, Rule 38(2)(1)* without the court's permission (an exception is having received an interim payment), doing so carries with it liability for the defendant's costs under *CPR 1998, Rule 38(6)* unless the court orders otherwise. QOCS protection (*q.v.*) applies absent one of the usual exceptions to it. Nonetheless, a consent order expressly recording that each side bears its own costs is appropriate to file so there is no debate. Outside of the QOCS exceptions, the court will only exercise its discretion to remove the QOCS shield and set aside the Notice of Discontinuance in exceptional circumstances of egregious conduct (*Excalibur & Keswick Groundworks Ltd v McDonald [2023] EWCA Civ 18*). At *para. 53, Nicola Davies LJ* said: *"What the defendant has sought to do … is to remove the substantive right of the claimant to the protection provided by the broad-based and mechanical provisions of the QOCS regime."* Nevertheless, it is best to investigate potential pitfalls in your case pre-issue to minimise the risk of discontinuance after proceedings are served.

Conclusion

The key point to take from this chapter is that it is necessary to ensure that your approach to costs and funding issues are proactive and not reactive. If you get the structure correct from the start, then it is much easier to maintain it throughout the life of the case. The losing party is fully entitled to take advantage of any aspect of the case which has not been properly prepared and the court will actively seek to maintain costs at a proportionate level. Accordingly, the winner needs to remove as many of the potential ambiguities which arise in practice by keeping clear, contemporaneous evidence that they provided proper advice to their client, acted reasonably and used their experience effectively.

CHAPTER TWO

CORE LEGAL PRINCIPLES

Introduction

The aim of this chapter is to consider how the legal principles underpinning clinical negligence cases tend to be applied in practice. Knowledge is power and this will help you to set up a process framework for the substantive law which you can apply earlier to plan each case more efficiently.

The *Bolam* principle is well known but its correct application remains difficult in contested cases and is no longer applicable across the board. Causation is equally problematic as a single weak link in the chain of causation can fatally undermine a case. Further principles are used to properly build the case on quantum within the set categories of loss. Ultimately, the courts judge the evidence adduced in the case against the prevailing legal tests and nothing else.

In any allegation of negligence, the following five areas need proving:

1. Whether there is a duty of care;
2. Whether that duty has been breached;
3. The extent to which any breach has caused an avoidable injury;
4. The nature and extent of that injury or loss; and
5. The valuation of the loss suffered.

Although in day-to-day practice the substantive law is rarely referred to, having a clear understanding of it is very useful because it reduces the chances of misdirecting yourself when applying the legal tests to the available evidence or of being outmanoeuvred by a more experienced or better prepared opponent. By the time the case is sent to counsel, it may be too late to turn matters around.

As every case turns on its own facts, clinical negligence cases tend to be won by applying the evidence effectively to the substantive legal principles. Thus, knowing your way around them can highlight a weak area in the case or help to give you enough of an edge to turn a seemingly impossible position into one resolvable by reasonable negotiation.

Misapplying the law can lead to a professional negligence claim or a formal complaint being upheld. Social media is already used to vent displeasure or spread the word about jobs well done. An overly technical approach to the case is unlikely to be appreciated by the courts or your clients and so the ability to explain these difficult legal principles simply and in plain English is essential in the modern era. All of these reasons provide the incentive to maintain your understanding of the principles underpinning clinical negligence actions.

Duty of Care

In the vast majority of cases, this will not be in issue because medical professionals and the institutions which provide medical treatment have a well-established duty of care not to injure their patients by their acts or omissions. The 'doctor-patient' relationship is sufficiently 'legally proximate' to fall within *Lord Atkin's* neighbour principle from *Donoghue v Stevenson [1932] UKHL 100* (see, for example, *Lord Dyson MR* in *Taylor v. A Novo (UK) Ltd. [2014] QB 150* at *paras. 25 to 27*; and *Paul & Others v The Royal Wolverhampton NHS Trust Rev 1 [2019] EWHC 2893 (QB), paras. 16-17)*. However, there are unusual sets of facts where it is necessary to establish the duty of care first (e.g. *ABC v St George's Healthcare NHS Trust & Others [2020] EWHC 455 (QB)* in respect of providing genetic information to a patient's children).

Where the duty of care is challenged, it may be necessary to prove that it falls within the ambit of *The Wagon Mound (No 2) [1966] UKPC 10* (i.e. that a reasonable clinician would foresee a real risk of harm at the time and guard against it). It is useful to remember that in this context foreseeability of a general risk of harm is required not of the specific injury sustained. Alternatively, it may be necessary to prove that a novel duty of care should be imposed by the courts. This means proving the three-stage test in *Caparo Industries plc v Dickman [1990] 2 AC 605*. This is that there must be (a) foreseeability of harm; (b) sufficient proximity; and (c) whether it is just and reasonable to impose liability for negligence.

A useful recent example of this is *Darnley v Croydon Health Services NHS Trust [2018] UKSC 50*. On the facts of that case, the duty of care on an NHS receptionist not to provide inaccurate information was not a novel duty (as had been successfully argued in the courts below). It came squarely within the duty of care owed by NHS Trusts to patients just as if the misinformation had been provided by a clinician (see *paras. 16, 17, 19, per Lord Lloyd-Jones*). It is important to note that the duty is not a positive one (i.e. to provide accurate information); rather it is not to provide misinformation. The applicable standard of care is considered further below.

Accordingly, it may be that superficially similar cases still require proof of the *Caparo* test (e.g. if the receptionist was not employed by a private clinic, was located elsewhere or the error was in providing information which was not otherwise inaccurate). As healthcare provision becomes more fractured, novel situations could well arise. Bear in mind, however, that *Lord Lloyd-Jones* also said (*para. 16*) that *"… it is not necessary to address, in every instance where the precise factual situation has not been the subject of a reported judicial decision, whether it would be fair, just and reasonable to impose a new duty of care. It is sufficient that the case falls within an established category in which the law imposes a duty of care."*

Breach of Duty

(a) Bolam

The issue usually encountered in practice is not just *what* the relevant standard of care is but whether the care in question *fell below* it. The starting point for establishing this is to clearly understand what the *Bolam/Bolitho* test requires and then to reassess its application to the changing strands of evidence at regular intervals during the case. It should always be possible to do this concisely (in a paragraph) in order to maintain a clear focus on what needs to be proved.

The two central cases are *Bolam v Friern Hospital Management Committee [1957] 1 WLR 583, at 586-7* and *Bolitho v City & Hackney Health Authority [1997] UKHL 46*. In summary:

1. The test is of the ordinary skilled medical professional practicing in that area of medicine;

2. This professional does not need to possess the highest expert skill – it is enough to exercise the ordinary skill of an ordinary competent practitioner in that area of medicine;

3. They will not be negligent if they acted in accordance with a practice accepted as proper by a responsible body of medics skilled in that particular area.

4. Evidence of an alternate body of opinion impugning the treatment is insufficient – it is not negligent to act in accordance with a minority opinion; however,

5. The proposed support for the treatment must be logical and capable of withstanding considered analysis.

This is so well known in general terms that it is relatively easy to forget some of the more specific parts of the test. Although the experts in the case will usually be consultants, it is not necessarily the case that the treatment will be judged against the standard of a consultant. A junior doctor can be judged against the standard of a reasonable similarly experienced doctor (rather than the standard of a reasonable consultant, see *Wilsher v Essex Area Health Authority [1987] 1 QB 730 per Mustill LJ* The applicable standard for a junior doctor is that of a specialist junior doctor (rather than the lesser standard of a well-informed junior doctor or the higher standard of a consultant): "… *This relates to the duty of care not to the individual, but to the post which he occupies. I would differentiate "post" from "rank" or "status". In cases such as the present, the standard is not just that of the averagely competent and well-informed houseman (or whatever the position of the doctor) but of a person who fills a post in a unit offering a highly specialised service. But, even so, it must be recognised that different posts make different demands. If it is to be borne in mind that the structure of hospital medicine envisages that the lower ranks will be occupied by those of whom it would be wrong to expect too much, the risk of abuse by litigious patients can be mitigated, if not entirely eliminated."*

In *FB v Princess Alexandra Hospital NHS Trust [2017] EWCA Civ 334, Jackson LJ* added (at *para. 59*): *"That involves leaving out of account the particular experience of the Doctor or their length of service. This analysis works in the context of a hospital where there is a clear hierarchy with consultants at the top, then registrars and below them various levels of junior doctors. Whether doctors are performing their normal role or 'acting up', they are judged by reference to the post which they are fulfilling at the material time."* With this in mind, should you receive a clinician's witness statement exhibiting their cv, it is worth asking why this is relevant to your case.

However, if the junior doctor ought to have been supervised by a consultant, then the role the consultant played would be assessed against the standard of a reasonable consultant in that area of medicine. In both cases, expert evidence is needed from a consultant, not a more junior doctor.

The alternative interpretations proposed by each side need to be proved to be logical. Merely asserting this without adducing suitably supportive evidence is insufficient. Sometimes, albeit rarely, there may be no published treatment standards or guidance and the prevailing practice is illogical. An example of this is where there is a known risk of injury (which is relatively easy to guard against) but the required frequency of the necessary investigations has never been set down (leading to the assumption that it is safe not to check for a prolonged period). More commonly, the issue arises in the context of the defendant's pleaded case asserting that the impugned treatment fell within a reasonable body of opinion on the assumption that it will be able to prove this at trial.

The seriousness of the harm which might be caused to the claimant is relevant to how a reasonable clinician might behave. Where the patient has some pre-existing vulnerability which creates a special risk of injury, then additional precautions must be taken to avoid an injury occurring (*Paris v Stepney Borough Council [1950] UKHL 3).* In practice, this usually comes within considering what a reasonable doctor would have done in the particular circumstances of this case but the rule itself is freestanding from *Bolam* and pre-dates it.

(b) Administrative Mistakes

The *Bolam* test applies to acts or omissions which occur as a result of the exercise of professional skill or expertise. Within the wide range of possible mistakes that can occur in the medical setting, some of these will not involve any professional skill; they will simply be administrative or clerical in nature. In these cases, there is no need to satisfy the *Bolam* test because the trial judge will be able to assess for themselves whether or not the mistake was accidental or negligent. These cases are no different to PI cases (where expert evidence on breach is not required).

In practice, it is important to carefully weigh up whether the alleged breach actually involved the genuine exercise of professional decision making. If there is evidence that it did not, then it may well be administrative in nature. In such cases, remember that what is needed is an administrative breach of duty which has then caused injury. If the injury is too remote or otherwise seemingly not clearly linked to the mistake, then it may be necessary to first prove that there is a duty of care (e.g. as was unsuccessfully argued in *Darnley (supra)*). Expert evidence does not assist in such cases because there is no professional error for the expert to apply their expertise to. A particular case may involve both administrative and professional mistakes. In such a case, proving the administrative breach may significantly simplify the case for your client.

If breach is not readily admitted, what amounts to a purely administrative mistake needs to be proved in evidence. The counterargument raised to an early invitation to admit liability is usually that the act or omission is one exercised within the impugned individual's professional duties and so *Bolam/Bolitho* applies and expert evidence is required. This then requires evidence as to what amounts to a reasonable standard of care.

In *XM v Leicestershire Partnership NHS Trust [2020] EWHC 3102 (QB)*, *Darnley (supra)* was cited on the issue of the applicable standard of care (rather than as to whether there was a novel duty of care). At *para. 25* of *Darnley (supra), Baroness Hale* stated: "... *The legitimate expectation of the patient is that he will receive from each person concerned with his care a degree of skill appropriate to the task which he or she undertakes. ... The standard required is that of an averagely competent and well-informed person performing the function of [their role].*" To put this another way, (a) how would the ordinary person in that role have performed the impugned task; and (b) does the trial judge really require expert evidence to answer this?

Baroness Hale was applying *Mustill's LJ* statement of the law in *Wilsher (supra)*. Accordingly, if the trial judge really does require assistance from experts, then this needs to cover (a) what specialist knowledge is applicable to this task; (b) how an averagely competent specialist in this role would approach it; without (c) imposing too high a standard for this task. Applying what is covered later in this book, knowing how many times your expert has actually done this task (or trained others to do it) themselves in NHS practice is an advantage.

Having the full quote to hand is a useful *aide memoire*. In *XM (supra)*, *Stewart J* (at *para. 363)* accepted the claimant's submissions "... *that there is one standard of care, regardless of the qualifications or post held by the health professional responsible for the task. ...*" At *para. 364* he rejected expert evidence to the effect that the act or omission would be split between 'administrative' and 'clinical' by the health visitor and GP, respectively. At *para. 365*, he rejected the defendant's submissions "... *that health visitors carry out a more mechanistic set of tasks, detailed in advance for them, and that essentially they go through a "tick box exercise". Tick box exercises can be of assistance. Nevertheless, they do not absolve health care professionals of their duties or from exercise professional judgement. ...*" As such, even a seemingly simple health decision or task requiring expert evidence to understand the applicable standard for making or doing it still requires evidence that it was performed with a degree of skill and care to be considered reasonable.

Accordingly, a reasonable approach to adopt is to consider whether the impugned act or omission was one which did not require the exercise of professional judgement. If so, then it is likely to be an administrative error in the normal sense of the word. If this is not accepted, then is it one which could be performed as a 'tick box'? From this point (and for more complex acts and omissions), what amounts to the usual professional standard for must be understood; i.e. it is not enough for the defendant to seek to argue that *Bolam/Bolitho* applies but then to say little real thought or exercise of judgement is applied in practice. Adopting this approach allows you to direct your investigations more efficiently and proportionately. The likely costs of pursuing such points can also then be better understood and explained to your client and the court.

(c) Reasonable Skill & Care

The 'reasonable skill and care' test is referred to by *McNair J* in *Bolam*, but subsequently was rather subsumed within his 'reasonable doctor' test. It has enjoyed something of a renaissance following *Muller v Kings College NHS Foundation Trust [2017] EWHC 128 QB*. In the cases discussed below, the standard is still of a reasonable clinician in that area at the date of the alleged negligence; the difference is that it is immaterial whether the impugned treatment enjoys the support of a reasonable body of similar specialists. This difference is pivotal.

It is easy to forget that clinical negligence occurred long before *Bolam* and that *McNair J's* 'test' was a direction to a civil jury (summarising the law from previous decisions) rather than a full judgement. In *Gladwell v Steggall (1839) The Lancet Vol 2, 13th April 1839 pp124-6*, the Defendant was found to have negligently treated an infection leading to an amputation. The test used was one of 'ignorant and unskilful treatment' with four surgeons being called for the Claimant against none for the Defendant. The roots of both tests can be seen here.

The reasonable care and skill test was set out in *Hunter v Hanley [1955] ScotsCS CSIH 2* as being *"such failure as no doctor of ordinary skill would be guilty of, if acting with ordinary care"* (per *The Lord President, Lord Clyde, 4th paragraph)*. In the penultimate paragraph of his judgment, his Lordship added: *"… and thirdly (and this is of crucial importance) it must be established that the course the doctor adopted is one which no professional man of ordinary skill would have taken if he had been acting with ordinary care."*

Penney & Others v East Kent Health Authority [1999] EWCA Civ 3005 confirmed that this standard is distinct from *Bolam* and applies to the mistaken interpretation of cervical smear slides. *Muller* then applied this to histopathology slides. *Lillywhite & Lillywhite v University College Hospital NHS Trust [2005] EWCA Civ 1466* and *XXX v King's College Hospital NHS Foundation Trust [2018] EWHC 646 (QB)* apply it to obstetric ultrasound scans. Accordingly, there is a very good chance that this is the test applicable to all cases where the central allegation is that a slide or scan has been negligently misinterpreted ('pure diagnosis' cases). Please note that although other scan types have not been specifically brought within this test yet, it seems logical to do so. More generally, in *O'Brien v Guy's & St Thomas' NHS Trust [2022] EWHC 2735 (KB) para. 21, Tindal HHJ* (sitting as a High Court Judge) cited *Penney* in support of stating *"… Bolam does not apply to fact-finding…"*.

The key point is that the slide (or scan) shows something as a matter of fact. Accordingly, whether the abnormality was there and was missed at the time is a matter for the trial judge to determine not the experts. The experts should only assist with interpreting what was (or was not) actually on the slide (or scan) without the benefit of hindsight. They should not be asked whether the impugned interpretation made was supported by a reasonable and logical body of opinion. Substituting the *Bolam* test would be abdicating the trial judge's responsibility to determine the facts.

In *Penney*, at *para. 27*, *Lord Woolf MR* explained that this is akin to asking whether the clinician interpreted the objective data wrongly. The main questions to be addressed are:

1. What is shown on the slide (or scan)?

2. Could the screener reasonably fail to see this at the time?

3. Could a reasonably competent screener treat the slide (or scan) as 'clear'?

Two further factual questions must also be answered: the specific training and knowledge the impugned screener had received at the time and how easy it was to discern what the judge found could be seen on the slide (or scan) (at *para. 28*). A sixth factual question is then relevant: what did the screener understand to be the correct procedure to follow in uncertain or borderline cases? Put another way, what were the consequences of getting it wrong?

This requires the screener to have been 'absolutely certain' of being right before declaring the slide (or scan) 'clear'. If the judge has found an anomaly on the slide (or scan) was present, then it is very unlikely that the screener could have been 'absolutely certain' and so did not exercise reasonable skill and care in declaring the slide (or scan) 'clear'. As a result of this, the defendant appears to be in a more difficult position than if the *Bolam* test was being applied. According to *Kerr, J* in *Muller (para. 95)*, it is irrelevant if the screener made an honest or uncharacteristic mistake or if it was made sincerely or in good faith. *"The standard is the objective one of reasonable skill and care, fixed by law" (para. 96).*

What if the slide or scan has been lost? In *Lillywhite*, *Jack J* tried to reconstruct the scan from the expert evidence and was persuaded by the fact that several experienced clinicians had made the same error when reviewing the same scan. However, the majority of the Court of Appeal disagreed with this approach and re-emphasized that the *Penney* approach should still be used even where there was little hard evidence. As *Latham LJ* explained at *para. 9* of the Court of Appeal judgment:

> *"The judge's task in evaluating this expert evidence was intrinsically difficult. The events were fifteen years in the past. There were some still photographs from the scans carried out by Mrs Wright. Otherwise there*

> *was no contemporaneous material other than the notes of Dr Meire and Professor Rodeck. It was a striking feature of the case that none of the photographs which had been taken of the scans by Dr Meire remained in existence, even though it was clear that Professor Rodeck, at least, had been seriously concerned about the fact that the diagnosis had been missed and had spoken to Dr Meire at the time. It was also unfortunate, to say the least, that even if none of those photographs had been kept, there was no evidence from Dr Meire or Professor Rodeck to the effect that those photographs had been examined by them after the event in order to determine why it was that the diagnosis had been missed. It should be stressed, however, that there has been no suggestion at any stage that this had been the result of any desire to brush what had happened under the carpet."*

As usual, it is best to address these issues early. Per *Buxton LJ (paras. 91-92):*

> *"If elementary steps had been taken of peer review and the re-reading of such of the images as were available before they were destroyed, the Trust would have been able to say then, and would have been able to tell the judge, whether it could explain what had occurred in terms that did not inculpate it as negligent. ... If there is indeed, as is now claimed, an explanation for those readings, it is very surprising that it was not readily apparent to two specialists anxiously considering the case ten years ago."*

Whilst *Latham* and *Buxton LLJ* were prepared to allow the appeal (on a clear *Penney* basis), *Arden LJ* was not. She preferred the view that *Jack J* had had the benefit of hearing and considering the evidence and his decision was not clearly wrong. Accordingly, that approach does have some judicial support for it. At the very least, claimant solicitors should be seeking to investigate whether such reviews took place and the defendant's legal team should be able to explain this in detail.

In *XXX* (*para. 12)*, the defendant contended that *Lillywhite* requires the claimant to be able to positively identify the scanning mistake that had been made to succeed. The fact that a mistake was made is not enough (i.e. the error must be identifiable, not just deduced). At *para. 20*, *Foskett J* stated that the key question is whether the anomaly is one which can be seen on the scan (or slide). As with *Lillywhite*, the case the defendant advanced was that an honest mistake had been made by a competent clinician (*para. 23*). However, it was held that the anomaly, although tiny, was capable of being seen on the scan (*para. 18*) and had been missed as a result of the scan technique being substandard (*para. 106*) and that this provided the most plausible explanation (*para. 109*). As to additional evidence which may have changed *Foskett J*'s mind, he said that positive evidence on whether this very experienced clinician had ever encountered and recorded this rare anomaly before and/or that he had received the recommended training on the scanning technique would have assisted (*paras. 108-9*). He does not appear to have been persuaded by the defendant's late attempt to reconstruct the relevant anatomy by commissioning a 3-D model (from the available images). These images were retained and the impugned clinician reviewed them when preparing his witness statement (*para. 49*) and gave further detail in oral evidence (*para. 53*). The possible reasons why the abnormality may have been missed were not supported by any evidence that they actually existed in this case (*para. 109*).

Brady v Southend University NHS Foundation Trust [2020] EWHC 158 (QB) illustrates that the courts are not yet willing to extend the reasonable skill and care test to mixed cases. *Bolam/Bolitho* remains the correct test where misinterpretation of the slides/scans combines with uncertainty as to the diagnosis. Although what the slides/scan show is a matter of fact for the judge, the overall question of whether the total error amounts to a breach is separate. However, it does not appear from this judgement that the 'absolute certainty' test was applied to the question of what the slides/scan showed.

Accordingly, it can be fairly said that concentrating on obtaining and understanding the factual evidence of what can be seen on the scan or slide early in the case is the best way of accurately assessing them. There is no harm in asking your expert to consider both tests (i.e. *Bolam* and *Penney*); in some cases, the interpretation of the slide (or scan) may also be unsupported by a reasonable body of clinicians in that field. If you choose this method, make sure you remember that there is a distinction and ensure that your experts set out each test correctly to avoid confusion.

An area to keep an eye on is whether the reasonable skill and care test is also applicable to surgical errors. The holotype is said to be an unnoticed iatrogenic surgical bowel injury during an uncomplicated and routine operation. Such an outcome is neither intended by the surgeon nor supported by a reasonable body of surgical opinion; but is it simply a known risk which arose purely accidentally? Following the usual surgical procedure with ordinary skill and care would not cause the injury.

At present, cases such as *Lillywhite* show that the issue is likely to be clouded by the evidential doctrine of *res ipsa loquitor*. As is set out in that section below, this is unlikely to assist the claimant. The facts will not simply speak for themselves; rather the defendant's evidence will need to be proved improbable. *Delaney v Southmead Health Authority [1995] 6 Med LR 355* provides an illustration. Although the defendant could not explain the cause of the injury, it was to a different part of the body to the operation site and the mechanism of injury was unrelated to the surgical technique.

In *Haughey v Newry and Maune Health and Social Care Trust [2013] NICA 78*, the injury to the ureter was anatomically more closely related to the bladder repair surgery and the issue was whether it was a rare complication or negligent. The court accepted the impugned clinician's evidence that he had performed the operation carefully and his experts' explanation as to how the complication is known to arise even with the exercise of reasonable skill and care.

In *Collyer v Mid Essex Hospital Services NHS Trust [2019] EWHC 3577 (QB)*, the hypoglossal nerve injury to the claimant's tongue was not only anatomically close to the laryngectomy but was also a previously unreported complication of this operation. It seems to be fairly close to the holotype case. Looking at this from the perspective of the factual enquiries set out in *Penney*, *HHJ Coe QC* found that the positioning of the relevant anatomical structures was not abnormal in this case (*para. 151*) and that the contemporaneous operation note showed that the surgery was uncomplicated involving the use of a standard technique and procedure with no obvious complications or difficulties (*para. 152*). It was also inherently unlikely that none of the surgical team (who all gave evidence) would have failed to notice the observable signs of a hypoglossal nerve injury if it had been caused by cutting it intraoperatively (*para. 174*). *"In the circumstances whilst it is not completely impossible that this is what happened I do not find that it is more likely than not to have happened. //... It is an unhappy situation for the court not to be able to identify the cause of an injury such as this. However, having given this matter careful consideration, my firm conclusion is that the cause of [the claimant's] injury remains unexplained."* (*paras. 175-6*).

Although *Bolam* was the test applied in all of these cases (and it was not suggested that *Penney* should be used in any of them), they illustrate the evidential difficulties that claimants face in the absence of clear, positive evidence of wrongdoing. However, that is an issue faced in the vast majority of clinical negligence cases. Perhaps the central issue in respect of this particular topic is to consider what 'objective data' (appropriating *Lord Woolf's* comment in *Penney*) the trial judge can point to in cases of surgical error? In the holotype case, this might be clear photographs or footage of the anatomy during the operation and a lack of any particular risk factors in the patient's medical history. Alternatively, rather than seeking a paradigm holotype, perhaps it is instead better to identify a case where applying the *Bolam* test results in an illogical result which is avoided by the *Penney* test.

A guiding principle here would be that the fewer choices or decisions the impugned surgeon had to make during the operation, the harder it is to explain how the injury 'just happened' in a purely accidental or unforeseeable manner. Taking a very simple example as a proof of concept, extracting the wrong (asymptomatic and healthy) molar instead of its decaying and painful adjacent neighbour probably meets the standard for both tests. However, if the contemporaneous record reversed the symptoms for these teeth, the case could fail under *Bolitho* if a reasonable dentist could make the same error in these circumstances. Is this really an issue that the trial judge needs to hear expert evidence on (i.e. whether a minority body of opinion was logical if the error could not have been missed) if the error was identifiable by careful observation of the teeth by the operating dentist?

All-in-all, the enquiries you need to make do not differ between the two tests (apart from formulating the correct test for the experts and highlighting the factual questions from *Penney*). Accordingly, the best practical advice is to concentrate on getting those right: if you have a case applying *Bolam*, you will also have a case based on *Penney*. *McGraw v Greater Glasgow Health Board [2022] CSOH 83* provides a useful reminder that it remains necessary to plead and prove the manner in which the clinician was negligent. In that case, this was (a) what the normal and accepted practice was at the date of the impugned treatment; (b) that the radiologist did not adopt this; and (c) that what the radiologist did or did not do was contrary to a reasonable body of opinion. As such, the factual question of what can be seen on the scan sits between questions which still require expert evidence.

(d) Gross Negligence

At the other end of the scale are those cases where the correct standard of care is more stringent than the *Bolam* test. This arises where the injury needing medical treatment was caused by someone else's negligence. The practical question is whether the negligent medical treatment breaks the chain of causation from the initial tortfeasor's point of view. This is answered from the breach of duty perspective and not a causation perspective.

Webb v Barclays Bank plc & Portsmouth Hospitals NHS Trust [2001] EWCA Civ 1141 confirms that the medical treatment needs to be grossly negligent. Gross negligence amounts to treatment which is so poor as to amount to a wholly inappropriate way of dealing with the injury sustained. It is far less clearly defined than the *Bolam* principle.

Practitioners need to be aware of this from the outset of their involvement in a case. Prospective claimants often equate a poor experience in hospital with sub-standard care and so understandably think that there are two separate injuries. They may already be bringing a PI claim where the instructed expert has prepared a report which criticizes the subsequent medical treatment (perhaps going so far as to as to call it negligent). This may lead to the claimant being (incorrectly) advised that they have a separate clinical negligence claim.

Alternatively, it may not be clear when a clinical negligence case is accepted that there was an earlier accident which might be someone else's fault. Whilst taking proper instructions should avoid this risk, it does occur relatively commonly. The risk is that considerable costs are then incurred investigating a case on the wrong basis and ultimately end up being irrecoverable.

A practical solution is provided by the causation elements of the case. In *Webb*, the court held that there was no break in the chain of causation but that the treatment was negligent applying the *Bolam* test. Accordingly, the hospital was required to make a contribution to the damages award. Nowadays, individual fee earners are less likely to run both PI and clinical negligence cases and there can be differing cost regimes for both. If you do still run both types of case, then you may still be able to investigate and pursue the case against both defendants. However, if you only practice clinical negligence, then it is more practical to allow the PI case to be investigated first. There is only likely to be a viable clinical negligence case if there is an additional, avoidable injury arising from grossly negligent treatment and the value of that injury is proportionate to pursue. If the claimant's PI expert raises the possibility of negligent treatment, then that does not mean the PI case cannot be settled at its full value. If the PI defendant raises the issue, then it can safely be invited to incur the expense of investigating whether the treatment amounts to gross negligence itself or to make a *Part 20* claim against the hospital. From the claimant's perspective, a clinical negligence case is likely to take far longer to include at a greater cost to them than the PI case without necessarily obtaining any higher damages award.

It will sometimes be unclear whether settling the PI case first prevents a clinical negligence case being brought (if there is no additional loss to be claimed). *Wright v Barts Health NHS Trust [2016] EWHC 1834 (QB)* follows *Appleby v Northern Devon Healthcare NHS Trust [2012] EWHC*

4346 (QB). In the absence of gross negligence, the PI defendant will probably still be liable for all of the consequential losses and there must be very clear evidence that the PI settlement was intended to settle the entire value of the claim. In *Wright* the reduction for contributory negligence in the PI case showed that it had not been intended to settle that case at full value and so the hospital could be sued for the balance subject to proving breach and that the amount of the additional loss that was caused from it. The key point is whether the defendants were liable for the same damage but for different losses. Analysing the specific losses sequentially may show that they arose from only one of the defendant's breaches such that the two defendants are concurrent tortfeasors rather than joint tortfeasors.

If you do find yourself advising in such a case, make sure that you fully understand and explain the costs consequences and PI and clinical negligence solicitors should discuss the issues before either agrees to a settlement.

(e) Consent

This is now another exception to the *Bolam* test. As with the reasonable skill test (*supra*), the factual questions for the judge (as to whether sufficient information was provided) sit between questions requiring expert evidence. There is also a distinction made between recommended treatment and treatment which has not been recommended.

It is well known that adults with sufficient capacity must be allowed to make their own decision when deciding whether they or their children undergo treatment. In *Chester v Afshar [2004] UKHL 41, para. 5, Lord Bingham* described it thusly: *"The existence of such a duty is not in doubt. Nor is its rationale: to enable adult patients of sound mind to make for themselves decisions intimately affecting their own lives and bodies."* Accordingly, it is necessary for patients to be given sufficient information by their treating clinicians to allow them to make this decision.

A useful starting point for investigating consent in children's cases is provided by *Bell & Another v The Tavistock and Portman NHS*

Foundation Trust [2021] EWCA Civ 1363. The Court of Appeal held that it was inappropriate for the court to impose guidance and restrictions on when Gillick-competent teenagers (see *Gillick v West Norfolk and Wisbech Area Health Authority [1985] UKHL 7*) should receive puberty blockers where it did not find the hospital's guidance unlawful or inappropriate. At *para. 92, Lord Burnett* said:

> *"...Clinicians will inevitably take great care before recommending treatment to a child and be astute to ensure that the consent obtained from both the child and parents is properly informed by the advantages and disadvantages of the proposed course of treatment and in light of evolving research and understanding of the implications and long-term consequences of such treatment. Great care is needed to ensure that the necessary consents are properly obtained. As Gillick itself made clear, clinicians will be alive to the possibility of regulatory or civil action where, in individual cases, the issue can be tested."*

(i) Recommended Treatment

For recommended treatment, the breach of duty test is set out in *Montgomery v Lanarkshire Health Board [2015] UKSC 11* and *Green J* has provided another helpful judgement setting out a logical method of analysing the available evidence in *Thefaut v Johnston [2017] EWHC 497 (QB)*. If the trial judge finds, as a matter of fact, that there was no consent, then they must also find a breach of duty and failing to do so is appealable (e.g. *Border v Lewisham and Greenwich NHS Trust [2015] EWCA Civ, para. 24*).

In essence, medical paternalism is a thing of the past. Modern patients are consumers with rights and have a better understanding of medical issues than earlier generations. The test is no longer whether the clinician exercised reasonable care in advising the patient of the risks associated with the procedure being considered because that implies that the clinician decides what is important. Instead, the duty on the clinician is to explain to the patient the material risks which are inherent to the procedure and to advise of the alternatives to it. This duty is retrospective (because court decisions clarify the existing law rather than creating new law) and the Supreme Court made it clear that their ruling reflected the position taken by the General Medical Council for many years.

The GMC's position means that this approach should already have been taken by clinicians and so the consent documentation in the records should be consistent with this test. In judging whether a particular patient wants to be told of these risks, and whether this occurred, are questions of fact to be decided by the judge and not by expert evidence.

If the clinician has recommended a particular treatment, then they must provide information on the pros and cons of it and of reasonable alternatives (along with the pros and cons of each). Adducing persuasive factual evidence is key. In *Pepper v Royal Free London NHS Foundation Trust [2020] EWHC 310 (QB)* and *McNab & Others v Greater Glasgow Health Board [2020] CSOH 53* factual evidence of what was actually said by the Consultant was found to be inadequate. In *NKX v Barts Health NHS Trust [2020] EWHC 828 (QB)* and *Williams & Others v Betsi Cadawaladr University LHB [2022] EWHC 455 (QB)*, the impugned midwife's and nurse's evidence (respectively) was preferred. In *Plant v El-Amir & Another [2020] EWHC 2902 (QB) Stacey J* held that there had been a failure to "*... share with* [the claimant] *any of what little research data there was about the limited benefits and risks of the proposed surgery...*" but there was also evidence that the 2nd defendant (a private clinic) had significant, relevant operational problems at the material time.

The risks of suffering the relevant injury should not be reduced to percentages and should be explained in a way that the patient can reasonably be expected to understand. Accordingly, lengthy consent forms containing a large amount of information may meet the *Bolam* test but may not necessarily be compliant with the new test. Equally, using percentages to assist in the explanation is not necessarily wrong – but a doctor who decides not to advise that a risk is a material one because it has a low percentage chance of occurring does appear to be failing in their duty.

It is therefore necessary to adduce evidence of what matters the patient felt were important, what questions they raised at the time and what research they did themselves before agreeing to the treatment being recommended (see also *Webster v Burton Hospitals NHS Foundation Trust [2017] EWCA Civ 62*). In essence, it is necessary to put the judge in a position where they can make a finding of fact and the relative risk of the complication occurring remains relevant as it goes to the credibility of the witnesses and the case being advanced. Whilst not a prerequisite, it is very helpful to adduce factual evidence showing a cogent, objective reason which explains why the clamant would have made this choice (such as in *Middleton v Ipswich Hospital NHS Trust [2015] EWHC 775 (QB); Hassell v Hillingdon Hospitals NHS Foundation Trust [2018] EWHC 14 (QB);* or *Kennedy v Frankel [2019] EWHC 106 (QB)*).

These cases continue to require careful preparation. The factual evidence may be sufficient to show that the risk was very low and/or that the claimant would have taken it had they been properly advised (e.g. *A v East Kent Hospitals University NHS Foundation Trust [2015] EWHC 1038 (QB); Tasmin v Barts Health NHS Trust [2015] EWHC 3135 (QB);* and *Clements v Imperial College Healthcare NHS Trust [2018] 2064 (QB)*).

Additionally, the claimant's motivation, desired outcome and whether the proposed alternative treatment is outmoded or experimental are all relevant considerations (see *Grimstone v Epsom & St Helier University Hospitals NHS Trust [2015] EWHC 3756 (QB)*). Being able to consider the oral evidence of the actual dialogue between the claimant and impugned clinician is of very great importance and this makes fatal cases more difficult (but not impossible; e.g. *Mossa v Wise [2017] EWHC 2608 (QB)*). The advice given ought to be in a language the claimant understands (e.g. *Rajatheepan v Barking, Havering and Redbridge NHS Foundation Trust [2018] EWHC 716 (QB)*); and as easy to understand as possible for that claimant so evidence that simpler language would have helped the claimant's understanding may tip the scales (e.g. *Mills v Oxford University Hospitals NHS Trust [2019] 936 (QB), para. 203*). The overall quality of the claimant's recollection of events (not just on the consent issues) will be weighed against the quality of the impugned clinician's and their contemporaneous records (e.g. *Cameron v Ipswich Hospital NHS Trust [2018] 38 (QB)*). The environment in which the information was given to the claimant is important and doing so in an unpressurised manner giving time to reflect found favour with the court in *Ollosson v Lee [2019] EWHC 784 (QB)*. However, the impugned clinician is under no obligation to give advice which they could not actually give (e.g. *Worrall v Antoniado [2016] EWCA Civ 1219*)

Furthermore, factual evidence on the hypothetical question of what the impugned clinician would have done had the claimant been given proper advice remains relevant to causation. This means that the claimant must prove that they reasonably would not have followed this advice (e.g. *Barrett v Sandwell and West Birmingham Hospitals NHS Trust [2015] EWHC 2627 (QB), paras. 160-163*) or what different treatment plan would have been actually agreed (e.g. *Crossman v St George's Healthcare NHS Trust [2016] EWHC 2878 (QB), para. 32)*. In answering these hypothetical questions, the trial judge is entitled to draw inferences from all the evidence rather than relying only on general assessments of witnesses' credibility (*Mordel v Royal Berkshire NHS Trust [2019] EWHC 2591 (QB), para. 152*).

Montgomery is not limited to prospective treatment or causing harm. It applies equally to the duty to inform the patient of the outcome of their treatment, the prognosis and to the requirements for any follow up or monitoring (*Gallardo v Imperial College Healthcare NHS Trust [2017] EWHC 3147 (QB)*). There is also a duty to warn of the signs and characteristic symptoms of potentially serious but treatable complications (e.g. *Spencer v Hillingdon Hospital NHS Trust [2015] EWHC 1058 (QB))*. Thirdly, it applies to where the treatment allegedly was pointless, of no real benefit at all, or did not cause additional harm (e.g. *Price v Cwm Taf University Health Board [2019] EWHC 938 (QB), para. 27*). However, the failure to disclose relevant information does not, by itself, create a right to damages (e.g. *Shaw v Kovac [2017] EWCA Civ 1028*, *Duce* (*infra*) and *Diamond v Royal Devon & Exeter NHS Foundation Trust [2017] EWHC 1495 (QB)*).

(ii) Treatment which has not been recommended

In all of these cases, the required information was in respect of recommended treatment. The position is somewhat different where it is alleged that there has been a negligent failure to provide information about alternatives to the recommended treatment. Where the clinician would not have given this advice then *Bolam/Bolitho* still applies. This issue is likely to be considered by the Supreme Court in 2023 as permission to appeal in *McCulloch & Others v Forth Valley Health Board [2021] CSIH 21* was granted in 2022.

Until then, the approach adopted in *McCulloch* is consistent with reported cases including recent ones such as *Malik v St George's University Hospitals NHS Foundation Trust [2021] EWHC 1913 (QB); Negus & Others v Guy's & St. Thomas' NHS Foundation Trust [2021] EWHC 643 (QB); and ABC v St George's Healthcare NHST & Others (supra).*

At *para. 40* of *McCulloch, Lady Dorrian* explained the rational as follows:

> *"Montgomery was about advising of the risks associated with a proposed course of action, which would of course include the risks if that course of action were not adopted. It does not follow that where a doctor concludes that a course of treatment is not a reasonable option in the circumstances of the patient the duty under Montgomery nevertheless arises. … The simple fact is that Montgomery has no application in the circumstances of the present case."*

The basis for this is that *Montgomery (supra, paras. 82 and 83)* distinguishes between "… *the doctor's role when considering possible investigatory or treatment options and, on the other, her role in discussing with the patient any recommended treatment and possible alternatives, and the risks of injury which may be involved. / The former role is an exercise of professional skill and judgment: what risks of injury are involved in an operation, for example, is a matter falling within the expertise of members of the medical profession…*".

This appears to create the risk that medical paternalism remains because the clinician makes this decision without having to inform the patient. As such, the patient does not know that another option has been considered and discounted by their clinician and so cannot decide whether they would like to try it out despite advice that it probably will not be successful.

Where *paras. 82 and 83* of *Montgomery* are cited, it can help to refer to the rest of *para. 83* and *para. 84* in order to ensure the evidence is not misdirected. *Para. 83* continues:

> *"But it is a non sequitur to conclude that the question whether a risk of injury, or the availability of an alternative form of treatment, ought to be discussed with the patient is also a matter of purely professional judgment. The doctor's advisory role cannot be regarded as solely an exercise of medical skill without leaving out of account the patient's entitlement to decide on the risks to her health which she is willing to run (a decision which may be influenced by non-medical considerations). Responsibility for determining the nature and extent of a person's rights rests with the courts, not with the medical professions."* *Para. 84* says: *"Furthermore, because the extent to which a doctor may be inclined to discuss risks with a patient is not determined by medical learning or experience, the application of the Bolam test to this question is liable to result in the sanctioning of differences in practice which are attributable not to divergent schools of thought in medical science, but merely to divergent attitudes among doctors as to the degree of respect owed to their patients."*

Patient autonomy remains important and so it remains open for the trial judge to weigh up the competing arguments as to whether the impugned act or omission does or does not fall within *Montgomery*. These paragraphs were considered in *Gallardo (supra)* to be *"significant"* in respect of the applicable standard of care *"beyond cases about consent to treatment" (para. 76)* where there was conflicting expert evidence as to when the claimant should have been informed of his diagnosis (and so make an informed decision as to his options).

In *Williams v University Hospitals of Morecambe Bay NHS Foundation Trust (2022) Unreported, paras. 30-48, HHJ Jones* referred to *Gallardo (supra)* and to *paras. 81-84* of *Montgomery* as well as *paras. 87, 89 and 90* demonstrating the benefit of referring the court to all relevant parts of the judgement. He rejected the defendant's submissions that a distinction exists between 'treatment' and 'investigations'. At *para. 43*, he stated that *"the essence of Montgomery is ensuring that the patient has control over his healthcare"* and (at *para. 44*) that the *"distinction between treatment and investigations reflect reality"* in circumstances where continuing a course of treatment was the alternative to considering investigations.

In *CNZ v Royal Bath Hospitals NHS Foundation Trust & Another [2023] EWHC 19 (KB), Ritchie J* utilised both *paras. 81-84* and *87* of *Montgomery (supra)* (at *para. 262*) and *McCullogh (supra).* He described *McCulloch* as considering the issue of what amounts to reasonable alternate treatment (*para. 265*). He held that the evidence showed that the alternative treatment (a Caesarean section delivery) was available but the defendant's doctors counselled against having it. However, he accepted that the mother could have chosen it notwithstanding the counselling and going against the clinical advice was a reasonable option within *para. 87* of *Montgomery* (*paras. 285-6*). However, he also found that the mother accepted the counselling and did not want an invasive birth and that the advice given was reasonable. So, there was no breach of duty (*paras. 287* & *396*). That said, *Ritchie J* also made it clear that *"... in other cases with other facts and with another mother the illogicality of the department's policy might produce a different result"* (*para. 288*).

Another useful aspect of this judgement is that *Ritchie J* considered how far back in time one can properly apply *Montgomery.* He wondered whether it was appropriate to apply it before the mid-1990s (but expressly did not decide this). *Montgomery* itself applied to events from 1999. Although he felt *"troubled"* to applying it to events from February 1996, he felt that there had been sufficient societal changes to probably permit this and that *Montgomery* itself did not permit him to apply a tapered or watered-down version of the test (all at *para. 264*)

Failing to remain informed of available literature is another relevant consideration. In *Webster v Burton Hospitals NHS Foundation Trust [2017] (supra)* (the first instance decision pre-dated the Supreme Court's decision in *Montgomery*) it was held that *Montgomery* did require the patient to be told of *"… emerging but recent and incomplete material showing increased risks of delaying labour in cases with this combination of features" (para. 40)* despite the defendant's submissions that the impugned clinician would not have given such advice (*para. 33*). *Para. 35* described the generality of the clinician's duty as being *"… to present the material risks and uncertainties of different treatments, and to allow patients to make decisions that will affect their health and well-being on proper information. The significance of the risks and uncertainties, including the possibility of alternative treatment, being sensitive to the characteristics of the patient."* The Court of Appeal did not specifically refer to *paras. 82 and 83* of *Montgomery* in their judgement.

The impugned clinician's evidence must also still be logical. In *Diamond v Royal Devon & Exeter NHS Foundation Trust [2019] EWCA Civ 565 & [2017] supra,* the defendant's expert accepted that the required advice should have been given whilst in *Mills v Oxford University HNHST (supra),* the experts agreed that it was a breach not to provide advice of alternatives to surgery.

(f) <u>'Independent Contractors'</u>

It may be necessary to consider whether the clinic or hospital was also responsible where private treatment is impugned. This need arises either because the clinician was not solely responsible for all of the breaches of duty or they have insufficient insurance in place to pay compensation (and costs). It is now relatively common to find that private doctors have a 'claims made' insurance policy. This will only provide cover if the insurer is notified of the potential claim during the lifetime of the policy. Whilst the GMC and National Midwifery Council require that clinicians have adequate insurance in place to allow patients to sue them, they are less keen to rule that these insurance policies are a breach of this guidance. A less commonly encountered problem is where the MDU, MPS or MDDUS withdraw cover under their discretionary insurance schemes. This risk should be reduced with NHS Resolution taking over indemnity for new cases of GP negligence from 2019.

The immediate hurdle that is faced is the assertion that the clinician was an independent contractor bearing sole responsibility for the claimant's injuries and so there is no cause of action against anyone else. Post-QOCS, the risk of unsuccessfully suing a party is reduced but has not gone away. You should not bring wholly unmeritorious claims. A well-targeted *Part 36* offer or having the case against the hospital struck out would remove this costs protection. There is little point incurring costs yourself which are unlikely to be recovered.

Carefully reviewing the evidence will usually show whether the clinician was genuinely independent of the establishment where the treatment occurred. The core document is the contract between the clinician and the establishment. Although this will probably say that the clinician is responsible for the treatment and needs his own insurance, it should also reveal the extent to which the hospital or clinic controlled the exercise of those duties. If it does not, then there should be other internal documents which do show this or the division needs to be explained in witness statements if it is not to be inferred by the court.

If the doctor is employed, then the claim proceeds against the hospital under the vicarious liability rules. If the clinician genuinely is an independent contractor then the treating establishment should be released or not pursued at all. In either case, the insurance position still needs to be established to avoid any nasty surprises. However, the answer should not be assumed without carefully considering the evidence and it may take protracted correspondence or pre-action or specific disclosure applications to obtain the requisite evidence.

The hospital has an increased likelihood of being concurrently liable for the breaches of the clinician in these scenarios:

(a) Different staff committed separate (actionable) breaches of duty.

Quite often, it is apparent from the medical records that the clinician's involvement was part of a longer chain of events. In particular, the consent process may well have initially been performed by a salesperson or receptionist and the nursing care is likely to have been provided by employed nurses rather than independent contractors. Accordingly, the treatment centre has concurrent responsibility for the acts and omissions of its staff as the clinician does for their surgery.

(b) The clinician could only perform their duties because the hospital provided them with the facilities to do so.

It is very often the case that the clinician is responsible for performing only the medical procedure itself. The facilities, equipment and support staff are all provided by the hospital or clinic. In this situation, it is possible to rely on *Rogers v Night Riders [1983] RTR 324 (CA)*. If full evidentiary disclosure shows the clinic or hospital was simply acting as a 'post box' to put the patient in touch with the clinician, then it would be unreasonable to hold it responsible for their negligence. However, this does not usually reflect what happens in the treatment given that healthcare is not ordinarily or legally provided by one person in isolation. Accordingly, the documentary evidence ought to show the extent to which the clinician was reliant on the availability of consulting rooms, operating theatres, administrative and medical support, medical equipment and clinical risk management procedures to safely perform the impugned treatment. The way this was provided does not need to be negligent because the provider is jointly and severally liable in negligence and contract for the negligence of the doctor under this rule. The Privy Council approved this decision in *Wong Mee v Kwan Kin Travel Services Ltd & Others [1995] UKPC 42*.

(c) There was a non-delegable duty of care on the hospital or clinic.

In respect of negligent medical treatment, the concept of a non-delegable duty has been known since *Gold v Essex County Council [1942] 2 KB 293* although it arose in the early cases as a series of *obiter dicta* in the context of employed clinicians' negligence (see also *Cassidy v Ministry of Health [1951] 2 KB 343* and *Roe v Minister of Health [1954] EWCA Civ 7*). The persuasive power of these views was enhanced in the leading judgement of *Lord Browne-Wilkinson* in *X (Minors) v Bedfordshire County Council [1995] 2 AC 633* when it was said that those running a hospital assume a personal (not vicarious) duty to people admitted as patients which can be breached even where the clinician themselves owed no duty of care. The requirement for an actual 'admission' to hospital is not necessarily a pre-requisite for this duty to arise but receiving 'treatment' is (c.f. *Darnley (supra)* where the Claimant left the A&E reception area voluntarily).

Another crucial pre-requisite is that you are not simply trying to show that there was a risk of injury arising from the delegation. A non-delegable duty of care is an exception to the general rule that independent contractors should be solely liable for their negligence. The ordinary principles of tortious liability are perfectly capable of addressing this (*Woodland v Essex County Council [2013] UKSC 66, per Lord Sumption; para. 22*).

Woodland takes the dicta from the earlier cases referred to above and formulates a legal rule which can be relied on in practice. The earlier dicta remain relevant because they show that *Woodland* does not need to be extended to cover clinical negligence cases; this rule arose (in part) from previous decisions in this area. What is needed is to apply this rule to the facts of each case in order to establish whether the non-delegable duty has been assumed by the hospital or clinic.

Lord Sumption sets out the test at *para. 23* of his judgement. To paraphrase it, it is necessary to prove:

(1) The claimant is a patient, child or is otherwise especially vulnerable or dependent on the defendant to avoid being harmed. Although 'patient' is not defined further (and so could be limited to someone lacking capacity), the other examples given are of a prisoner or care home resident. Accordingly, it appears to apply to patients who have been

'admitted' and cannot simply leave hospital to avoid an injury arising from the negligence.

(2) There is an 'antecedent relationship' between the patient and the hospital. This not created by the alleged negligence but by virtue of there being a degree of control being exercised over the patient by the hospital or clinic:

  (i) The hospital placed the patient in its care, charge or custody; and

  (ii) It is possible to infer that the hospital has assumed a positive duty to protect the patient from harm. This is more than the usual duty to refrain from conduct which will create a reasonably foreseeable risk of harm.

(3) The patient has no control over how the hospital chooses to exercise this duty.

(4) Some integral, practical aspect of this duty has been delegated to the clinician. They then have to exercise the elements of custody or care and control over the patient in order to deal with the aspect delegated to them.

(5) The clinician has negligently performed this delegated aspect rather than been negligent in some ancillary aspect.

Whether or not the hospital has control over the circumstances which caused the injury is irrelevant. What distinguishes these cases from those where the duty can be safely delegated is that the hospital has retained control over the patient (*para. 24*). Accordingly, cases where the hospital just arranges or pays for the treatment (e.g. *Myton v Woods (1980) 79 LGR 28*); where it has contracted out the care to another hospital (e.g. *A (Child) v MoD [2004] EWCA Civ 641*); or where an independent laboratory is contracted to analyse investigation results (e.g. *Farraj v King's Healthcare NHS Trust [2009] EWCA Civ 1203*) are all examples where there is a delegable duty for this reason.

In one respect, a non-delegable duty requires more from the tortfeasor than the *Bolam* test (*Armes v Nottinghamshire County Council [2017] UKSC 70*). *Lord Reed* (at *para. 31*) explains it as: "*... not merely to take personal care in performing a given function but to ensure that care is taken. The expression thus refers to a higher standard of care than the ordinary duty of care. Duties involving this higher standard of care are described as non-delegable because they cannot be discharged merely by the exercise of reasonable care in the selection of a third party to whom the function is delegated.*" Since this type of tortious liability is the exception rather than the rule, it must be kept within reasonable limits (*para. 32*).

Accordingly, *Gallardo (supra)* applied this in imposing liability on an NHS Trust for failing to properly inform its patient before he moved to private care. "... *The Defendant owed the Claimant a duty to advise him of the outcome of his surgery, of his prognosis, and of the need for follow-up. The surgery had been carried out on the NHS. The histopathology had been obtained on the NHS. The duty arose in consequence of his treatment. It was a necessary component of it. / The duty had not been discharged by the time the Claimant moved to the private wing of the hospital" (paras. 92-3),*

The issue of patients receiving NHS care externally was considered further in *Hughes v Rattan [2022] EWCA Civ 107* in the context of NHS general dental treatment. The Court of Appeal upheld the trial judge's decision that there was a non-delegable duty of care on a dentist who was the only named treating clinician on the personal dental treatment plan (*para. 69*). At *para. 71*, *Bean LJ* summarised the application of the *Woodland* criteria as follows:

1. 'Patient' includes any patient receiving treatment. It does not require actual admission. It remains to be seen whether it also includes consultations where no treatment has occurred.

2. The necessary antecedent relationship between the clinician and patient is established when the most recent patient dental

treatment plan was signed. It was important that the dentist was also the practice owner. The duty owed was personal to the clinician and was a positive duty to protect from injury (rather than a duty not to avoid acting in a way that foreseeably causes harm). This created the necessary degree of control.

3. The claimant had no meaningful control over how the defendant chose to perform his duties. The general right to refuse medical treatment and the more specific one to express a preference as to which associate dentist she was treated by were insufficient.

Drawing all of these issues together, it would appear that a non-delegable duty is more likely to arise where the negligence occurs whilst the claimant is undergoing treatment either as an inpatient or outpatient (including undergoing day surgery). The negligent treatment seemingly needs to be both 'reasonably foreseeable' (for the case against the clinician) and within the assumed positive duty to 'protect the patient from harm' although it would be sensible to use the evidence to distinguish between these two alternatives by showing how the harm arose in each situation. The rule seems less likely to apply where either the patient was attending a consultation only or the negligence occurred off-site or outside of the NHS (depending on the degree of control being actually exercised by the defendant and claimant). A clear understanding of the factual evidence proving all the circumstances of the Claimant's care provision is key.

Whilst it may seem trite, care is required when pleading this issue. In *Gulf View Medical Centre Ltd. v Tesheira and Roopchand v Tesheira [2022] UKPC 38, Lords Stephens and Pentland* held that a non-delegable duty had been admitted. *"The Board considers that the use of the word "ensure" in paragraph 23 of the amended statement of claim was a way of alleging a non-delegable duty of care in the context that this was not an absolute duty but still required fault to be established on the part of those caring for the deceased.*

Several [Commonwealth] *judgments delivered prior to the date upon which the amended statement of claim and the amended defence were filed articulated a non-delegable duty as a "duty to ensure"" (para. 61).* The amended defence did not deny responsibility for the acts of others but contended that it had met the requisite standard of care and that those to whom it had delegated the duty it owed had not been negligent *(para. 63)*. The 'duty to ensure' is the same duty as in *Armes (supra)*.

(d) <u>Vicarious Liability*</u>

Although they are entirely separate (see *Fitzgerald v Hill [2018] QCA 283, per McMurdo P* (Supreme Court of Queensland), *para. 66* cited in *Gulf View (supra)* and *X (Minors (supra))*, the potential overlap between the non-delegable duty of care and vicarious liability is neatly illustrated by the Irish case of *Morrisey & Another v Health Service Executive & Others [2020] IESC 6.* Here, the HSE was found to be primarily liable for the negligent failings in cervical screening. It had retained sufficient control over the program as a whole that the ordinary person would believe they were overseeing it. They had a non-delegable duty of care but were not vicariously liable.

The apparent expansion of vicarious liability in England & Wales has seemingly been slowed in *Wm Morrison Supermarkets plc v Various Claimants [2020] UKSC 12* and *Barclays Bank plc v Various Claimants [2020] UKSC 13.* In practical terms, the factual evidence produced remains very important. There is a 2-stage test for imposing vicarious liability. Firstly, there must be a relationship between the parties which makes it proper to impose vicarious liability. Secondly, there must be a sufficiently close connection between this relationship and the alleged breaches of duty. Accordingly, the impugned actions must further the employer's business interests in some way. This was reiterated in *Ali v Luton Borough Council [2022] EWHC 132 (QB)* in a data breach scenario.

Applying these decisions to a medical scenario, where they are closer to independent contractors, the correct test is whether the impugned clinician was in a relationship akin to employment or carrying on their own business in respect of the alleged negligence (*Barclays Bank*). Where the impugned clinician can properly be seen as an employee, then their actions probably need to fall within the scope of activities they were authorised to take as part of their employment (*Wm Morrison*).

The factual evidence of the link between the employment and the wrongful act or omission is crucial. In *Ali (supra, para. 47),* the court stated that the *"... wrongful acts were not related to friction, confrontation or intimacy inherent in the Defendant's enterprise. This factor seems to me to most readily applicable in cases of ... interaction between the individual tortfeasor and a third party..."* As such, the clinician-patient relationship may well still qualify. *Chell v Tarmac Cement and Lime Ltd [2022] EWCA Civ 7* considered the decisions in *Wm Morrison* and *Barclays Bank* in the context of a PI claim where the tortfeasor caused injury to the claimant by a misguided practical joke. The Court of Appeal declined to overturn the first instance decision that there was a close connection between the employment and the horseplay in light of the trial judge's careful factual findings.

If these hurdles can be passed, then the further legal principles from the wider authorities such as *Lister v Hesley Hall [2001] UKHL 22* (which also approves of the Canadian Supreme Court decisions in *Bazley v Curry (1999) 174 DLR (4th) 45* and *Jacobi v Griffiths (1999) 174 DLR (4th) 71*) will need to be applied.

Hughes v Rattan (supra), overturned *"with some hesitation"* (*para. 91*) the trial judge's decision that associate dentists whose relationship was more akin to employment than in *Barclays Bank (supra)*, it nonetheless failed that test. There were more factors in favour if the relationship not being sufficiently close than against (*paras. 88-90*) and these provide a useful indication for the sort of facts the evidence needs to address.

(g) Res Ipsa Loquitor

In a small proportion of cases, this evidential doctrine can be used to prove negligence; the facts literally speak for themselves without requiring further evidence. One of the pre-requisites is that the claimant does not know what happened. However, this does not mean that a lack of medical knowledge justifies its use. For example, if the claimant was unconscious at the time the injury occurred and the injury would not normally be associated with the treatment being received at that time, then the doctrine is probably applicable.

If it is, then it is for the defendant to explain what happened. However, the presumption of proof can be rebutted if the defendant can provide evidence of a non-negligent explanation for the injury. This then takes the claimant to back to having to prove breach of duty in the normal way meaning that it rarely advisable to pursue a case only on a *res ipsa* basis.

As was seen above, 'reasonable skill & care' cases appear to overlap with *res ipsa* cases. However, the facts there require proof of what was seen on the slides (or scan) even where the misreading was a glaring error.

In *Ratcliffe v Plymouth & Torbay Health Authority [1998] EWCA Civ 2000, Hobhouse LJ* made it clear that the doctrine had little real application in medical negligence cases where expert and factual evidence on breach has been called. Accordingly, the approach the claimant takes needs to be planned out carefully. *Thomas v Curley [2013] EWCA Civ 117*, seems at first to contradict this because *res ipsa* was considered at trial. However, the trial judge was careful to emphasise that his decision was made one the basis of *Bolam* rather than *res ipsa*. The injury sustained was evidence of sub-standard practice because of the particular anatomical layout of this patient and not because there was no other possible explanation available to him. *Sardar v NHS Commissioning Board [2014] EWHC 38 (QB)* shows that judges can take the view that adducing insufficient evidentiary support for all parts of the case on liability can expose a claimant to looking as if they are trying to prove that the injury is evidence of breach. So, *res ipsa* can be used indirectly by defendants to illustrate gaps in the claimant's case. In practice, expert evidence can be used to consider both alternatives for the benefit of the trial judge.

Collyer v Mid Essex Hospital Services NHS Trust (supra) is an example of a 'near *res ipsa*' case; i.e. one where there is a strong inference of negligence from the facts. However, it was not contended that the maxim applied in such cases and *HHJ Coe QC* said (*para. 142*): *"This is not to say that res ipsa loquitur applies. It does not apply here. Res ipsa loquitur has a very limited application in cases where each side calls evidence."*

In practice, therefore, a case based solely on *res ipsa* is unlikely to succeed at trial and is likely to require preparation on the usual basis.

<u>Causation of Damage</u>

> *"The outcome of litigation can be brutal and, despite having crossed many of the hurdles, the claim fails on the issue of causation"*

HHJ Kelly succinctly enunciated the importance of establishing causation thusly in *Richins v Birmingham Women's and Children's NHS Foundation Trust [2022] EWHC 847 (QB), para. 155)*. The importance of not considering it fully were set out by *Jay J* in *Saunderson & Others v Sonae Industria (UK) Ltd [2015] EWHC 2264 (QB)* at *para. 466*:

> *"There are clear lessons to be learned from this litigation. The Claimant's legal team should have worked out the science at a much earlier stage. Working on a reasonable best case scenario (as I have done), … they should have investigated whether the case stacked up. Instead, at all material times, the Claimant's legal team appears to have wanted to make a virtue out of uncertainty – perhaps because they clung to the notion that the case would settle. Alternatively, they believed that the judge would not be interested in the science, and/or they placed undue faith on the likely cogency of the lay evidence."*

Since we have the benefit of requiring expert evidence, it is inadvisable to leave this to them. It is for the courts to determine causation, not the experts and this often requires investigating factual, medical, legal and generic causation (e.g. *CNZ (supra)* gives a very detailed example of this).

(a) Basic Principles

It is necessary to establish both (a) the nature and extent of the injury resulting from the breach of duty and (b) what would have happened if no breach of duty had occurred. In *Tahir v Haringey Health Authority [1998] Lloyds Rep (Med) 104, Otton LJ* provided useful guidance on what the claimant must prove:

1. It is a question of past fact determined on the balance of probabilities (*Mallett v McGonagle [1970] AC 166*);

2. The Claimant will be fully compensated if they can prove that the breach was (a) the sole cause; (b) a substantial cause; or (c) it materially contributed to the injury (*Bonnington Castings v Wardlaw [1956] UKHL 1* and *McGhee v National Coal Board [1972] UKHL 7*);

3. However, if they fail to cross this threshold, then they will not recover any damages (*Barnett v Chelsea & Kensington Hospital Management Committee [1969] 1 QB 428*);

4. The lost chance of making a better recovery does not, by itself, amount to an actionable injury (*Hotson v East Berkshire District Health Authority [1988] UKHL 1*).

Accordingly, if the claimant can prove that there is more than a 50% chance of proving causation, they get 100% of the compensation. It is not reduced to reflect the risks of not proving it (although the parties may wish to take this into consideration when considering the overall litigation risk). Similarly, if the prospects of proving causation are below 50%, the value of the claim is nil.

(b) Factual causation

This often causes the most practical difficulties. The claimant must prove that 'but for' the breach of duty, they would not have suffered an injury. So, if they would have suffered the same injury anyway, their case fails. However, as long as the avoidable injury is more than *de minimis*, then factual causation is made out (*Cartledge v E Jobling & Sons Ltd [1963] AC 758, pp771-2 per Lord Reid*) and liability ought to be admitted (subject to considering legal causation). For an excellent breakdown of how judges analyse the evidence in respect of the causation of individual symptoms and the consequential losses arising therefrom, see *Snow v Royal United Hospitals Bath NHS Foundation Trust [2023] EWHC 42 (KB).*

The 'injury' suffered "... *does not mean simply a physical change, which is consistent with making one better, as in the case of a successful operation, or with being neutral, having no perceptible effect on one's health or capability" (Rothwell v Chemical & Insulating Co Ltd [2007] UKHL 39 per Lord Hoffmann, para. 7)*

This factual element should be sub-divided into those facts which can be proved using the factual evidence and those which can only be proved using expert opinion. So, 'factual causation' can also mean the part of causation proved using the documentary and lay witness evidence and 'medical causation' used to describe those facts requiring expert evidence. *CNZ (supra),* is an example of a case where the court explains how several different types of documentary evidence and the witness evidence was relevant to its fact-finding process.

It is important to keep the part each type of evidence plays clear in your own mind so that the case you are presenting does not become confused. The sequence of events that *did happen* can be drawn from the records and the witness statements whereas the events which *would have happened* come from asking the witnesses what they would have done in the absence of the errors made; from the documentary evidence of how the medical condition should be treated; and from the available treatments and facilities which were actually available to treat the condition. The experts can then base their opinions more persuasively rather than making assumptions which may be unfounded.

(c) Legal Causation

"The law requires that the wrongdoing is the effective or substantial cause of a loss before the defendant is liable to compensate for the loss by payment of damages. This concept used to be referred to as the "causa causans"…" (*Khan v Meadows [2021] UKSC 21 per Lords Hodge & Sales at para. 55*). The probable factual cause of the claimant's injury will become the legal cause if it does not fall foul of one of the control mechanisms limiting the *extent* to which the defendant should be held responsible:

(i) Remoteness & the 'Egg-Shell Skull' doctrine;

(ii) *Novus actus interveniens*; and

(iii) Contributory negligence.

In most clinical negligence cases, these concepts are more rarely encountered than issues over factual causation.

(i) Remoteness of Damage & the 'Egg-Shell Skull' doctrine.

The primary injury complained of is usually fairly clearly within the range of injuries which the clinician ought to have had in mind when a breach relating to treatment occurred. However, if the breach of duty is in respect of an administrative act or an alleged systems failure, then the primary injury sustained may not have been sufficiently proximate to the breach to fall within what a clinician in that situation would have considered to be reasonably foreseeable.

The issue is more likely to arise where it is asserted that the chance of the injury occurring is so small as to be negligible or further down the chain of causation in respect of some of the secondary injuries or consequential losses being alleged. Applying the basic test in *The Wagon Mound (No 1) [1961] UKPC 2* (that the damage must be reasonably foreseeable) is useful in delineating which injuries and losses should and should not be recoverable. It is also useful to remember that the direct consequence test (under *Re Polemis [1921] 3 KB 560*) is the wrong test to apply although lay clients often find that easier to understand. If a loss was directly caused by the breach but was not reasonably foreseeable to the clinician at the time of the breach, then it will be too remote and there will be no legal causation. Where the patient had an underlying condition which resulted in their suffering more harm than would usually occur, then the tortfeasor must pay for that additional damage even if this was not reasonably foreseeable. This is the 'egg-shell skull' doctrine (see *Smith v Leech Brain & Co Ltd. [1962] 2 QB 405 per Lord Parker CJ at 415*). The type of injury must be reasonably foreseeable but the amount of harm does not; the defendant takes his victim as he finds him. It is no defence to say that they should only be liable for the 'ordinary' injury.

(ii) *Novus Actus Interveniens*

New intervening causes are encountered where the claimant has suffered another injury after the negligent treatment. As *Collins MR* explained in *Dunham v Clare [1902] 2 KB 292*:

> "*The question of whether death resulted from the injury resolves itself into an inquiry into the chain of causation. If the chain of causation is broken by a novus actus interveniens, so that the old cause goes and a new cause is substituted for it, that is a new act which gives a fresh origin to the after consequences.*"

Accordingly, it is necessary to prove (a) the factual causative impact that both injuries have had (and will continue to have) on the claimant; and (b) the legal causative impact of whether the second injury has actually intervened to limit the impact of the first.

In cases where an unrelated, pre-existing injury has occurred, it is also necessary to establish the extent of the injury caused and what its prognosis was so the effects of your case can be properly distinguished. In *Zeb v Frimley Health NHS Trust [2016] EWHC 134 (QB)*, there was sufficient factual evidence for the court to conclude pre-trial that the impugned treatment was unlikely to have caused a more than *de minimis* injury. The 'but for' test applied as this is not an example of a new intervening cause (*para. 32*). If both events are tortious, then the second may be a supervening cause with joint liability (ibid, *para. 33*).

In cases where the medical treatment was needed to treat the effects of someone else's wrongdoing, then *Webb v Barclays Bank* (*supra*) applies. Assuming that the breach of duty test is met, then it is necessary to determine the extent to which each defendant's negligence contributed to the overall injury and whether the clinician's breach has added to the original injury sustained. Where the claimant was responsible for the 'intervening' injury, then the causative effect of this needs to be proved. In *Zeb (supra),* the evidence was sufficiently clear for this to occur pre-trial but in *Dunham (supra)* the case was remitted to the trial judge.

Reeves v Commissioner for the Police of the Metropolis [1997] EWCA Civ 2686 shows that the defendant cannot escape liability if the act was one they were supposed to protect against. If it was not, then it is necessary to look at the reasonableness of the claimant's actions leading to the injury in the context of the defendant's overall care. If they can truly be said to have been independent of that care or acted contrary to all good sense, then their conduct can properly be characterised as a true intervening cause (e.g. *M'Kew v Holland and Hannen Cubitts (Scotland) Ltd (1969) UKHL 12* and *Sabri-Tabrizi v Lothian Health Board (1998) SC 373*). However, misjudging the level of risk (in the absence of criminal or otherwise morally blameworthy intent) is unlikely to be sufficient (see *Hicks v Young [2015] EWHC 1144 (QB)*)

The issue can also arise in respect of multiple medical defendants or clinicians within the same Trust. Accordingly, the potential liability of all possible defendants will need to be carefully considered. If (for any reason) this is not done, there is another risk that the treatment provided by a third party will be later considered to break the chain of causation (possibly after limitation has expired). In *Wright v Cambridge Medical Group [2011] EWCA Civ 669* the court emphasised the need to allow the court to make the decision as to whether each of the defendants was liable not the parties. This does not sit well with the costs consequences of unsuccessfully suing co-defendants but the effects of this are now potentially ameliorated by QOCS protection (see Chapter 1).

(iii) Contributory Negligence

In most instances, although it may seem that a patient has contributed to their own injury in some way, the courts are very reluctant to agree especially where the claimant has sought the care of experienced clinicians. However, in *Zeb (supra)*, *Garnham J* was willing to find (if he was wrong that 'but for' test had not been met) that the claimant's failure to inform her doctor that the alleged medical condition had already been diagnosed abroad, he would have made a deduction of 50%. This case is also an example of where contributory negligence was alleged as an alternative to novus actus.

If it is alleged, then the burden of proving this shifts to the defendant and must be pleaded. Patients are often reliant on the professional expertise of the clinicians and ambiguity in the advice they have been given usually mitigates against a finding of contributory negligence (e.g. *Spencer v Hillingdon Hospital NHS Trust [2015] (supra))*.

However, *Pidgeon v Doncaster Health Authority (2002) Lloyds Rep Med 130* does show that the courts are prepared to make such a finding where there is evidence that the claimant acted unreasonably in failing to follow clear advice and that more than minimal harm resulted (it may be pleaded as an alternative to it also breaking the chain of causation). What is required is clear evidence and so any such assertion needs to be properly analysed. As such, contributory negligence remains the exception rather than the norm.

(d) Material Contribution & Material Increase in Risk

The strict application of the 'but for' test can cause injustice where a breach of duty causes harm but other competing factual causes exist which prevent it being proved that the breach probably caused either the injury complained of or all of it. In effect, it cannot be said to be the legal cause of the injury because it is not the probable factual cause – the claimant cannot prove that 'but for' the negligent treatment, they would not have suffered the avoidable injury. This particularly resonates in cases where the claimant is receiving different treatments with their own recognised risks; where they have several underlying medical conditions; or where a single injury has multiple contributing factors to it.

Bonnington Castings v Wardlaw [1956] (supra) permits causation to be proved where the 'negligent' event materially contributed to the overall injury. *Fairchild v Glenhaven Funeral Services [2002] UKHL 22* allows it to be proved where the breach of duty has materially increased the risk of the injury occurring. The key requirement is that the total injury cannot be divided up. However, few clinical cases qualify. In *CNZ (supra), Ritchie J* held that materially contributing to the overall risk of the injury *"does not directly apply to the claimant's case on proof of brain injury because brain damage caused by PHI* ['progressive haemorrhagic injury'] *is not a trigger disease and the material contribution to the risk test is not the relevant test" (para. 364)*.

In respect of causation of damage, in *Leigh v London Ambulance Service NHS Trust [2014] EWHC 286 (QB),* the material contribution test was applied where a negligent delay of about 1/3 of the total arrival time materially contributed to the injury sustained. Medical science was insufficient to prove that the delay caused the injury using the 'but for' test but the contribution made was more than negligible. The defendant was required to compensate for all of the injury.

Conversely, in *Reaney v University Hospital of North Staffordshire NHS Trust & Another [2015] EWCA Civ 1119,* material contribution did not apply on the facts of this case because the 'but for' test was sufficient to prove causation. The award of damages in a case where the negligent treatment worsened the consequences of an earlier, non-negligent injury is the value of the additional injury only. The clinician does not take the patient as he finds him (i.e. the egg-shell skull rule does not apply) where the original condition is not itself worsened by the breach of duty.

Material contribution is not universally popular as it is seen as an unjustified departure from the purity of the 'but for' test by some. In contrast, it is seen as the only means of avoiding the inherent injustice arising from the slavish application of the 'but for' test by others. In *Bailey v MOD [2008] EWCA Civ 883*. At *para. 46 Waller LJ said:*

> *"In a case where medical science cannot establish the probability that 'but for' an act of negligence the injury would not have happened but can establish that the contribution of the negligent cause was more than negligible, the 'but for' test is modified, and the claimant will succeed."* *This comes down on the side of the 'inherent injustice' school of thought.*

Williams v The Bermuda Hospitals Board [2016] UKPC 4 has bought additional clarity to the issue (although this is also not without its critics). The issue was whether the additional sepsis caused by a relatively short delay in treating appendicitis could be said to be the legal cause of the overall injury. A considerable amount of documentary evidence was adduced by the defendant and the NHSLA (which intervened due to perceived importance of this issue) in a concerted attempt to sideline *Bailey*. However, *Bonnington Castings* was applied and *Bailey* endorsed with the additional gloss that it did not, in fact, represent a departure from the 'but for' test at all. Instead, it is an example of a case where it was found that the totality of the injury had been caused by the defendant's negligently weakening the claimant's condition.

Not every case which could be a material contribution case is (e.g. *Arksey v Cambridge University Hospitals NHS Foundation Trust [2019] EWHC 1276 (QB), para. 99*). Much will depend on how the evidence develops. If the evidence shows that the totality of the injury was caused by either a negligent or a non-negligent cause (and not by a combination of the two mechanisms), then *Hotson* (supra) applies to defeat the claimant's case on normal 'but for' principles. In *DS v Northern Lincolnshire & Goole NHS Foundation Trust (Rev 1) [2016] EWHC 1246 (QB)*, a delay in delivering the baby of 6-9 minutes would have been insufficient to avoid his cognitive injuries. Where there are several possible factual causes, then material contribution cannot be used to prove that the negligent cause is the probable cause (*Wilsher v Essex Area Health Authority [1987] UKHL 11*).

The effect of failing to prove material contribution may be that only a far more modest causal link can be proved. In *Wardlaw v Farrar [2003] EWCA Civ 1719*, the trial judge found that the negligent delay had not materially contributed to the patient's death and so awarded damages only for the PSLA suffered during the week-long delay (*para. 5*).

In respect of causation of consequential losses further down the chain of causation, it seems that the defendant must adduce persuasive evidence to show how much of the injury was unavoidable if it wants to persuade the court to limit damages using material contribution on the basis that there would have been some injury caused in any event (*John v Central Manchester & Manchester Children's University Hospitals NHS Foundation Trust [2016] EWHC 407 (QB)*). At *paras. 97-100*, it was held that material contribution applies where it is impossible to precisely apportion the amount of injury the competing factors have had. If it is merely difficult to do this, then the unaltered 'but for' test must be used.

Material contribution does not have to apply to both causation of damage and consequential losses within the same case. In *CNZ (supra), Ritchie J* stated that *John* provides the correct test for brain injury cases caused by clinical negligence (*para. 382*). However, previous decisions did not provide the complete answer in the specific case *"... where the functional outcome cannot be apportioned or divided because none of them address it head on"* (*para. 381*). The specific question in *CNZ* was therefore framed as being *"... the claimant's cerebral palsy has been caused by one noxious factor: acute PHI* (progressive haemorrhagic injury), *and where the agreed medical evidence is that every minute of PHI caused increasing brain damage, the scientific gap is how to attribute the breach PHI (or each minute of brain damage) to each or any functional deficit"* (*para. 383*).

Accordingly, material contribution was not required to prove causation of damage: *"... the material contribution test is not appropriate in relation to deciding the issue whether the breach caused the brain injury because all of the experts in this case advised that, on the balance of probabilities, every minute of acute PHI caused damage to the claimant's brain cells after the 10th minute. I consider that the but for test is sufficient and is satisfied"* (*para. 389*).

In contrast, material contribution was required to fairly decide causation of consequential losses: *"... it was agreed by all of the experts that such proof was scientifically impossible. In my judgment a reasonable and fair quantification of the claimant's functional outcome on the but for scenario for each minute of negligently caused acute PHI is impossible not merely difficult. So the Claimant shall recover 100% of her damages" (para. 393).*

Williams also provides guidance on the related issue of 'doubling of the risk of injury'. This is another contentious issue in this area and is discussed further in Chapter 6. As the law presently stands, a doubled risk does not necessarily amount to a material contribution as the doubled risk may still be very small.

(e) <u>'Sherlock Holmes' Causation</u>

Where there are competing causes, the 'but for' test remains the correct test. If there were a finite number of known competing possible factual causes, it is not enough to eliminate all but one and then conclude that the remaining possibility was logically the 'most likely' of them and so that it must be the 'probable cause'. The 'but for' test cannot be met by a process of eliminating the possibilities; the factual cause must be proved to be more than 50% likely (see the line of authority arising from *The Popi M [1985] UKHL 15. Pollock v Cahill & Cahill [2015] EWHC 2260 (QB)* reiterates that the alternative factual causes must be genuine possibilities with some evidentiary support and that any expert evidence on causation cannot take the place of inconsistent factual evidence.

This was cited in respect of evaluating witness evidence (*q.v.* Chapter 6) in *Pomphrey v Secretary of State for Health & North Bristol NHS Trust [2019] EWHC (QB), 2019 Med LR Plus 25 (para. 33 per Tomlinson LJ)*. This paragraph is itself also cited in *Richins (supra, para. 94)*; *HTR v Nottingham University Hospitals NHS Foundation Trust [2021] EWHC 3228 (QB) (para. 83)*; and *Muyepa v MoD [2022] EWHC [2022] 2648 (KB), para. 11.*

The conclusion drawn is based on fully analysing the facts of the case; there is no rule of law stating that the 'most likely' remaining cause is 'the likely' cause of the injury (*Datec Electronics Holdings Ltd. v UPS Ltd [2007] UKHL 23)*. Applying this, in *O'Connor v The Pennine Acute*

Hospitals NHS Trust [2015] EWCA Civ 1244, Jackson LJ said (at *para. 64*): *"The mere elimination of A, B and C is not itself sufficient. The court must step back and, looking at all the evidence, consider whether on the balance of probabilities D is proved to be the cause."* In *Collyer v Mid Essex Hospital Services NHS Trust [2019] (supra), HHJ Coe QC* preferred this approach in rejecting the contention that the fact that a claimant had suffered an injury which had never been seen before and so would not usually happen with the exercise of reasonable skill and care was itself powerful evidence of negligence. The claimant must still prove that the impugned treatment was the probable cause of their injury *(paras. 142-3)*.

Ide v ATB Sales Ltd [2008] EWCA Civ 424 and *Graves v Brouwer [2015] EWCA Civ 595* endorse this approach. *Graves* also demonstrates that it is also insufficient to attempt to show that *res ipsa* provides a method of proving the 'likely' cause; that the instructed experts must consider all of the potential competing causes; and that the foreseeability of the injury being guarded against and the steps which were in fact taken to prevent it occurring mitigate against that potential cause being elevated to the status of the legal cause.

Accordingly, the law does not support *refutation* as a means of proving legal causation. It is important to remember this when assessing expert evidence because, in science, refutation is *"an effective way of reducing the number of alternatives to be considered before seeking additional evidence"* (https://www.epa.gov/caddis-vol1/about-eliminating-improbable-causes).

(f) Gregg v Scott

Gregg v Scott [2005] UKHL 2 primarily concerned the treatment of cancer but is also useful in causation generally. In essence, where the claimant's survival chances have been reduced by the breach of duty, it is necessary to prove that these have been lowered from above 50% to below 50%. If they have, then the 'but for' test has been satisfied; otherwise, it has not (even of the lost chance is substantial, say 45%).

In assessing this survival chance, particularly when applying it to non-cancer cases, it is important to bear in mind that the true survival chance may be the aggregated chance of survival from more than one treatment method. For example, it may be necessary to add the survival chance had the breach of duty not occurred to the survival chance of the average patient with that condition. In this context, published survival rates in clinical studies may be misleading because they are not necessarily comparing like with like – the claimant may fall within only a small proportion of the patients studied given the particular facts of the case you are dealing with. It is also important to remember that the definition of a 'cure' can well be different in non-cancer and/or non-fatal cases.

Gregg v Scott effectively prevents recovery in a substantial number of scenarios where the breach of duty has increased the risk of death (or, arguably, harm). In a relatively small tranche of cancer cases, however, it may possible to circumvent it at the cost of a significant proportion of the full value of the case. In some types of cancer, medical science has advanced to the point where the cancer's progression has been studied in sufficient detail for life expectancy to be predicted quite accurately. In *JD v Mather [2012] EWHC 3063 (QB)*, recovery was allowed for the reduced life expectancy (as opposed to loss of survival chances) of 3½ years. However, this was not allowed in *Oliver v Williams [2013] EWHC 600 (QB)* because the available statistical data for the type of cancer in that case was not as comprehensive as in *JD*. The value of these claims is effectively a small proportion of the value of the loss of survival claim reflecting the much shorter period and so proportionality considerations do apply to them.

(g) Chester v Afshar

In *Chester v Afshar (supra)* their Lordships considered whether it was necessary for a claimant to prove that they would *never* have had the operation had they been properly consented to it. The 'but for' test is satisfied in the sense that the claimant may be able to prove that they would not have had the operation if they had been warned of the risk of this injury occurring. However, it is not satisfied if the failure to warn of a risk which then materialises (in the absence of further negligence) as it would have arisen at any future point in time when the surgery was eventually performed. The risk was inherent in the operation itself and so did not change as a result of waiting. Accordingly, reliance was placed on the policy consideration that *"The function of the law is to enable rights to be vindicated and to provide remedies when duties have been breached. Unless this is done the duty is a hollow one, stripped of all practical force and devoid of all content"* (*per Lord Hope, para. 35*).

The main practical consideration is proving that the claimant would have delayed the operation if they had been told of the risk. The practical difficulties are well-illustrated in the cases since *Chester* and have been repeated post-*Montgomery (supra)*. In a nutshell, the lower the risk of the complication arising is, the harder it is for the claimant to persuade the court that they would have chosen to take the time to think about whether to take it. In *Correia v University Hospital of North Staffordshire NHS Trust [2017] EWCA Civ 356, Simon LJ* commented (at *para. 28*): *"... it seems to me that if a claimant is to rely on the exceptional principle of causation established by Chester v. Afshar, it is necessary to plead the point and support it by evidence."* It is often necessary for the claimant to be able to point to some very specific reason to support their assertion (e.g. *Duce v Worcestershire Acute Hospitals NHS Trust [2018] EWCA Civ 1307*) and for this to be supported by factual or medical evidence (e.g. *Diamond* (supra)).

If this hurdle is overcome, then the defendant is liable for the avoidable losses caused by the avoidable injuries.

(h) <u>'Scope of Duty' Cases</u>

There is a subset of cases where the losses appear to be caused by the breach of duty in the sense that they would not have occurred had the breach and initial injury not occurred. They tend to be 'indirectly' related to the breach of duty which leads to the possibility that they could fall outside of the impugned treatment or consultation's reasonable purpose. Applying *Chester v Afshar (supra)* logically leads to the defendant potentially being liable for all of the reasonably foreseeable avoidable losses 'but for' the negligence.

However, *Khan v Meadows (supra)* confirmed that these losses must be within the scope of the duty of care which was owed by the defendant (*South Australian Asset Management Corporation v York Montague Ltd "SAAMCO" [1997] AC 191*). It is necessary to consider the connection between purpose of the treatment or consultation, the risks associated with it and the harm, injury and/or losses said to flow from the breach of duty. These are matters of fact which need to be ascertained and proved. The narrower or more specific the purpose was, the less likely it is that the connection to 'indirect' losses will be strong enough to impose liability.

In *Khan, Lords Hodge and Sales* set out "*... a helpful model for analysing the place of the scope of duty principle in the tort of negligence... . ... Application of this analysis gives the value of the claimant's claim for damages in accordance with the principle that the law in awarding damages seeks, as far as money can, to place the claimant in the position he or she would have been absent the defendant's negligence*" (*para. 28*). To paraphrase, the six questions are:

1. Actionability: Is the harm actionable in negligence?
2. Scope of duty: What are the risks of harm which the law requires the defendant to guard against?
3. Breach: Did the defendant breach this duty of care by an act or omission?
4. Factual causation: Is the loss in question a consequence of the act or omission?
5. 'Duty nexus': Is there a sufficient link ('nexus') between the risk of harm, the harm suffered and the specific duty owed?
6. 'Legal responsibility': Is a particular element of the harm irrecoverable because it is too remote; it is a novus actus; there has been a failure to mitigate it; or the claimant ought to have reasonably avoided it?

These can be considered in a different order or together (*para. 29*). This also helps to show how the specific scope of duty questions (2 and 5) fit into the wider analysis of a case.

Although the decision in *Khan* was unanimous, *Lords Burrows* and *Leggatt* also gave judgments which did not specifically endorse this six-question approach.

Lord Burrows (who emphasised that his judgment should be read in conjunction with his lengthier opinion in the concurrent appeal in M*anchester Building Society v Grant Thornton UK LLP [2021] UKSC 20)* set our three principles covering how to apply *SAAMCO* to the facts of this clinical negligence case (at *para. 77*). To paraphrase:

1. The specific purpose of the information advice or treatment was crucial. Here, the evidence showed that the claimant had sought advice from her GP only about the risk of her being a carrier of haemophilia.

2. The purpose informs the court about the scope of the duty of care. This meant that the defendant should fairly be responsible for the risks of the child being born with haemophilia but the mother retained responsibility for other risks associated with pregnancy (such as autism).

3. SAAMCO involves asking the counterfactual question: would the loss have been incurred if no breach occurred? If the answer is unchanged, the loss is outside of the scope of the duty of care. If the mother not been a haemophilia carrier then she would still have given birth to an autistic child.

He summarised five points from his judgement in *Manchester Building Society* (at *para. 71*). To paraphrase:

1. The SAAMCO/scope of duty principle covers asking whether a factually proved loss is within the scope of the professional's duty of care.

2. It is usually regarded as being distinct from remoteness of damage and *novus actii*.

3. The scope of the duty is a question of law underpinned by the policy of achieving a fair and reasonable allocation between the parties of risk of the overall loss that has occurred.

4. The counterfactual test operates as a useful cross-checking mechanism to achieve this.

5. There is no rigid distinction between 'information' and 'advice'. The more limited the information or advice that is provided to the claimant, the more useful the counterfactual test is likely to be.

Lord Leggatt also refers the reader to his judgment in *Manchester Building Society* (at para. 89). To paraphrase:

1. The rationale is that it would be unfair or unreasonable to impose liability for adverse consequences which would have occurred even if no breach had occurred (*para. 90*).

2. Context is important. There were a number of relevant or potentially factors which were likely to influence the claimant's decision (including personal, social, economic and medical) A defendant is not necessarily responsible for all of these without evidence (*para. 91*).

3. There was no causal link between the purpose of the claimant's concern (possessing the haemophilia gene) and the cause of the 'indirect' losses (autism) (*para. 93*).

4. If there is such a causal link, the counterfactual question then to be asked is whether the same loss would have been suffered in the absence of negligence (*para. 94*).

5. The application of scope of duty to other types of cases (such as surgical errors) has not yet been determined (*para. 96*).

6. He understands 'duty nexus' to be analogous to 'causal connection' in cases involving advice or information provision (*para. 97*).

In *Khan* itself, the claimant could recover the costs associated with her child having haemophilia but not the far higher costs of associated with his autism even though both were avoidable applying the 'but for' test and reasonably forseeable. In practice, the distinction will often not always be as clear cut as their Lordships felt it was in *Khan*.

In *Kennedy v Frankel [2019] (supra)* the defendant sought to argue for the first time at trial that the claimant's impulse control disorder fell within the scope of the duty of care whilst her subsequent psychosis did not. *Yip J* deferred these considerations to the quantum stage with a direction that the parties could return to court if they were unable to resolve them proportionately. Accordingly, *Yip J* appears to have seen this issue as part of the causation of consequential losses rather than causation of a more than minimal injury which prevented liability being imposed. Accordingly, taking *Khan* and *Kennedy* together, this issue will not prevent early admissions of liability being made for the part of the injury and loss that was within the scope of the duty of care. The advice provided to undergo specific treatment then led to that treatment; both of which appear to have caused the avoidable injury.

Whilst we await further decisions, a practical approach to this issue is to combine these *Montgomery*, *Chester* and *SAAMCO* issues into your analysis of the factual evidence contained in the medical records and in preparing your witness statements. The experts can be asked to comment on this evidence to better inform the position but their evidence is not determinative. These issues can then be canvassed in the Letters of Claim and Response thereby maximising the opportunity to consider them pre-action and settle liability proportionately.

(i) <u>Pure Psychiatric Injuries Cases</u>

In some cases, the breach of duty causes a psychiatric injury but no physical one. These cases have additional control mechanisms governing whether the psychiatric injury was legally caused by the breach. The starting point remains *McLoughlin v O'Brian & Others [1983] 1 AC 40.* The psychiatric injury must be a recognised illness arising out of a shocking event arising from the breach of duty. The claimant must be someone of 'reasonable fortitude'. It is possible that hindsight does apply to whether the risk of harm was reasonably foreseeable (*Page v Smith [1995] UKHL 7*, per *Lord Lloyd*). The psychiatric illness must have been reasonably foreseeable, and this gives rise to the differing positions between 'primary' and 'secondary' victims.

(i) <u>Primary Victims</u>

A primary victim in a clinical negligence case is required to prove that a sudden stressor event has caused the psychiatric injury. The stressor must have arisen suddenly from the negligent treatment itself rather than gradually from it or in dealing with the consequences of it. The leading cases remain *Alcock v Chief Constable of South Yorkshire Police [1991] UKHL 5 (per Lord Ackner)* and *Page v Smith (supra).*

The difficulties which tend to arise in practice are more to do with differing expert views on what has caused the psychiatric injury and when the stressor occurred. This is especially so if it is the apprehension of suffering physical injury which has caused the psychiatric injury given that the recognised risks of the operation are explained in advance. It should be borne in mind that a seemingly innocuous breach of duty can lead to a serious psychiatric injury and that not everyone wants to, or immediately does, seek medical treatment or counselling.

This can cause difficulties as the apprehension of harm needs to be immediate. For example, in *Harford v Electricity Supply Board [2021] IECA 112*, the Irish Court of Appeal allowed an appeal where the trial judge had erroneously found that the stressor arose from a sudden 'shock' at the time of the breach (when the danger was being faced). In fact, the stressor had arisen more gradually starting approximately 8 hours or so as the claimant came to appreciate how close to death he had been at the time when he realised the error. Although the claimant relied on an Australian High Court case which supports the contrary position (*Tame v New South Wales; Annets v Australian Pty. Ltd [2002] HCA 35, 211 CLR 317*), this does not represent the law in England & Wales (or Eire).

(ii) Secondary Victims

These are close relatives of the person who was injured as a result of the allegedly negligent treatment. In theory, liability may arise where there is no primary victim (*Alcock v Chief Constable of South Yorkshire Police (supra) (per Lord Oliver at 15th para.)*. A duty of care does not automatically arise in these cases and so should not be assumed. Foreseeability of injury alone does not automatically give rise to the duty of care because there are potentially many people who could then fall within it. Public policy is therefore against allowing this. Five control mechanisms were set down in *Alcock* which nowadays can be summarised as follows:

1. There was a close relationship of love and affection between the primary and secondary victims;

2. The stressor was shocking, sudden and unexpected;

3. The psychiatric injury arose from witnessing the traumatic injury to the primary victim;

4. The secondary victim either witnessed the negligent treatment or its immediate aftermath; and

5. There must be a close temporal connection between the injury and the secondary victim's perception of it.

These five elements *"apply as much to clinic negligence cases as they do to accident cases"* (*Paul & Another v The Royal Wolverhampton NHS Trust & Other Appeals [2022] EWCA Civ 12, per Sir Geoffrey Vos, MR at paras. 12 & 96*). Each of these elements must be proved and elements (iv) & (v) can be taken together as requiring sufficient 'proximity' between the secondary victim and the tortfeasor. Although the 'event' can be stretched to cover a period of treatment (see *North Glamorgan NHS Trust v Walters*

[2002] EWCA Civ 1792), the nature and timing of it necessarily varies from case to case. In practice, it remains very difficult to prove this. *Paul* is due to be heard in the Supreme Court in May 2023.

Taylor v A Novo (UK) Ltd (supra) emphasised that the breach of duty may cause a distinct injury to the primary victim such that the secondary victim's psychiatric injury is not part of the seamless series of events envisaged in *Walters. Taylor v Somerset Health Authority [1993] PIQR 262* reached the same conclusion in the clinical negligence context. *Paul (supra)* reconsidered these elements and the relevant authorities and reached the conclusion that *Taylor v A Novo (supra)* precludes recovery where the secondary victim's psychiatric injury was caused by *"a separate horrific event removed in time from the original negligence, accident or first horrific event" (para. 96 per Sir Geoffrey Vos, MR)*. As to what *Taylor v A Novo (supra)* says about the length of the interval between the two events, *"the ultimately decisive feature was simply that there had been an interval of time between the breach of duty, whether or not it occasioned injury at the time, and the shocking event"* (*Paul (supra) at para. 104 per Underhill LJ*). Interestingly, the Court of Appeal felt that *Taylor v A Novo* merits reconsideration by the Supreme Court.

Until then, Wild & Another v Southend University Hospital NHS Foundation Trust [2014] EWHC 4053 (QB), Brock v Northampton General Hospital NHS Trust [2014] EWHC 4244 (QB), Baker & Others v Cambridgeshire & Peterborough NHS Foundation Trust [2015] EWHC 609 (QB), Owers v Medway NHS Foundation Trust [2015] EWHC 2363 (QB), Wells v University Hospitals Southampton NHS Foundation Trust [2015] EWHC 2263 (QB) and *Shorter v Surrey & Sussex Healthcare NHS Trust [2015] EWHC 614 (QB)* all also demonstrate the difficulties that claimants have in proving these elements at trial and that none of them can be safely ignored post-*Taylor*. In *YAH v Medway NHS Foundation Trust [2019] EWHC 2964 (QB)*, the claimant succeeded as a primary victim but would have failed as a secondary victim because her shock did not amount to the legal definition of shock under *Alcock* (at *para. 86*)

What amounts to a 'shocking' stressor event was explored in *King v Royal United Hospitals Bath NHS Foundation Trust [2021] EWHC 1576 (QB)*.

A distinction was made between events which meet the ordinary dictionary definition of 'horrific' or 'shocking' and those which go beyond this. Only the latter is likely to qualify. In this case, a father who was told without warning that his newborn son was seriously ill and then witnessing his death was something which, whilst 'horrifying', fell within the range of possibilities a father could reasonably expect to encounter (*para. 41*).

Pursuing a secondary victim claim may well result in the case being struck out (as originally occurred in *Paul & Others v The Royal Wolverhampton NHS Trust (Rev 1) [2019] (supra)* and so both sides ought to plan for this.

The best practical guidance that can be given is to focus on carefully analysing the factual evidence against a careful review of the current law before going to the expense of obtaining expert evidence (which is unlikely to assist in proving whether the legal tests are met but will assist the court in fully understanding the triggering events of the condition involved). *RE & Others v Calderdale & Huddersfield NHS Foundation Trust [2017] EWHC 824 (QB)* did succeed at trial and otherwise unreported settlements can also be found online.

<u>Quantum</u>

A detailed exposition of quantum issues can be found in other excellent practitioner textbooks. In order to know how much you can reasonably and proportionately spend on dealing with the issues of breach and causation you need to be able to put a fairly accurate value on the case from the outset. This also has the benefit of helping your client's expectations and setting an appropriate reserve on the case.

A useful guideline is to remind yourself that every claimant is entitled to full (100%) compensation for the *avoidable* injury suffered The compensation award needs to attempt to put them back in the position they were before they were injured (see *Wells v Wells [1999] AC 345* at *382-3* and the authorities referred to therein). Accordingly, any item of loss needs to be assessed against this standard first rather than accepting it at face value.

Next, it is useful to keep in mind the general principles governing recoverability which have developed at common law. To summarise, these are:

1. Whilst each loss claimed must be caused by the breach of duty, the defendant takes his victim as he finds him. Applying the tests referred to above, any loss which was reasonably foreseeable is recoverable even if it is disproportionate to the injury suffered.

2. However, it must still have been reasonable to incur that item and amount of loss to recover all of it. The loss itself can be 'proportionate' under the egg-shell skull rule but the amount can be 'disproportionate' if the cost was unusually high or cheaper alternatives were unreasonably ignored (so the lowest cost alternative is not automatically the most reasonable choice). The loss is net of any necessary deductions is the recoverable amount. A deduction covering the contingency (or risk of any item being incurred in any event) is appropriate.

3. In terms of past losses, the item must actually have been incurred whereas, for future losses, the item just needs to have a more than speculative chance of being needed. If it does, then the whole of that item's value is the starting point, not the percentage chance of it actually arising. Once that is known, the percentage chance of it being incurred is applied to that cost.

4. Although claimants are expected to attempt to mitigate their losses, where doing so worsens the position, those additional costs are recoverable by the claimant (and the defendant gets the benefit of any reduction resulting from the mitigation itself).

5. Interest is awarded on past losses in order to compensate the claimant for being kept out of their money. The period over which this is payable and the rate of interest is at the discretion

of the court and so delays to the progress of the litigation are relevant considerations. Conversely, future losses are discounted in order to take proper account of the fact that the claimant is receiving the damages early and so double recovery would otherwise result. The law assumes that the claimant will make up the deduction for accelerated receipt of these items by investing them at a rate of return at least equivalent to the discount rate (currently -0.25%) over the term each item of future loss is needed. Pursuant to the *Civil Liability Act 2018 Sch 1A4(3)(c)-(d)* it is now assumed that the ordinarily prudent investor does accept a 'low risk' in their investments and so will not necessarily invest only in Index-Linked Gilts issued by the government (a 'very low risk' investment). The outcome of the government's January 2023 consultation into multiple discount rates may result in further changes (https://www.gov.uk/government/consultations/personal-injury-discount-rate-exploring-the-option-of-a-dualmultiple-rate/personal-injury-discount-rate-exploring-the-option-of-a-dualmultiple-rate).

6. Some losses are irrecoverable if either criminal law or public policy has said so. It is also the case that the deliberate exaggeration of a loss or malingering by the claimant could prevent the full recovery of those losses. With the introduction of the concept of fundamental dishonesty, however, there is now the significant risk that the entire claim would fail.

Accordingly, the burden of proof applies as much to each item of loss as it does to proving that an avoidable injury has occurred at all. It is helpful to distinguish between the basic 'causation of injury' and the 'causation of consequential losses' to avoid making the mistake that proving the injury equates with proving the losses arising from it.

All past and future losses must be proved to be reasonably incurred or needed and this requires evidence. It takes a full and proper investigation of the facts of each case and careful consideration of that evidence in order to ensure that the court can reach a reasonable conclusion as to how much compensation is needed to put the claimant back in the position they would have been in had they not been injured. As the test is one of reasonableness, any ambiguity in the evidence or case law tends to create a broader reasonable range of settlement rather than a narrower one.

In this context, 'item of loss' denotes both individual medical symptoms and financial losses and expenses. Accordingly, this approach applies as much to proving that any given case comparator is the closest to your case as they do to the individual heads of special damage.

'Reasonableness' in terms of quantum must be determined by the evidence in each individual case because the judge is ultimately being asked to make a series of findings of facts. These facts will be assessed by the specific support provided for them in the medical records, expert evidence, witness statements and documentary evidence covering the factors mentioned above. This includes all relevant factors, including evidence of the claimant's pre-negligence history and future wishes.

However, as seen in the previous chapter, 'reasonableness' in terms of costs recovery is subordinate to proportionality and 'necessity' is disregarded entirely. The practical difficulty that this causes is recovering the costs of investigating and pursuing quantum 'reasonably' where the overall value of the case is not increased by a sufficiently 'proportionate' amount. The substantive law has not been reduced to account for this change in the procedural rules.

The issue is less pressing in catastrophic injury cases than in more modestly valued ones, however, the defendant is justifiably entitled to expect the claimant to prove all aspects of their case. The suggested starting point should always be cross-referencing the claimant's comments with their friends and family and the entries in the contemporaneous medical records. Commonly used ways of then obtaining the necessary supporting evidence cost-effectively include the use of questionnaires, diaries, keeping all receipts, internet research and utilising national statistics before seeking the input of the various experts. However, it should always be remembered that the base evidence needs to be admissible and so needs to be included in witness statements or exhibited thereto after standard disclosure.

In appropriately high-value cases, there is a tendency to assume that periodical payments are mandatory or that a particular care regime or life pathway is inevitable. It must always be borne in mind that the wishes of the injured claimant provides powerfully persuasive evidence and should not be allowed to be undermined unintentionally in the attempt to obtain the fairest settlement.

The evidence obtained can then be used to assess and explain the relative complexity of the quantum investigations both for the benefit of the claimant and the court. Often, the minutiae of a quantum claim makes a considerable difference to the claimant's quality of life even where the cost of obtaining that amount appear to be prima facie disproportionate to the amount claimed. By focussing on the likely supporting evidence at an early stage in the case, you can avoid falling into the trap of slavishly following a detailed checklist covering all possible losses when only a few are applicable. Such checklists are, however, very useful in maximising damages and so getting as close as possible to the goal of putting the claimant back in the position they would have been in had the Defendant not negligently injured them. For example, *Whittington Hospital NHS Trust v XX [2020] UKSC 14* permits the cost of commercial surrogacy abroad. However, *Lady Hale* made it clear that claimants must prove that the use of a surrogate, the extent of the surrogacy costs, the arrangements for the foreign surrogacy and the decision not to use non-commercial surrogacy in the UK are all reasonable on the facts of their case (*paras. 40-54*).

Fundamental Dishonesty

Although this has not yet become a major battleground (as it has in some areas of PI litigation), it cannot be safely ignored by clinical negligence practitioners.

Wright v Satellite Information Services Ltd [2018] EWHC 812 (QB) makes it abundantly clear that the claimant must understand the factual basis for each head of loss being claimed. Accordingly, careful advice is required to ensure this before the schedule of special damages is signed and the current, correct statement of truth reduces the scope for misunderstandings still further.

The problem is what amounts to 'fundamental dishonesty' has increasingly moved away from 'intentional fraud'. In *Ivey v Genting Casinos (UK) Ltd (t/a/ Crockfords) [2017] UKSC 67*, the test was set rather low: *"Dishonesty is a simple, if occasionally imprecise, English word"* (per *Lord Hughes at para. 63*) and the claimant's own honest belief that their error was not dishonest does not mean that the conduct itself was also honest (*para. 75*).

In *Ivey*, the impugned conduct was cheating at cards. However, in *Wright*, it was that the claimant acknowledged under cross-examination that his care expert had significantly overstated the amount of care he required. At *para. 27, Yip, J* said *"... [The schedule] needs to be supported by sufficient narrative to explain the case being presented by the claimant."* At *para. 28*: *"Claimants will be fixed with knowledge of and taken to certify the truth of its contents. It is very important that the lawyers draft the schedule in such a way that the facts to which the claimant is attesting are clear. Failing to do so is failing in their duty both to the client and the court."* At *para. 29*, schedules *"... need to be drafted by lawyers with sufficient experience and skill to properly present the claim as it will be presented at trial. [This case] highlight[s] the dangers of treating the schedule as little more than a number crunching exercise."* Although the evidence showed that the claimant had not understood the schedule and so was not fundamentally dishonest, this is unlikely to be the case again following *Yip, J*'s trenchant comments.

The implications of a finding of fundamental dishonesty might not be immediately obvious from the wording of the *Criminal Justice and Courts Act 2015, s57(1)(b)* says that the standard is the civil balance of probabilities (not the criminal one) and can be made in respect of either the primary case or a related claim. If so, under *s57(2)*, the primary claim must be dismissed (unless, unusually, this creates substantial injustice) and this includes the elements where the claimant has not been fundamentally dishonest (*s57(3)*). *Howlett v Davies [2017] EWCA Civ 1696* illustrates that QOCS protection is lost and the defendant's costs order can be enforced more easily. On top of that, the claimant can expect to face separate proceedings for contempt of court and imprisonment. *CPR 1998, Rule 81.9* and the *Contempt of Court Act 1981, s14* provide for a maximum penalty of 2 years imprisonment and/or a fine, confiscation of assets and any other penalty allowed by the law.

In *North Bristol NHS Trust v White [2022] EWHC 1313 (QB)*, committal proceedings were brought under *CPR 1998, Rule 32.4* and provides a useful guide as to the process which is followed. The defendant received an immediate 6-month prison sentence. The same length of imprisonment was imposed in *Calderdale NHS Trust v Metcalfe [2021] EWHC 611 (QB)*. In *George Eliot Hospital NHS Trust v Elder [2019] EWHC 1813 (QB)*, the sentence was 5 months imprisonment. In *Calderdale NHS Trust v Atwell [2018] EWHC 2537 (QB)* and *Hull NHS Trust v Colley [2022] EWHC 854 (QB)*, suspended sentences were considered fair. Relevant features of these cases include exaggerated case valuations or symptoms which proved to be significantly inconsistent with social media or surveillance evidence, documents signed by statements of truth and/or expert evidence.

LOCOG v Sinfield [2018] EWHC 51 (QB) shows that the value of the related claim does not have to go to the root of the case to trigger these consequences and peripheral amounts can be sufficient.

In light of this, it is prudent to advise claimants of these consequences and fully understand what publicly accessible information they are self-publishing on social media about themselves early in the case (e.g. *Sammut v The Dudley Group NHS Foundation Trust (2019) (QB, unreported, 12KBW website)*).

Carefully interrogating the evidence as a whole; cross-referencing it with your client's pleaded case; and identifying and planning for the effects of a change in the evidence is the best way to head off these problems. Repeating this process against any allegations subsequently made then makes it more likely that you will identify relevant weaknesses in them. Not all allegations of fundamental dishonesty are sustainable.

In *Preater v Betsi Cadwaladr University Health Board (2022) (unreported, Wrexham County Court),* the allegation failed despite social media and video surveillance evidence where the trial judge was able to weigh up all of the specific evidence for and against it. Similarly, in *Elgamal v Westminster City Council [2021] EWHC 2510 (QB)*, it was emphasised that there must be a causal link between the exaggeration and the reduction in the claim's value. At *para. 124*: *"The claim has not been shown to be related to the exaggerations relied upon by the defendant. In any event, the experts had agreed upon the need for the relevant care and assistance, and the claimant advanced a case based upon that evidence. The substantial reduction… was not a consequence of the failure of the claimant's case where there had been exaggeration"* (*per Jacobs J*).

When doing so, remember that all of the evidence is relevant. In *Roberts v Kesson & Another [2020] EWHC 521 (QB)*, the claimant accepted in cross-examination it that parts of his first witness statement were dishonest. *Jay J* held that *"… the claimant would have persisted his false claim had his insurers not called him out" (para. 56)*. In *Walkden v Drayton Manor Park Ltd [2021] EWHC 2056 (QB)*, the adverse findings were upheld notwithstanding that the trial judge had given permission to appeal his findings of fact on the degree of exaggeration and his finding of fundamental dishonesty. *Michael v I E & D Hurford Ltd & Another [2021] EWHC 2318 (QB) "[t]he case turned on the credibility of the [claimant]… This case is an illustration of the importance of live evidence and the power of the trial process to establish the facts and ensure a just outcome for both parties"* (*per Stacey J, para. 56*).

To summarise, asking the right questions of your client when preparing their case, ensuring that they understand the importance of their claims being congruent with their lifestyles and planning for possible changes to the evidence are key habits to develop.

Conclusion

The increasingly powerful downward pressures on legal costs in clinical negligence claims genuinely risks causing injustice. If no one wants to pay for a reasonable investigation of a case because it is 'simple' or 'low value' it seems likely that meritorious cases will fail, unmeritorious cases succeed, and cases will be over- or undervalued by lawyers on both sides. The courts risk being burdened with poorly prepared cases.

As the burden of proof remains unchanged, it remains necessary for the parties' lawyers to apply the traditional tests to breach of duty; causation of damage and consequential losses; and quantification. This requires a thorough understanding of how to apply these complex legal principles practically in an increasingly time-constrained environment.

A reasonable approach to adopt is to focus on developing daily actions and behaviours which lead to habitually improved practice in these areas:

1. Focussing your investigations on the central allegations;

2. Testing these central allegations against all the factual and expert evidence;

3. Using this to provide clear advice to your client on strategy and settlement; and

4. Closing cases which do not continue to have sufficient prospects of success.

Having set the foundation out in this chapter, the remainder of this book examines how to apply them to the various stages of a clinical negligence case from initial investigations to trial or settlement.

* NB: At the time of finalising this book, the Supreme Court's decision in *The Trustees of Barry Congregation of Jehovah's Witnesses v BXB [2021] EWCA Civ 356* is awaited. This may affect the law in respect of whether a relationship akin to employment exists to justifiably impose vicarious liability.

CHAPTER THREE

PRE-ACTION PREPARATION

<u>Introduction</u>

The previous two chapters set the framework for clinical negligence cases. Although the substantive law remains as complex as ever, costs must be kept reasonable and proportionate if the loser is to be made to pay a reasonable proportion of them. These competing interests are not easily reconciled in all but the highest value cases.

The pre-action period needs to be used to build a lean, efficient and winnable case by:

1. Identifying those cases which are likely to succeed and those which are not;

2. Planning cases effectively by clearly and accurately identifying the central issues;

3. Obtaining a clear indication of your opponent's case and narrowing the remaining issues to be litigated; and

4. Attempting to negotiate a settlement before issuing proceedings.

The reason for doing each item of work needs to be clearly recorded. Remember that 'necessity' is irrelevant to costs recovery and 'reasonableness' is trumped by 'proportionality'. The overall approach to the investigation and preparation of your case needs to be objectively proportionate to the *CPR 1998, Rule 44.3(3)* criteria of value, complexity, importance or the conduct of your opponent. Pursuing investigations which are reasonable but disproportionate is inefficient even if technically correct (see Chapter 1).

Accordingly, the period between initial instructions and commencing court proceedings is vital to the success of your client's case. The quality of the evidence obtained during this period heavily influences the outcome. Front-loading a case affords the claimant the opportunity to produce a watertight case before serving a letter of claim or being subject to costs budgeting. Conversely, clinical governance and the duty of candour gives the defendant the opportunity to investigate the circumstances of the adverse incident thoroughly and produce decisive evidence before the claimant even seeks legal advice.

Allowing for the stages in the *Pre-Action Protocol for the Resolution of Clinical Disputes*, claimants should be aiming to have sufficient evidence to issue proceedings in many cases about 10-12 months after instructions and defendants should be in a position to respond to served proceedings at that point. Proportionality is a two-way street; what one party does is likely to impact upon the other.

Basic Approach

The starting point is to accurately assess every new case by:

(a) Applying the substantive legal tests on breach of duty, causation of damage and limitation to the facts you are presented with; and

(b) Forming a view on whether the case can be run at a proportionate cost to value.

Once the central issues have been understood, the core factual evidence can be properly assessed and then expert evidence obtained on liability issues. At this point, the skeleton of the case is known and a decision can be taken as to how best to deal with the other side.

Once your opponent's case has been set out, it becomes desirable to consider what the likely settlement parameters are and to open negotiations. These will typically be aimed at narrowing the issues to be litigated or at an outright settlement. If negotiations break down, then a reasoned decision as to whether court proceedings should be commenced or whether further investigations are needed can be properly taken.

Risk Assessment

The quality of your initial risk assessment fundamentally influences how the case is run. Your aim should be to clearly identify the allegations on breach of duty and causation of damage and to assess whether the impugned treatment is likely to have been sub-standard and caused avoidable harm. It should not be to cover off every possible outcome or to postpone a decision on these central issues pending further evidence.

Every law student who has passed tort possesses the necessary basic legal knowledge to make this decision. What comes with experience is having the confidence to apply this knowledge and of having a greater chance of having run a case on similar facts to the one being assessed. In the absence of such experience, the ability to find and apply the relevant treatment standards and recognised risks of any given treatment is important.

The initial instructions provided are often of variable quality because non-lawyers have little real understanding of the relevant legal tests. Lay claimants and lawyers alike are unlikely to understand the underlying medicine. Given downwards costs pressures, the claimant's lawyers need to know the likely prospects of success and a proportionate and progressive investigation plan before the case is accepted. Given the wide availability of QOCS protection (*q.v.*), defendant lawyers need to assess whether their client is likely to be facing a substantial costs risk (both own client and adverse costs) if a case is unsuccessfully contested. Part of their assessment involves whether QOCS protection is likely to be lost by the claimant.

There are various methods of achieving this risk assessment, depending on individual firms' practices. Efficiency includes having a clear idea of your acceptable risk profile. This can be calculated from the proportion of historically accepted cases that have gone on to be costs-bearing and then deciding whether this shows that too many or too few have been accepted or knowing the trigger points at which a case will be defended or settled. Cash-flow factors which ought to be taken into account are the amount of unrecovered profit costs; the value of disbursements written off; and case duration and locked-up work in process. Once the risk profile has been generated at the management level, the percentage of cases which need to be accepted to make the desired profit is known. What is then needed is an accurate risk assessment process for new enquiries.

Clinical negligence cases are generally complex and the importance to the patient, their family and the clinicians involved (of feeling that they have been let down by trusted clinicians or unfairly criticised) cannot be overlooked safely. A complete risk profile system should allow for exceptions as long as the lawyer taking the decision is suitably experienced in winning difficult clinical negligence cases.

In many cases, defendants do not have the same commercial considerations as claimants and are entitled to wait and see whether any adverse incident is pursued in litigation (and whether the claimant can then get their case off the ground) before commencing their own investigations into the clinical negligence allegations that are then made. These might be different to the issues raised in previous investigations into the incident. It is then entitled to see whether the claimant commences court proceedings within the statutory limitation period and serves them properly. At some point, however, it must assess the relative merits of the case against the established legal principles. The longer it leaves this assessment, the more it risks having lost too much ground to the claimant's advisors.

The best approach for either side to adopt is to immediately identify the central allegations on breach of duty, causation of damage and causation of consequential losses. It is usually possible to do this even on relatively brief instructions. However, it is essential to avoid getting side-tracked by extraneous information. Whilst taking a detailed account is important, it should not detract from developing the discipline of clearly identifying the central allegations at the start.

The central allegations are those which go to the heart of the case and which must be proved in order for the claimant to succeed. Ancillary or supporting allegations should be placed to one side for risk assessment purposes and allegations going to service standards complaints or which have not caused an appreciable injury can be disregarded. What is left should be a brief, crystal clear statement of what needs to be proved.

This is then used to assess the facts you have been presented with and this helps considerably in efficiently assessing the risks. It is advisable to avoid falling into the trap of assuming that you need more information. You may well do in order to win the case, however, at present, you are simply assessing whether the case is *likely* to be won or lost.

Having applied the law to the facts, you must then make a decision on the likely view that the experts to be instructed in due course will take. This part of the assessment is seemingly harder because most lawyers do not have the requisite degree of knowledge that a specialist in this field of medicine has. The risk of getting it wrong can be managed in several ways. 'Pseudo-experts' (in the form of in-house clinicians applying generalised knowledge) can be asked to provide an overview of the medical issues involved. Secondly, this information can be available from expert evidence obtained on similar, previous cases because medical science and practice does not tend to change quickly. Thirdly, the availability of online or in-house clinical practitioner texts or guides are useful because experts will often refer to them in order to support their opinions. What is needed at this stage is a general understanding of what amounts to standard medical practice in this area of medicine, what the recognised risks of the provided treatment are; and whether the claimant was likely to have suffered substantially the same injury in any event.

Having assessed this, proportionality should be considered. Although it is inefficient to perform a detailed quantum assessment at this stage, it is necessary to establish whether the likely costs of investigating the case fully and then running it to trial are going to outweigh the likely amount of compensation. Costs include both the recoverable and irrecoverable costs (see Chapter 1). If the severity and duration of the avoidable injury (together with any otherwise avoidable financial losses and expenses) are exceeded by the likely costs, then a plan is needed to run the case at a proportionate cost to value if it is to be accepted.

Next, the limitation position needs accurately assessing. Generally, the three-year period for bringing clinical negligence cases (*Limitation Act 1980, s11(4)*) runs from either the date when the *cause of action* accrued (*s11(4)(a)*) or from the later date of knowledge (*s11(4)(b)*). The cause of action is not necessarily the date of the breach because, fundamentally, it arises when the breach causes a more than minimal injury (e.g. *M'Mullan v Lochgelly Iron & Coal Co [1933] UKHL 4*). This injury may arise sometime later.

The date of knowledge is usually later still. It is necessary to assess how likely it is that the claimant did not have constructive knowledge earlier than they believe. The legal test is primarily objective but with a subjective element: would a reasonable patient in their position have thought their case needed to be investigated? (see *Limitation Act 1980, ss14(1)-(3)* and *Collins v Secretary of State for Business Innovation & Skills and Others [2014] EWCA Civ 717*). This is a rather low bar for the defendant to jump and it is dangerous to assume that constructive knowledge will not be earlier. Evidence that the treating clinician has not been upfront about what has happened can justify the postponement of the limitation clock under *Limitation Act 1980, s32*. However, the duty of candour may well provide clear evidence of a very early date of knowledge.

In a fatal case, limitation runs from the date of the patient's death (*ibid., s12(2)(a)*) or the claimant's date of knowledge (*ibid., s12(2)(b)*) unless the patient's limitation date had expired before they died (*ibid., s12(1)*). The death must have been caused by the alleged breach but foresight here is not needed (*Haber v Walker [1963] VR 339*).

You need to decide if there is enough time to prepare the case before limitation expires or whether there is a reasonable chance of persuading the court to exercise its discretion (under *ibid., s33*). By the time this issue reaches court (usually as a preliminary issue), a considerable amount of expense has already been incurred in dealing with liability and quantum issues. Accordingly, it is best to address the *Limitation Act 1980, s33(1A)(3)* checklist before the case is accepted (see *Collins*, *supra*).

Where the injured person is child, limitation expires on their 21st birthday. Where the injured person is unable to manage their own affairs, then the limitation clock does not start to run until they attain legal capacity. This can result in an unlimited limitation period. However, it is necessary to assess whether they are likely to recover sufficient capacity or have experienced intervals of lucidity. If they have, then the clock continues to count down towards the original limitation date from the point they regained capacity to litigate and so progression towards the three-year period can 'stop and start' in this way without extending the original limitation date (see *Masterman-Lister v Brutton & Co [2002] EWCA Civ 1889*). The extent to which the defendant is likely to contest a lack of capacity also needs assessing because the test is issue-specific (*Bailey v Warren [2006] EWCA Civ 51*).

Finally, it should be confirmed that all of the parties and the allegedly negligent treatment occurred within the jurisdiction. It is usually imprudent to assume that you can sue a defendant outside of England & Wales. Local rules apply and, even where the foreign defendant can be sued effectively here, enforcing any judgement against them abroad may be extremely problematic. Local lawyers may be unwilling to accept instructions or to agree a lien on costs. The issue is not just limited to treatment occurring within the British Isles. Where visiting foreign clinicians fly in to provide treatment it can prove difficult to trace and sue them here and it is sometimes cheaper or otherwise desirable for patients to have treatment abroad. Where extra-jurisdictional issues arise, they should be specifically highlighted from the start so that additional care is taken, specialist advice sought and properly budgeted for. *Roberts v SAAFA & Others [2020] EWHC 994 (QB)* helpfully summarises these and shows that foreign time limits can be disapplied on public policy grounds. Specialist jurisdictional advice should be obtained.

Funding

If the case enjoys a reasonable prospect of success, then funding arrangements suitable for the client need to be considered. This is covered in Chapter 1.

Form of the Risk Assessment

The above considerations can be usefully structured and distilled into one page of A4. This can then be easily referred to later and to focus the initial investigations.

Initial Investigations

The purpose of the initial investigations is to establish whether the core evidence supports the central allegations being made. This evidence comes in three main parts: factual documentary evidence; factual witness evidence and expert opinion.

The initial assessment is not set in stone and the risks are relative. One lawyer's concept of risk differs to another's and so both sides can reasonably believe that they will win. Whether the prospects are 45% or 55% can come down to fine lines and both sides are likely to be considering different evidence at this stage. Accordingly, it is important to test both sides of the case by performing regular re-assessments at key stages as new evidence becomes available. Typically, these will be when the medical records are received, upon receipt of expert evidence, witness statements, the letter of response and pre-issue. After proceedings have been issued, risk assessments ought to be done when the defence has been received; after the exchange of documentary, witness and expert evidence; and pre-trial. These re-assessments do not always need to be lengthy, but they do need to be effective.

The best way to avoid missing a crucial piece of evidence is to remain focussed on the central allegations and to build the case around these. It is good practice to advise your client of the initial assessment, the investigation plan and of the re-assessments.

The purpose of the pre-action period is to establish whether there is sufficient evidentiary support to justify issuing proceedings. It should be used to test out the assumptions made in the initial risk assessment, to notify the defendant of the case it faces and to attempt to reach a settlement if possible.

Complaints Documentation

An important source of background evidence is the initial investigation carried out by the treatment provider. The duty of candour under the *Health & Social Care Act 2008 (Regulated Activities) Regulations 2014, Regulation 20* provides an investigative framework which should already have occurred (but can be triggered by the *Pre-Action Protocol*, see *para (2.2(b))*. It runs in conjunction with the NHS Complaints Procedure (under *The Local Authority Social Services and National Health Service Complaints (England) Regulations 2009*); the Welsh Redress scheme (under the *National Health Service (Concerns, Complaints and Redress Arrangements) (Wales) Regulations 2011*); and more general clinical governance measures.

Not all clinical negligence cases fall within the duty of candour; but the majority do. Documents are triggered if a 'notifiable safety incident' has occurred. Under *regn. 20(7)* of the English regulations, this is an injury which causes more than moderate harm and is wide enough to cover most physical and psychiatric injuries requiring some form of treatment or re-assessment. The harm must have been either unexpected or unintended but, of course, not all 'carelessness' is 'negligent' (*Moorgate Mercantile Co Ltd v Twitchings [1977] AC 890*). Thirdly, the adverse incident is notifiable if in the reasonable opinion of a healthcare professional, it could (or did) result in harm. There is no requirement that this decision be made by a consultant in the same area of medicine and so it may be considered that the underlying condition (not the impugned treatment) caused the injury so no investigation was needed. That said, the wording uses 'could' and not 'would' and so the harm need only be 'possible' not 'probable'.

NHS England's *'Serious Incident Framework – Supporting Learning to Prevent Recurrence' (27th March 2015)* and NHS Improvement's *Patient Safety Incident Response Framework* webpage provide useful guidance in respect of how internal investigations should be conducted. The underlying purpose of the investigation is to establish the facts which led to the serious incident so that similar incidents can be prevented. The aim is to apply the 'human and systems factors approach' developed in high-risk sectors (such as space and aeronautics and motor racing) to clinical care. Individuals should not be blamed, instead they are seen as part of the overall organisation where individual errors are part of a failure in the risk prevention system.

Serious incidents include those within the duty of candour definition of a notifiable incident. A serious incident does not automatically imply negligence but there is a very considerable degree of overlap. The investigation itself requires the medical records to be reviewed and witness statements to be obtained. Such statements do not need to be signed because they are taken as *aides memoire*. A root cause analysis is performed to establish the central cause of the incident. An independent expert is intended to be involved.

The serious incident investigation is not intended to take the place of civil, criminal or regulatory proceedings but nonetheless requires a robust investigation into the facts with documents prepared before litigation is contemplated. As such, it provides an invaluable source of contemporaneous information. The early disclosure of this evidence ensures that both sides have access to the same information and so serves to keep costs proportionate.

Para. 3.2(c) of the *Pre-Action Protocol* encourages the early disclosure of the documents produced as part of the defendant's complaints investigation. Accordingly, disclosure should not wait until standard disclosure. However, the *Protocol* itself does not impose any requirements on whether or how internal investigations should be performed (see *para. 2.3*) so whether one has been done needs establishing.

The documents produced are a written record of the initial verbal notification to the patient of the incident. This must be kept securely and must include all of the facts known at the time and what further enquires will be made (*regns 20(2)(a); 20(3) and 20(3)(e)* of the English regulations). This information must then be sent to the patient together with the results of those further enquiries (*regn. 20(4)*). Copies of attempts to contact the patient and copy correspondence with them should also be kept (*regns 20(5)(b)* and *(20(6)*).

The NHS Complaints Procedure is triggered by a complaint made within 6 months of the treatment (with a discretion to investigate later complaints). The complaint will be investigated and either a report (such as a root cause analysis or serious incident report) or letter setting out how the patient's complaint was considered, the conclusions reached and when any remedial action will be taken.

The Welsh Redress system generates similar-style reports but can also include a formal review by the scheme's panel and an offer of compensation which is open for 6 months. During this time, the claimant's reasonable legal fees will be paid. The compensation limit is £25,000.

Modern clinical governance also promotes the use of treatment guidelines, analyses, protocols and policies along with encouraging the reporting of adverse incidents to help improve clinical practice. *Para. 3.2(c)* of the Protocol also requires disclosure of such documents where they are relevant to the likely issues in the case. Chapter 6 covers how these can form part of the relevant evidence in a case.

Accordingly, these procedures provide the defendant with ample opportunity to have investigated the care provided to the claimant contemporaneously and before litigation is contemplated. Whilst the purpose is to be open and honest with patients, it inevitably provides prospective defendants with the opportunity to marshal this evidence and to review the pertinent medical records. Accordingly, the prompt provision of this non-privileged evidence, serves to save time and avoid unnecessary costs being incurred; is in keeping with the spirit of the protocol and assists in the proportionate investigation of the case.

Medical Records

The purpose of obtaining the claimant's medical records is to assess how well the notes made at the time of the impugned treatment matches the claimant's instructions and allegations and the treating clinicians' recollection of events. Breach of duty, causation of damage and limitation all need critically assessing as soon as is possible. All potential ambiguities or differing interpretations of what has been written need to be noted for future reference. The importance of this cannot be underestimated: an entire case can turn on the correct interpretation of the contemporaneous records.

The starting point for the claimant's solicitor is to obtain the relevant medical records. Strictly speaking, it is not necessary to use the form found at *CPR Annex B of the Pre-Action Protocol for the Resolution of Clinical Disputes* because *para. 3.2(a-c)* is drafted widely enough for other forms containing similar information to be used. However, it is good practice to do so. It is important to remember that the information in the form of authority is disclosable and so an incautious description of the impugned treatment can prove detrimental later in the case.

These are usually provided within 6-8 weeks of the request rather than the 40 days stipulated in the protocol (*para. 3.4.1*). Some providers try to insist that the claimant collects the records in person, but this is not required under the BMA's guidance:

> *"A patient can authorise their solicitor, or another third party, to make a SAR on their behalf. There are very few circumstances when a GP will be able to lawfully decline.*
>
> *Provided the solicitor has given the GP the patient's written consent for the disclosure of the full medical record, the SAR from the solicitor should be treated in the same way as if it was made directly by the patient.*

> *Past medical histories are highly relevant in compensation or insurance claims."*

(Source: https://www.bma.org.uk/advice-and-support/ethics/confidentiality-and-health-records/access-to-health-records; 2nd June 2021 update)

Although the *Pre-Action Protocol* 'allows' applications for pre-action disclosure under *CPR 1998, Rule 31.16* (see *para. 3.7*), the usual rules apply. Thus, the defendant would be entitled to its costs of the application unless the claimant can show that its conduct was unreasonable. By the time the delay becomes objectively unreasonable and the application is heard, the records will usually have been provided so this sanction provides only 'long-stop' protection.

It is worth noting that medical records are often 'signed off' by the treating clinicians before they are provided and so the claimant's legal team should assume that this has occurred and that the treating clinicians have had the opportunity to review their records.

The records you need to request initially depend on both the issues you have identified and proportionality concerns. In some cases, it is reasonable to obtain only the proposed defendant's records and the GP records (for comparison). The GP records provide a useful benchmark by which to assess the defendant's records so, if the GP is the defendant, the secondary care records would take on that role. It is sensible to have a clear idea of the claimant's previous medical history and ongoing care and rehabilitation needs. However, records covering only condition and prognosis issues or seemingly unrelated treatment can be postponed for the time being. The core sets will usually provide enough information to re-assess the central allegations identified in the initial risk assessment.

Once the first round of records has been received, they need to be carefully sorted and paginated so they can be properly understood and used. If the factual matrix is complicated, then a chronology of events should be prepared for ease of future reference. Even with experience, this is a time-consuming task. Introductory training courses are available and can be helpful. Other alternatives are to use an external pagination company or to employ in house nurses. The *Pre-Action Protocol* (*para. 3.5*) and the standard directions order both require that the claimant's solicitor prepares and maintains a legible bundle of medical records. Although not expressly stated, this means a logically ordered and paginated indexed bundle on single-sided sheets of A4 (except for continuous CTG traces) with no duplication or incompletely copied pages. Whilst electronically provided records are useful, the records contained within the electronic .pdf files need to be easily sorted using appropriate software.

The Second Risk Assessment

This ought to occur about 3 months after initial instructions for the claimant but can be omitted from the defendant's initial investigations. The issues identified in the first risk assessment need to be tested against this new evidence to ensure that the case still has a reasonable prospect of success. The exact wording of the relevant entries should be considered. Medical abbreviations and unfamiliar terms can be looked up online. Where illegible handwriting is encountered, you can do little more than highlight this for future review by the experts if the case progresses. The facts contained in the medical records form the foundation of any later expert evidence. In general, the evidence they contain is likely to be ambiguous and so it is unsafe to assume that the meaning which helps or undermines your client's case is necessarily the correct interpretation. The clinicians involved may already have provided clarification in the complaints documents but can be expected to provide witness statements explaining what their records say later in the case (after proceedings have been issued and served). The relative quality of the records is important and ought to be considered by the experts in due course.

The evidence in the core records ought to be reasonably consistent with the central allegations of negligence. The more incongruent or ambiguous they are with the case you have identified, the harder it is to prove your case. The accounts of the key lay witnesses need to be considered and cross-referenced with the content of the records and any inconsistencies discussed with them or highlighted to cover later (depending on the importance of the inconsistency). The complaints documents will usually have been prepared with reference to these entries and so these also need to be carefully cross-referenced in this matter.

These medical records will usually help you to build up a clearer picture of the factual matrix which underpins the core allegations. If this supporting evidence is weak or full of holes, then it is unlikely that any expert evidence will be supportive or, if it is, persuasive.

Key barriers to maximising this step are the amount of medical records and the complexity of the information they contain. Relying on the accuracy of the initial risk assessment and being able to identify the key records swiftly are therefore pivotal to arriving at a reliable second risk assessment. Doing so should result in a much clearer understanding of whether the allegations on liability and quantum are likely to be made out and make the instructions to the expert much clearer. Limitation also ought to be reviewed at this point because the contemporaneous evidence is a very good indicator that this has been assessed accurately.

Since expert opinion needs a firm factual basis to be persuasive, if you cannot find evidence to get around a perceived fundamental problem at this early stage, it is unlikely that further evidence will help to solve these basic issues with the case. Accordingly, it is likely to be better in the long-term for your client to know of these problems (and how you propose to deal with them) sooner rather than later. Rejecting a case on the basis of the records (and complaints documents) is a reasonable option if you have clearly identified the issues at the start of the case and carefully reviewed this updated evidence.

Preliminary Witness Statements

Witness evidence is considered in more detail in Chapter 6. The purpose of taking early witness statements is to get a clear idea of the key witnesses' evidence. However, witness statements present something of a practical dilemma given proportionality. It is unarguably necessary and reasonable to obtain the factual evidence from witnesses as soon as is practicable as their recollection tends to fade with time. How long any one witness statement takes depends on the quality of the witness and of the person taking it; the complexities of the events being covered; whether documentary evidence is being cross-referenced; and how thoroughly the core issues have been identified. The number of witnesses required to prove the facts in dispute tends to be higher the longer the time period being dealt with is and the less the issues in dispute have been narrowed.

Thus, as a general proposition, taking statements at the start of the case is likely to be a more disproportionate exercise than leaving it until later. Conversely, leaving them to later risks being more unreasonable because key evidence may be missed, forgotten or contaminated with the effluxion of time; or the witness may have died or become untraceable. Attempting to find the middle ground by regularly updating witness evidence risks duplication and producing previous inconsistent statements.

None of these approaches are inconsistent with the costs budget. The *Precedent H* phase is divided between incurred and anticipated costs. By the time it usually comes to be prepared (by court order after the defence has been filed), significant costs will have been incurred in preparing this evidence because the number and identity of the witnesses and the issues they will be addressing needs to be included in the Directions Questionnaire and the page limit of each statement needs to be included in the standard directions order.

However, the time already incurred on witness statements (up to the costs CMC) can be used by the court to limit what is allowed for the future, anticipated time. The impact of this depends partly on whether the CCMC occurs before the exchange of witness statements. If it does, then a party can find that the time they want to spend on updating the statements following documentary disclosure or any additional costs incurred for updates arising from an extension to the exchange date, are not permitted. Furthermore, it risks reducing the chances of any amendment to this phase being allowed later.

If you have properly identified the central issues requiring proof, then you ought to be able to focus efficiently on the facts any given witness can assist with. The fee earner conducting the interview needs to have sufficient experience and training to understand these matters and to have an effective interviewing style involving the appropriate use of open questions to elicit the broad answer followed by closed questions to get to the bottom of it. On assessment, it is likely that the costs assessor will want to see evidence that a competent junior lawyer was used with any more senior input being reserved for objectively difficult issues and progressive (and non-duplicative) supervision. For this to work, the team needs to understand the central issues in the case. You must be able to assess whether the witness has come up to proof as making several attempts at taking the same statement is probably duplicative and disproportionate.

The use of witness questionnaires (in place of a preliminary statement) is 'proportionate' in terms of costs in the short term. However, there is a tendency to then not to prepare the statement themselves which risks fatally undermining the case. If the decision not to take a preliminary statement is taken, then a date should be diarised to reconsider this later in the pre-action period, probably before a Letter of Claim is sent and certainly before proceedings are issued.

Preliminary Expert Evidence

Expert evidence is considered in more detail in Chapter 7. The purpose of obtaining expert evidence is to test out the central allegations on breach and causation. To achieve this purpose, an experienced expert (usually of the equivalent to a consultant) who was in NHS practice at the time of the alleged breach(es) of duty is required. It is almost always necessary to have an expert who practices in the same discipline as the impugned clinician, but the requirement is actually to have an expert with the correct *expertise (e.g. C v North Cumbria UHNHST (infra))*. Accordingly, in certain circumstances, medical disciplines overlap sufficiently closely to justify using an expert with the correct degree of experience but who is in a different discipline. If you are unsure, check with the proposed expert before instructing them.

In most cases, you will want to instruct an expert on breach issues before one on causation issues. However, if breach of duty appears straightforward, then it can be acceptable to instruct the causation expert first. Be careful with this, however. Breach of duty may be more complicated than first thought and it is rarely obvious. Whilst asking your causation expert to comment on breach may assist initially, relying on their opinion in the mid- to long-term is likely to mislead your case preparation.

(a) Selection

This remains a pivotal step in any clinical negligence case. Getting the right experts greatly increases the chance of getting a persuasive and supportive opinion which stands up to thorough scrutiny. Getting the wrong expert means you are likely to be relying on someone who will not come up to proof.

Ideally, what you want is an expert whose evidence has been preferred at a previous clinical negligence trial. A quick search on *www.bailii.org* can show up very useful judicial comments on the experts heard at trial. These comments can help to show whether you want to use that expert and areas of their evidence that might need additional work in your particular case.

The second criterion is actual experience of the treatment being impugned in your case. In respect of breach of duty, this goes to properly assessing the correct standard of care. In respect of causation, it goes to their ability to think through and explain the likely consequences of the breach, what would have happened in any event and of any alternatives. Considering the expert's cv will often help to show what their day-to-day practice entails. For example, an orthopaedic expert who actually specialises in spinal treatment is unlikely to be as persuasive as a hand/upper limb orthopod in a complex wrist fracture case(e.g. *Robinson v Liverpool University Hospitals NHS Trust & Mercier (infra, Chapter 7)*).

Certain commonly used databases (including the AvMA one) rely on practitioners keeping it updated whilst others may be subscription-based.

Accordingly, it should not be taken as read that an expert's inclusion on a database means they are a reasonable choice. Proportionality requires efficiency and you do not want to be wasting time trying to shore up a weak report, or worse, trying to find another expert later in the case.

It is best to resolve any doubts about the choice of expert at this stage. Once you have the report, then changing experts is likely to be seen as an attempt at 'expert shopping'. If you have not served the report or otherwise disclosed the identity (or sometimes the discipline) of the expert, then you are unlikely to recover the costs of both reports. If you have disclosed the identity of the expert, then you are likely to have to disclose the report as either a pre-condition or condition of being granted permission to rely on the further expert (e.g. *Edwards-Tubb v JD Weatherspoon plc [2011] EWCA Civ*).

This significantly increases the risks of undermining your client's case as there is a presumption that full information is required (e.g. *Vilca & Others v Xstrata Ltd & Another [2017] EWHC (1582) (QB)*). Here, there was not *"any sound basis for concern about undesirable expert shopping"* (*para. 29*) and *"no sound basis for any suspicion of abuse of process"* (*para. 30*) because the expert was genuinely unwell and this was properly evidenced. Ordering disclosure of the previous expert's reports was refused and was also not considered to be needed as a deterrent to others (*paras. 32 & 33*). At *para. 32, Stuart-Smith J* added: *"The principles are now well established: anyone competent to conduct litigation knows that, if there is a hint of undesirable expert shopping or that significant relevant material is being withheld, the imposition of the condition will be the usual order"*.

If the need to change experts later does arise, then it is necessary to do this as soon as is practicable and to act reasonably and openly, In *Burke v Imperial College Healthcare NHS Trust [2019] EWHC 3719 (QB), Tipples J* held (*paras. 58-9*):

> *"The defendant by choosing to raise this as an issue for the very first time towards the very end of the CCMC came under a very clear obligation to make full disclosure of all material information relating*

> *to the application concerning the change of expert, which it failed to do. The information which was provided by the defendant's counsel to the Master was incomplete and wrong and, as a consequence, misleading.*
>
> *As I have just said, it is quite clear to me that there is a more than a hint of expert shopping in relation to the evidence which is now available. This is a case in which it is clear to me the usual condition should be applied."*

It is always wise to make an attendance note explaining why an expert has been selected in case maters do not go to plan. Once the choice(s) have been made, the expert can be approached.

(b) Approach

Practice varies as to how detailed the letter of approach should be. Some practitioners prefer to send a detailed letter (approaching the detail found in the letter of instruction itself) to several experts. This does have the advantage of allowing the expert to make a fully informed choice as to whether they can safely accept instructions. The disadvantages are that it takes more time to prepare the letter (at a time when all that is needed is to find a suitable expert) and that it risks disclosing confidential information about your client's case before instructions have been accepted.

The alternative is to send a brief letter of approach setting out just enough information for the proposed expert to understand what sort of report is needed; a summary of the central issues; whether they are conflicted from acting (i.e. they know the clinician or have links with the defendant); any limitation issues; and the amount of documentary evidence they will be sent. You should also include how they will be paid and request a copy of their current fee structure and c.v. It is also helpful to ask them if they can suggest any suitable alternate experts if they are unable to act; however, some experts balk at making such recommendations so sometimes need persuading to do so. Such a letter should be no more than 1 page at most.

It is reasonable to approach more than one expert at once, even though the losing party will often object to this when it comes to costs. The additional cost of making several approaches at the same time is not great with a short letter and is proportionate when weighed against the delays which occur when a proposed expert belatedly says they cannot assist. It is always better to have more than one iron in the fire.

If the expert's current cv and fee structure is acceptable, then you can proceed to instruct them.

(c) Instruction

Proportionality makes it even more important not to waste time and energy by sending experts unnecessary documents or woolly instructions. Having identified the central issues and considered these in the context of the core medical records and complaints documents, preparing a proper set of instructions proportionately is a less daunting prospect.

The aim is to prepare a clear and comprehensive set of instructions which concisely presents the proposed case to the expert. Your best chance of getting back as clear and comprehensive report as possible, is to clearly set out the relevant evidence and to set out your views on how the factual evidence relates to the central issues. The expert can then focus on addressing these in their report.

Practice differs as to the sort of report requested at this stage. Broadly speaking, the report is necessarily provisional because it is requested at a time when the evidence is incomplete. A brief screening report has the benefit being quicker and cheaper to obtain and so seems more proportionate if the report is unsupportive. However, the downside is that the opinion may not have been thought through fully. This is not necessarily a fatal flaw at this stage of the case as long as it is recognised. If it is not, then the case can be fatally undermined. Asking for a fully detailed report at this stage minimises this risk but carries with it the risk of incurring a much higher level of irrecoverable disbursements (if either the case turns out to be of a modest value or across your file load)

The letter of instruction remains of pivotal importance and should cover the following points:

- A summary of what you want them to report on;
- List of enclosures;
- A summary of the relevant facts;
- An explanation of the central issues they are to report on;
- Any specific questions you want them to answer;
- A summary of the *CPR 1998, Part 35* requirements.

If you have a standard format of instructions, this should always be checked to ensure it is relevant to the case in question. Whilst practice varies in respect of whether to send a paginated set of records, best practice is to comply with the standard directions order well in advance and to paginate the records as soon as is possible and this makes it easier to discuss the case with the expert later.

The letter itself needs to include a summary of the expert's duty under *CPR 1998 Part 35*. This can be fairly standard in nature and safely form part of a template. The key point is that the expert must be independent and so you need to have evidence that you summarised this. Summarising the *CPR 1998, Part 35* duty and legal tests the claimant needs to meet is the safest way to do this.

Secondly, it is advisable to provide a detailed summary of the factual background and medical history. Building this around the central allegations identified earlier helps to focus the chronology of events more efficiently. This summary should, as far as is possible, be neutral and cover the relevant aspects of the claimant's previous medical history, impugned treatment and how they have responded to treatment. Aspects which are not central to the type of report being considered can be summarised more briefly.

Thirdly, the allegations on breach of duty or causation then need to be set out. In order to progress the case, the central allegations can now be broken down into smaller parts in order to focus the expert's mind on what will be needed at trial. To do this, consider the constituent elements of the allegation(s) and what steps were taken (or not) in the claimant's case. If the serious incident investigation report is available and critical of the impugned treatment but liability has not been admitted, it is important to ask the expert why this might be justifiable. Finally, it is important to ask the expert to consider what arguments your opponent's expert can raise to ensure that your expert has considered all relevant angles.

The instructions should be accompanied with a paginated bundle of documents (either digital or paper). Consistent pagination is critical so you, your client and the expert can know which piece of evidence is where. This saves a considerable amount of time. Imaging (radiology) cds need to be checked before despatch to ensure that they have not become corrupted and that the password still works.

In order to keep your client updated, a copy of the instruction letter should be sent to them to confirm their instructions. If the position seems clear, then the instructions themselves can safely be sent at the same time with any additional comments or evidence from your client being sent along afterwards in order to minimise the reporting time. There is also the temptation in the face of downwards costs pressures to skimp on the instruction of the experts. Doing so, creates the risk that they will not consider the relevant issues, stray outside of their areas of expertise and/or misunderstand the evidence being sent.

CPR 1998, Rule 35.10 and *PD35 para. 5* provide that the instruction letter is not disclosable where the expert has accurately summarised the scope of their instructions. However, some experts do annex the letter to the report and this needs to be addressed with them before service. References in the report to other documents (e.g. other reports or draft statements) can prove problematic. These do not need to be disclosed unless the expert has actually relied upon them in forming their opinion. However, the reference to them can cause difficulties because it draws your opponent's attention to their existence. Accordingly, it is prudent to address such issues before them become a problem in the letter of instruction.

(d) Considering the Report

Ideally, the report will clearly answer the questions contained in the instruction letter and in sufficient detail to cover both the central issues in the case and the more important of the ancillary questions. However, unfortunately, this cannot be assumed and the report must be checked carefully to ensure that the expert's opinion fits the facts of the case. Due to the technical nature of expert evidence, it is surprisingly easy not to realise that an expert has formed their opinion based on an incomplete understanding of the evidence they have been sent or simply tried to side-step or gloss over a fact which does not fit in with their opinion.

Accordingly, it is necessary to critically and carefully assess each report by thinking the position through logically and cross-referencing the facts relied on by the expert with the known facts already obtained. This does not mean that you should go back and reconsider the medical records and other evidence reviewed before the expert was instructed. Such an approach is likely to result in the work done being considered to be duplicative and disproportionate. What it does require is for you to be able to make use of the clear notes of the evidence made previously to help assess the quality of the opinion now being expressed.

If the report is unsupportive, then your client is likely to want to ask questions and perhaps even provide additional evidence. It is therefore important that you fully understand why the expert has said what they have and how it relates to both the central issues and the evidence. By doing so, you may arrive at the entirely reasonable conclusion that the expert has covered all of the reasonable angles. In this case, the proper course is to advice that your client's case is unlikely to succeed and that the expert has arrived at a reasonable and logical opinion. In such cases, it usually difficult to persuade external funders to pay for the cost of an additional report form a different expert in the same discipline.

Even where such an opinion can be obtained (technically allowing the case to continue), it is likely that your opponent will obtain an opinion which is reasonably consistent with the unsupportive opinion you have first obtained. With the advent of QOCS protection (*q.v.),* is this as much of a concern for claimants as it used to be, pre-Jackson? The second report shows that the case could meet the legal criteria but you also know that there is another and seemingly-logical body of opinion to the contrary. There is no real evidence that defendants have become more risk averse as a result of QOCS (*q.v.*) and so a reasonable conclusion would be that the case is more likely to go to trial. Accordingly, this could justify advice that the case is too risky to proceed. However, it may also be reasonable to use the unsupportive report to test out your supportive one. There is no need to disclose the unsupportive report, because you need only paraphrase the matters raised by the first expert to the second (including any perceived differences in their relative experience). With the introduction of costs budgeting, however, the existence of two experts may become clear at that stage if the reports are charged for separately as they would be in the final bill. However, there is no particular need to make that distinction at that stage and it is arguably not in your client's interests to do so (but see the section on expert shopping, *supra*). Defendants are not in the same position because they do not have to prove anything; they simply need to stop the claimant doing so. In that context, an initial unsupportive report does not have the same impact as it does for the claimant. However, post-Jackson, it ought to impress upon them that this is a case which they ought to be settling on the best terms (i.e. before the claimant's costs increase). This does not necessarily mean making an admission of liability but ought to involve assessing the relative settlement range and the scope for making partial admissions on certain issues or facts.

Where the report is supportive, then it is still necessary to consider whether further evidence is required for the expert to finalise their opinion. Such reports should be marked as a 'preliminary report, not for disclosure' by the expert but this is not always clear. Such reports can be relied on to help draft the letter of claim or response but the expert should be consulted before the report is disclosed.

Where the expert recommends that additional reports be obtained from experts in other disciplines, it is necessary to consider whether it is reasonable and proportionate to do so. If the proposed further report only deals with a very narrow issue, then it may not be. The point was illustrated in *Hobbs v Guy's & St Thomas' NHS Foundation Trust (supra)* where the costs of the work relating to the instruction of the consultant anaesthetist was not allowed because his instruction was unreasonable because his opinion simply echoed that of the consultant plastic surgeon (although the argument made was slightly more nuanced). The practice point to be drawn from this is that the instruction of further experts must stand up to objective scrutiny. In many cases it will do because the first expert may at the initial effects of the injury but will then transfer the patient to another discipline for ongoing treatment and follow up. As each case must be judged on its own facts, the decision must be made on each case – there is no universal rule that limits the number of experts based on likely value, for example. Considering the evidential points which the further reports are likely to cover helps considerably in deciding whether the costs involved are likely to be reasonable and proportionate.

When advising the client on the report, it is good practice to do so clearly and with empathy for the client. Often, this will be the first time when (near) definitive advice can be given. Using plain English to explain legal and medical terminology and concepts is a must. You should anticipate as many of the questions that the client will want answered as possible in the letter. It is not advisable to simply regurgitate the report or to summarise it very briefly and you should put yourself in a position to discuss the issues directly with your client. Depending on the complexity of the issues, the importance of the case to your client, the value of the case and the proximity of limitation, it may also be prudent to discuss the issues with the expert before finalising your updated advice. Experts are not infallible.

It may be possible for the expert to amend their views to support a case on the basis that the claimant's factual evidence is preferred but not to support the case if the defendant's factual evidence is preferred.

Identifying these cases early on helps to focus minds on the tactical approach to be taken in the case.

Letters of Claim & Response

(a) Early Notification Letter & Letter of Claim

The *Pre-Action Protocol* allows for a notification letter to be sent to the defendant before a full letter of claim; the idea being that this will avoid defendants being given later notice of claims. Doing so gives the defendant more time to start their investigations. Whether such a letter is reasonable and proportionate in each case depends on the relative complexity of the case. If a detailed complaints investigation has been conducted and disclosed, then the defendant already has sufficient notice of the case and the intended litigation can be suitably notified when the medical records are requested. In cases where a more detailed investigation is required to properly particularise the core allegations on breach and causation (and it is also reasonable and proportionate to do so), then a sufficiently detailed notification letter is very helpful and may successfully narrow the issues being investigated.

Template letters of notification and claim are found at *Annexes C1 and C2* of the *Pre-Action Protocol*, respectively. Strict adherence to them is not required. A copy of the letter should be sent to the relevant defence organisation even though the claimant may not have a reference at this point. The sanction for the defendant not promptly commencing an investigation after receipt of these letters is modest; the *Pre-Action Protocol, para. 3.12.2* says only that *"The court may question requests for extension of time limits if a Letter of Notification was sent but did not prompt an initial investigation."* This has little practical impact.

The template letters are similar in their section headings. Accordingly, in practice a sizeable number of cases can simply proceed straight to a letter of claim where prompt investigations have sufficiently identified the issues to get the ball rolling. One interesting aspect of the template letter of claim is the reference to a *Part 36* offer. Although this is clearly stated to be optional, it can have its uses. Firstly, it is extremely unlikely that the defendant will be in a position to respond to a monetary offer in full and final settlement of the case within 21 days of receiving the letter of claim. Practically speaking, the acknowledgement letter to the letter of claim is often not received by then. However, it may well be that detailed negotiations have already taken place and a genuine opportunity for final settlement has arisen. In other cases, making a monetary *Part 36* offer with the letter of claim tends to be seen as an overly aggressive tactic which only serves to antagonise the defendant. In such circumstances, the defendant is best served by responding with a request that the offer either be withdrawn or the relevant period of 21 days be extended pending the letter of response. This helps to maintain the prospect of negotiations whilst still giving the defendant sufficient time to properly investigate its case without being under the spectre of facing a reasonable *Part 36* offer. If the claimant refuses, then it risks appearing unreasonable when the issue of costs comes to be determined even if it beats its offer. *Part 36* offers are considered further in Chapter 8.

This is not to say that it is inherently unreasonable to make a monetary *Part 36* offer with the letter of claim in low or modestly valued cases. If the claimant's solicitor is sufficiently experienced to have recognised that the case has proportionality issues and has been able to arrive at an accurate broad-brush valuation, this is one of the few options open to them to keep costs down. It is surprising, however, how few defendants appreciate this. Although the defendant is entitled to investigate the position fully, this is not always congruent with acting proportionately. It is important to be alive to the twin likelihoods that this is the best opportunity to get the most proportionate balance between costs and damages and that the impugned clinicians' time would be better spent treating patients. Even if they are incorrectly seen as 'mere' witnesses (as opposed to clients) the time taken to prepare their evidence and keeping them properly informed increases their dissatisfaction and leads to increased feelings of being wronged. The potentially cogent argument that a clinician has been forced to fully defend a case in order to protect their reputation is misplaced where the claimant has tried to reach a reasonable settlement early on. There is no easy way to find out if a clinician has been sued in negligence (contrast the GMC's professional misconduct decision list). Accordingly, if the clinician's reputation is of such importance to them that their professional indemnity insurers to do not wish to negotiate, then this is a relevant consideration in costs under *CPR 44.3(5)(e)*.

Secondly, 'partial' *Part 36* offers can be made, and these are of more useful practical significance in seeking to narrow the issues and thereby avoid incurring unreasonable or disproportionate costs. Typically, the perceived reasonableness of this will depend on the extent to which they are consistent of any complaints investigation, inquest or disciplinary tribunal's findings of fact. Although such investigations proceed on a different basis to the adversarial system for negligence claims, it is likely that the contemporaneous documentary evidence will have been assessed and the relative veracity and persuasiveness of the key witnesses weighed in the balance. Accordingly, these factors ought to be taken into account when considering whether it is reasonable and proportionate to litigate the issues to which this evidence goes to. Are you genuinely likely to be able to obtain different but consistent evidence to the contrary and at what cost? Is it reasonable and proportionate to incur costs finding out? If you do succeed, is your opponent likely to then incur additional costs to address these issues? It is no longer simply a case of having a free hand to challenge unsupportive evidence. Instead, informed decisions must be made regularly as to what issues genuinely need to be pursued (from a substantive or evidential law standpoint) and which ought to be pursued (from a procedural and commercial standpoint)

The template letter of claim does not include anything on disclosure of further documentation. It is a useful point at which to request missing medical records if these remain relevant. *Para. 3.2(c)* of the *Pre-Action Protocol* does say that the medical records request can include *"a request for any relevant guidelines, analyses, protocols or policies and any documents created in relation to an adverse incident, notifiable safety incident or complaint."* There is no reason why the request cannot be made in the letter of claim, especially where local guidelines might apply or a specific issue as to the cogency or congruency of the complaints response letter or SII/RCA report has been raised by your expert. It is right to investigate this further. Similarly, proportionality does not require omniscience and so it may have been entirely justifiable to investigate the central issues against the factual content of the medical records in order to save time and money. Another justifiable reason for not requesting these documents is that they may be superseded by any admissions made in the letter of response. Accordingly, the request can be usefully prefaced by saying that disclosure is only required if liability (or another discrete issue which they go to) is to be denied.

However, admissions can also deflect you from pursuing requests for disclosure (please see further below and in Chapter 6). In *Snow v Royal UH Bath (supra)*, *HHJ Roberts* made detailed findings in respect of the defendant's 'failure' to disclose documents referred to in the relevant NICE Guidelines. These stipulated: *"Therefore, this procedure should only be used with special arrangements for clinical governance, consent and audit or research" (para. 70).* At *para. 71* he noted: *"Whilst I acknowledge that the Defendant admitted that it was negligent in the consenting of the Claimant for a TaTME* [the impugned operation], *the Defendant has not disclosed documentation showing that special arrangements for clinical governance, consent and audit or research were put in place prior to the Claimant's operation"* At *para. 73*:

> *(c) "The Defendant has not disclosed any documentation evidencing special arrangements for clinical governance, consent and audit or research, as recommended by NICE, or any standard framework, as required by the Defendant's own process for the introduction of new interventional or diagnostic procedures. In particular, there are no documents from the Defendant showing a policy on information to be given to patients undergoing a TaTME, including the provision of written information, for which NICE had already provided a clear working model;*
>
> > *i) A pro forma to record patient selection, which should be copied to the patient's records;*
> >
> > *ii) A policy to keep records of patients undergoing a TaTME* [the relevant procedure] *and for regular reviews;*

iii) A training policy to include supervision and mentoring or proctoring.

At *para. 76*: "[Counsel] *said that the governance documents had been lost but the Defendant did not disclose any witness statements or documents referring to governance documents being lost.*" At para. 77:

> *"Initially, [Counsel] said that it was not proportionate to disclose documents relating to governance procedures because the Defendant had admitted that the Claimant had not been properly consented. This position subsequently changed to being that there were documents relating to governance and procedures for implementing TaTME at the Hospital but they had all been lost. I find this unconvincing. In the absence of any witness statement or documentary evidence from the Defendant that it put in place special arrangements for the introduction of TaTME at the Hospital, I am unable to accept that all of the documents have been lost as this is implausible. There would be documents relating to approval from the local ethics committee or the local clinical governance committee. Furthermore, my findings below strongly suggest that there was a systemic failure by the Defendant to put in place special arrangements for the introduction of TaTME."*

It is helpful to see a trial judge's view of both the potential relevance of these documents and the arguments advanced for not disclosing them. In particular, admitting liability; proportionality; a lack of relevance; and an explanation that none were required in the absence of supportive witness evidence were all found to be unpersuasive. In practice, evidencing your requests for these documents (and critically assessing the responses to them) should be started as early as possible.

(b) Letter of Response

The response time of 4 months from receipt of the letter of claim is one of the main practical considerations affecting when best to send the letter of claim. Many claimants (especially those who have been through the complaints process) do not appreciate why the defendant then has another 4 months to investigate matters. Conversely, defendants often need this time (and more) to investigate the case. The 4 months runs from the date the letter of claim was received and so it is prudent to send it to the defendant's professional indemnity organisation to prevent delays arising from the defendant failing to send it on. The time does not run from the date medical records were received or the date when any perceived lack of clarity was provided. However, it is useful in practice to raise and deal so far as is possible with such matters by agreement as early on in the process as you can.

The *Pre-Action Protocol* allows the defendant to ask for an extension of time to provide the letter of response and for the claimant to deal with this reasonably. *Para. 3.25.2* only requires that the defendant provides an explanation of why the extension is necessary and *Para. 3.25.3* requires the claimant to adopt a reasonable approach. In practice, the most common reasons given are either that expert evidence is still required or that further medical records are needed. Increasing the *Pre-Action Protocol* response period from 3-4 months was intended to reduce the incidence of the first of these reasons and the *Pre-Action Protocol* itself allows the defendant to request additional records in its letter of response.

Annex C3 sets out the template and the way that this sets out makes it plain that an apology can be made without any admissions and that what is intended is a reasoned response where:

(a) Any full or partial admissions are clearly set out (including whether they are intended to be binding);

(b) Any denials are clearly explained with the defendant's case being set out clearly. This includes any response to a *Part 36* offer;

(c) The disciplines of the supportive expert evidence being relied upon and which relates to breach of duty and which to causation of damage;

(d) Confirmation as to whether copies of any medical records are required at this stage and supplying copies of any other documents being relied upon; and

(e) Confirmation of any non-NHS insurer should be provided and the defendant should inform the claimant of any other potential defendants to the claim.

The *Pre-Action Protocol* envisages that the defendant will set out the next steps. These are not usually seen as alternatives which the claimant can choose from. Instead, the claimant will usually be invited to discontinue their claim because the defendant feels that it has a strong case breach and/or causation or liability will be admitted and details of the claimant's case on quantum will be requested. More rarely, ADR will be attempted by way of a monetary *Part 36* offer but any form of ADR is permitted. Rehabilitation and resolution without an admission being made are also permitted but are rarely encountered.

Under the *Pre-Action Protocol*, the defendant should make it clear whether any admissions made are intended to be binding. Accordingly, if this is not clear, then it ought to be confirmed in writing. *CPR 1998, Rule 14.1A(4)* and *PD14* set out the procedural requirements. To briefly summarise, they come within this rule where made before the letter of claim is sent if the admission expressly refers to *CPR 1998, Part 14*. Accordingly, if this is not clear, it ought to be confirmed. *CPR 1998, Part 14* does not need to be expressly referred to if a letter of claim has been sent. Since admissions can also be withdrawn (either by consent or by court order), they are considered further below in Chapter 4 with summary judgements. At this stage, it is prudent to confirm in writing that you rely on the admission and are ceasing further enquiries into breach and/or causation in light of it (depending on the extent of the admission made); but remain aware that further evidence may come to light which may justify the admission being withdrawn. It is important that admissions can be relied upon but it also dangerous to assume that the court will always refuse permission to withdraw an admission. A further practice point to remember is that *CPR 1998, Rule 14.1(4)* specifically refers to *CPR 1998, Rule 21.10* as requiring the court's approval for any compromise, settlement or payment. Although the wording of this rule specifically refers only to full admissions of liability or partial admissions for a specific sum of money, it is also possible that 'any compromise' includes any admission of part of the claim because that part would then be compromised on one party's favour. It is prudent in any event to have the admission included in the order for directions or first available order after the admission is made.

Pre-Issue Review

The *Pre-Action Protocol* recommends that the parties take stock after the letter of response has been served. If it is likely to take the claimant more than 6 months to decide whether to proceed, then they ought to advise the defendant of this (*ibid., para. 3.29*). *Para. 5.1* reiterates that litigation should be last resort and so it is advisable to use the post-response period to engage in ADR of one type or another and *para. 5.4* reminds the parties that they *"may be required by the courts to provide evidence that ADR has been considered."* It does not require it, however, "*It is expressly recognised that no party can or should be forced to mediate or enter into any form of ADR, but a party's silence in response to an invitation to participate in ADR might be considered unreasonable by the court and could lead to the court ordering that party to pay additional court costs.*" Settlement is considered further in Chapter 8.

Part of the reason for this is the position regarding expert evidence. Expert evidence does not need to be disclosed and neither party will see the substance of each other's instruction letters. Accordingly, it is commonplace to encounter the situation where both parties say that they have supportive expert evidence. Negotiations either do not take place at all or do so with one or both sides adopting the position that their reports are not in a disclosable format. In practice, therefore, litigation is not the last resort, it is the only way in which the case can progress.

The *Pre-Action Protocol* recognises that the parties need flexibility in respect of expert evidence; that jointly instructed experts are often not a realistic option; and that experts' fees are expensive. It says only that parties should co-operate in selecting the disciplines to be used; whether they should be jointly instructed and whether early disclosure should be made. It certainly does not require any of this to occur and neither side should feel obliged to do so because such decisions are likely to have a significant impact on the viability of a contested case at a time when the evidence is incomplete and the pleadings still to be drafted.

Although the court cannot prevent a party obtaining expert evidence, it can refuse permission to allow them to rely on it at trial. This therefore limits a party's ability to expert shop (i.e. to obtain reports from different experts in the same discipline, *supra*) or to obtain reports on minor, ancillary issues which do not proportionately progress them. As we have seen already, the court can also refuse to allow the costs of such reports (*Hobbs, supra*).

Since QOCS protects losing claimants (*supra* and see further Chapter 8), there is less costs risk to them of issuing proceedings prematurely. However, the risk of losing the case (i.e. of the claimant getting no compensation) is not so reduced. Both parties therefore ought to take the time to use the period following service of the letter of response to carefully reassess the strengths and weaknesses of both side's respective cases to save time and money later on.

The quantification of the case is an area which often does require a considerable amount of further thought before proceedings are commenced. The extent to which this can be finalised before the case issued depends not only on the claimant's prognosis but also on the availability of documentary evidence from the parties. Pre-Jackson, it was usually considered unreasonable to incur the costs of detailed enquiries before liability issues were determined. That remains the case and it is likely that the detailed quantum investigations needed the value the case will only start after the letter of response has been served.

Pre-Action Applications

Before issuing proceedings, the claimant's legal team needs to be satisfied that the case has a reasonable prospect of success. This decision will usually be taken either in the face of a clear denial of liability and the failure of negotiations or where there has been insufficient time before limitation expires to fully investigate the case.

Whether the case can be safely issued can be assessed against the legal test for successfully making a pre-action disclosure application. Broadly speaking, if such an application is likely to fail, then there is sufficient evidence to plead the case with the accuracy needed for litigation.

The situation may also arise where it is believed that one party possesses documents which would help the other side assess its case. *Para. 3.7* of the *Pre-Action Protocol* states that the claimant should apply for pre-action disclosure of medical records only where the defendant has failed to disclose them or provided an explanation for any delay within 40 days of the request. *Para. 3.8* allows either party to apply for third party disclosure under *CPR 1998, Rule 31.17*. For the defendant, the *Pre-Action Protocol, para. 3.17* requires the claimant to disclose 'relevant' records and to provide copies *'if possible'*. Otherwise, *para. 3.18* states that *"[s]ufficient information must be given to enable the defendant to focus investigations and to put an initial valuation on the claim."*

As the *Pre-Action Protocol* promotes the early exchange of information, it might be thought that it follows that applications for pre-action disclosure are relatively straightforward. Unfortunately, that is not the case. Moreover, the line of authority at common law is mainly derives from high value and complex commercial litigation which can make the case law heavy going and the finer principles difficult to filter out.

The test is set out in *CPR 1998, Rule 31.16* and the related case law. A useful analysis in the post-Jackson era is set out in *Marine Services (Grimsby) Ltd. v Associated British Ports [2014] EWHC 4254 (Admlty)*. There is a two-stage test: (1) the jurisdiction to hear the application; and (2) the discretion as to whether to grant it (*Phoenix Natural Gas Ltd. v British Gas Trading Ltd [2004] EWHC 451 (Comm)*). These can overlap, especially when it comes to the desirability of allowing the disclosure (*CPR 1998, Rule 31.16(3)(d)*).

To summarise, the court will have jurisdiction to grant the pre-action disclosure if:

(i) The applicant and respondent are likely to be parties to the court action if it is issued (*CPR 1998, Rule 31.16(3)(a)&(b)*);

(ii) The documents being requested pre-action would fall within the definition of standard disclosure if court action was started (*CPR 1998, Rule 31.16(3)(c)*);

(iii) Disclosing the documents pre-proceedings would be desirable to dispose fairly of the anticipated proceedings, and/or assist the dispute to be resolved pre-proceedings; and/or save costs (*CPR 1998, Rule 31.16(3)(c)*)

The first of these is often not troublesome. The medical records are likely to have made it clear whether the correct defendant has been identified and the claimant wishes to bring a claim. The issue more usually encountered is really whether the claimant has enough information to bring proceedings. A distinction needs to be drawn between where medical records are needed and where other documents are being sought.

In *Phoenix Natural Gas (supra), Cooke J* made it clear that documents set out in a *Pre-Action Protocol* are to be seen on a similar footing to medical records whereas the pre-action disclosure of other documents ought only to be made in exceptional circumstances. *Cooke J* proceeds on the basis that following the *Pre-Action Protocol* implies that the parties have been acting reasonably and so 'additional' disclosure should normally be dealt with in the pre-trial period. *Tomlinson J*, made similar points in *Trouw UK Limited v Mitsui & Co (UK) plc [2007] UKCLR 921.* Since almost every case arguably would benefit from one party seeing additional disclosure in order to achieving settlement or saving costs in some other way, this is not a sufficient reason to make the order (*Pineway Limited v London Mining Company Limited [2010] EWHC 1143 (Comm) per David Steel J; Marine Services (Grimsby) Ltd v Associated British Ports [2014] (supra)*)

The applicant must also show that the pre-action disclosure is 'strictly necessary' in order to make a pleaded case against the respondent (see *Steamship Mutual v Baring Management Ltd. [2004] 2 CLC 628* and *First Gulf Bank v Wachovia Bank National Association [2005] EWHC 2827 (Comm)*). Fairly crucially, *Rix LJ* explained in *Black v Sumitomo Corporation [2001] EWCA Civ 1819* that *"The purpose of the rule is not just for the assistance of a prospective claimant to improve his prospective pleading but also of those who need disclosure as a vital step in deciding whether to litigate at all or as a vital ingredient of the pleading"* but that *"[t]here is a clear distinction between a personal injury action on the one hand and speculative commercial actions."* However, a *"wide and woolly"* request is still likely to fail because *"every application for pre-action disclosure should be crafted with great care, so it is properly limited to what is strictly necessary" (per Morison J* in *Snowstar Shipping Co Ltd v Graig Shipping plc & Another [2003] EWHC 1367 (Comm)*)

When applying the line of commercial cases on pre-action disclosure, it is important to remember that commercial cases often involve documents of considerable financial sensitivity. That is unlikely to be the case in clinical negligence but this does not mean that the case law is irrelevant or unpersuasive. In both types of cases, the documents sought may be privileged. In order to be disclosed pre-action, they need to (a) fall within standard disclosure; and (b) be so crucial to the case that it is justifiable to order their disclosure pre-proceedings. *Rix LJ* (in *Black v Sumitomo (supra)*) suggested that this can be assessed by addressing these questions:

(a) Whether the injury sustained is clear and requires examination of the documents being sought;

(b) Whether the documents requested were narrowly focussed and bore directly on the injury complained of and on the responsibility for it; and

(c) Whether the documents would be decisive on the conduct or event going to the heart of the existence of the litigation.

This is not the same thing as it being desirable to disclose the documents but does influence it. *Rix LJ* highlighted that this causes some confusion in practice. Jurisdictionally, there must be a real prospect in principle of the main litigation being avoided, of disposing fairly of the proceedings or of saving costs. If so, then the desirability of allowing pre-action disclosure must be considered on all of the available facts (including those listed in the preceding paragraph and the opportunity the applicant has to make his case without allowing pre-action disclosure). This is far more involved than doing so 'in principle'. Practitioners should not be misled into conflating the two elements because *"... [i]n many if not most cases it will be possible to make a case for achieving one or other of the three purposes, and...each of the three possibilities is itself inherently desirable" (para. 82)*.

In *Hussein v MDU & Another [2020] EWHC 157 (QB)*, despite the claimant satisfying all of the tests under *CPR Rule 31.16(3)* and having several points in favour of allowing disclosure, the judge still refused to exercise his discretion. Permission was refused, inter alia, because the limited disclosure already made was enough for him to be persuaded that the defendant had acted 'reasonably' and 'suggested' that the reasons for the claimant believing he had had his legal rights breached might be misconceived. The remainder of the documents being sought could reasonably (but not definitively) form part of standard disclosure.

Accordingly, these principles show that careful consideration is needed to particularise the description of the documents being requested and how it would be unjust to refuse disclosure. Where core medical records going to the heart of the case on breach of duty or causation of damage are at issue, then the disclosure is very likely to be allowed. However, where the documents go to supporting issues which do not prevent the statements of case being finalised, then it will not be (e.g. *Corbyn v Evans [2021] EWHC 130 (QB), para. 60*). QOCS influences this by removing a significant part of the costs risk of commencing proceedings making it more desirable to leave questions of evidence to standard disclosure. At this point, the parties will know precisely what facts have been pleaded and what evidence is needed to prove them, thereby making the costs of disclosure lower and more proportionate.

There is a difference having obtained sufficiently supportive evidence to prepare the particulars of claim or defence and winning the case. This is really the difference between deciding how much to front load the case. Front-loading a case involves doing much of the work that would be done post-proceedings. It has the benefit of filling in the evidential gaps which could prevent the case being won and is therefore considered good practice. However, doing so before the case issues have been formalised in the pleadings tends to mean that the work done has less focus and so is arguably much less proportionate.

Conclusion

The combined purpose of proportionality and QOCS is to reduce the amount spent on legal costs by limiting the amount of those costs recoverable from the loser. This creates a risk that the lay client themselves (on either side) will be expected to cover any shortfall.

It is therefore in your clients' interests that the correct balance is struck between protecting or pursuing their legal remedies against the risk of incurring significant irrecoverable costs. Lay clients are increasingly looking to their advisors for advice on how this balance is best struck on their case and lawyers need to be able to provide a value-for-money service.

If one party's pre-action investigations are cursory, then the risk of losing the case increases significantly. If they are too detailed, then the costs involved risk being irrecoverable from the losing party. If both parties adopt the same strategy (i.e. either too much or too little work) then the risk multiplies.

The goal is to get as clear an idea of how the case is likely to look at trial as soon as is possible. The work done needs to focus on and move quickly between the key stages of the pre-action process. These are: the initial risk assessment; obtaining and considering the preliminary factual evidence and then expert evidence; sending the letters of claim and response; narrowing the issues and negotiating; and reviewing the case before proceedings are commenced.

Both parties need to adopt a proactive approach if they hope to successfully argue later that their opponent acted disproportionality. Evidence of what has happened needs to be kept to persuade the court and your client that a reasonable balance was struck. Wherever possible, a genuine attempt at settlement by making a realistic *Part 36* offer is highly desirable (for both parties) to avoid the costs, delays and risks of commencing court proceedings. Claimants should not rely on being able to use pre-action disclosure to give them access to potentially relevant documents outside of the core medical records.

CHAPTER FOUR

ISSUE & SERVICE OF PROCEEDINGS

Introduction

Commencing court proceedings carries with it the decision that the case will proceed to trial. Although it may well settle one way or another before trial, starting court proceedings on the assumption that settlement will be achieved carries with it the danger that the case will be improperly prepared in one or more areas. If it does not, the service of the proceedings should trigger the realisation that the case is now one which risks being tried no matter how far advanced settlement negotiations may be.

The current level of court fees has a significant impact on whether to commence court proceedings if there is a reasonable prospect of either (a) reaching a negotiated settlement before limitation expires; and (b) of the parties agreeing a limitation amnesty. Since the court is only able to exercise its costs management powers after proceedings have been served, consideration ought to be given to whether proportionality is best served by delaying the issue of proceedings on a case-by-case basis.

The chapter is broadly divided into three sections: commencing, serving & responding to proceedings; drafting the statements of case; and clarifying the pleaded case.

Commencing Proceedings

In order to commence court proceedings, it is necessary to file a correctly drafted claim form at court with the correct court fee. For limitation purposes, it is the date that the claim form was received at the court's office that is important and not the date it was sealed and issued (*CPR*

1998 PD7A, para. 5.1). However, for cases falling within the mandatory County Court Damages Claims Portal (pilot running until 30th April 2024), then the relevant date is the date the claim is issued (not received) under *CPR 1998 PD51ZB, para. 2.2(4).*

Accordingly, it is advisable to leave plenty of time before limitation expires. Correctly uploading the claim form to the online issue platform is not necessarily intuitive for everyone and there can be a delay of several hours before you find out if it has been successful (the High Court and County Courts also have different systems). Despite the online nature of the issue process, it remains advisable to make a clear attendance note (preferably counter-signed by a colleague) as to when the claim form was sent. In practice, this tends to mean it is advisable to leave extra time if you are not very familiar with the online issue process as receiving a rejection email after limitation expires is to be avoided. Since there can be a delay of several hours before the confirmation email is received and, if rejected, you will still need to leave time to correct the mistake, re-file the claim form and wait another confirmation. Unless the circumstances are exceptional, you should avoid leaving the issue of proceedings to the last day.

The claim form itself needs to be correctly drafted. Although an individual court may not pick up on all of these requirements, the following should be done in every case:

- Avoid putting initials in the claimant's name because the full name is required. As not everyone has a middle name, either put the full name or a first name and surname.

- The address must be within the jurisdiction; i.e. in England or Wales. If your client resides outside of the jurisdiction, then an English or Welsh address must be given for service. This can be the address of their solicitor (at the bottom of page 2 of the form).

- The full name of the defendant is not strictly necessary because the acknowledgement of service is used to clarify the correct name.

However, getting the name wrong can mean the wrong defendant has been sued and so care is needed to be as accurate as is possible. If the name cannot be easily discerned from the pre-action papers, then evidence of the steps taken to verify that the name was correct should be kept on file in case it is necessary to prove that you acted reasonably.

- The brief details section is designed to provide the defendant with enough information for them to identify the incident complained of. Accordingly, it is necessary to include:

  (a) That the claimant claims damages from the defendant (including its employees or agents, if appropriate);

  (b) Arising from the relevant cause of action (i.e. negligence, breach of statutory duty and/or breach of contract)

  (c) The dates of the alleged breaches;

  (d) The location of the alleged breaches (including the address);

  (e) That there is a claim for interest pursuant to statute.

  It is also helpful to state the date of any admission made and any limitation 'amnesty' agreed between the parties.

- The statement of value section is intended to confirm that general damages are expected to exceed £1,000 and to confirm that total damages are within the prescribed limits for the High Court (£50,000+; *CPR 1998 PD7A, para. 2.2*) or County Court. It is best to ensure that this is based on the current available evidence and evidence that it was is likely to be relevant if you late need to apply to increase the value of the case. The High Court may return a claim form unissued if it falls below £50,000 and has no other reason to justify its issue there.

- The address for service box at the bottom left-hand corner of the claim form is intended to contain the name and service address of each defendant. This can cause difficulties where there are multiple defendants. In such cases, it is permissible to refer to an appendix annexed hereto if there is insufficient space. Although all addresses need to go onto the court's and claimant's copies, each service copy can contain just the address for that defendant. Again, the address must be within England & Wales. If it is outside of the jurisdiction then the claim form cannot be validly served without taking the additional steps set out in *CPR 1998, Part 6 III* (which are outside the scope of this book but depend on whether the defendant is in Scotland, Europe or the rest of the world. Similarly, special rules pertain to suing a government department (also set out in *CPR 1998, Rule 6.10*).

- The bottom righthand side of the claim form requires you to state the value of the claim; the amount of the court fee; the amount of any costs and so the total amount claimed. The court fee is now 5% of the value of the case up to a £10,000 fee. The solicitor's costs should normally 'to be assessed' and the total value 'to be confirmed'.

- On page two of the official template, you are asked to confirm your preferred County Court Hearing Centre. For High Court cases, it is probably advisable to make it clear you are requesting either the Royal Courts of Justice or the local District Registry. Following this is a section asking for details of any vulnerable witnesses (including proposals for how these vulnerabilities should be dealt with). There is then a check box at the top asking whether the claim involves a human rights claim. The purpose is to put the court on notice of this additional element so it can allocate additional resources and requires forward planning to properly address these issues. At a CMC in the High Court, you may need to justify why a case valued under £200,000 should remain thee and a brief explanation can be put here (as well as in the Directions Questionnaire later).

The vulnerability provisions can be found in *CPR 1998 Rule 1.1(2)(a)* which require that the parties are on an equal footing and can participate fully in the proceedings. *Rule 1.6* and *Practice Direction 1A* set out the detail of how this is to be achieved.

AXX v Zajac [2022] EWHC 2463 (KB) contains helpful guidance on applying these provisions. There is also an accessible language summary in the headnote written to ensure that the judgement can be understood by readers with an average reading ability. in the headnote (reflecting the claimant's Flesch score).

Vulnerable clients may also benefit more from remaining anonymous. Helpful guidance on how the court assesses applications for anonymity orders can be found in *Dixon v North Bristol NHS Trust [2022] EWHC 1871 (QB)*. In *GKE v Gunning [2023] EWHC 332 (KB)*, (where anonymity was granted) shows that care is required not to create inequality of arms where the vulnerable witness order permitted the one side to take instructions on the written questions to be put to their client. At *para. 84, Ritchie J* observed:

> *"It is my view that giving the questions to the Claimant in advance created [sic] was not fa ir to the Defendant and created an unlevel playing field and degraded her evidence. The Defendant was not provided with the cross examination questions from the Claimant's counsel in advance. When this issue arose and during his closing submissions the Defendant expressed his astonishment and disbelief that this occurred and submitted in the strongest possible terms that it was unfair. I have sympathy with that submission. As a result, I have taken great care to approach the Claimant's cross examination answers with the unlevel playing field in mind."*

Vulnerable clients may also require litigation friends to act for them. Useful guidance on how the court approaches exercising its duties in regularising the appointments of litigation friends is provided by *Hinduja v Hinduja & Others [2022] EWHC 1533*

(QB). Ideally, capacity to litigate will have been assessed pre-action but the position can change (e.g. *Masterman-Lister, (supra)*). Useful guidance on both the test for legal capacity to conduct proceedings and the effect of settling a claim where it was not recognised that the patient lacked capacity can be found in *Dunhill v Burgin (Nos. 1 & 2) [2014] UKSC 18*. At *para. 18*, *Lady Hale* stated: *"I would hold, therefore, that the test of capacity to conduct proceedings for the purpose of CPR Part 21 is the capacity to conduct the claim or cause of action which the claimant in fact has, rather than to conduct the claim as formulated by her lawyers."* Any settlement must be approved by the court under *CPR 1998 Rule 21.10* to be valid and, in this case, the litigation friend ought to have been appointed when proceedings were commenced.

Coles v Perfect & Others [2013] EWHC 1955 (QB) provides an example where the evidence of capacity at settlement remained equivocal and neither side asserted that the claimant lacked capacity. *Teare J* was reluctant to order a trial to determine capacity in these circumstances and held that the court has an inherent jurisdiction to approve settlements and, by doing so, it ought to prevent the settlement being held to be invalid under *CPR 1998 Rule 21.10* if the claimant is later found to have lacked capacity (*para. 13*). This is useful to bear in mind where a claimant has capacity to litigate but expert evidence states that they lack capacity to manage their financial affairs, for example.

- Page three is the section asking you to set out the particulars of the claim. Most cases will require a separate document and there is the option to say that the particulars will be served separately. Previously, only particulars served with the claim form formed part of the public record and so could be obtained by the press whereas those served separately could not. The present rules are that separate particulars can be obtained but the press must make an application on notice to do. The court will take into account suitable representations from the parties to the case.

- Pages 4 and 5 contain the statement of truth and contact details for the claimant or their solicitor (if instructed). The statement of truth's standard wording no longer refers to particulars of claim and so it no longer needs to be amended to 'claim form' if the particulars are not being sent to the court for service. If the solicitor is signing the claim form then they ought to use the options on the form to show that they are signing the statement of truth on their client's behalf and are duly authorised to so do.

Issuing online, you will download the claim form for service. There is now no 'original' sealed copy (i.e. one bearing a physical ink court seal); rather there is an 'official' copy held at the court digitally. Where you have the option of a free text box or can upload a covering letter, you should make it clear what is being enclosed, what you want them to do (e.g. issue and serve or issue and return to you); the limitation date and an invitation to discuss with you if there is any problem. This latter point reduces the risk of the claim form being returned for some minor error. On this note, the *Human Rights Act 1998, Article 6* right to a fair trial has been interpreted as precluding the court from returning an unissued claim form due to an error when doing so would result in limitation being missed. The correct procedure in such cases is for the court to issue the claim form within limitation but to require an appropriate amendment to be made before service.

In terms of paying the correct fee, you should retain evidence on the file as to why you reasonably believed that that the value of the case was the amount you have set out in the claim form. The statement of truth verifies this amount but it is increasingly common to see defences pleading that the amount given limits the amount that can be recovered. The alternate argument is that the amount of damages is determined by the trial judge's discretion having heard the evidence before them and so they cannot be fettered by a procedural matter. However, deliberately or recklessly undervaluing the case so as to pay a lower court fee is clearly a matter which risks the ire of the court. Evidence of your thought process can be relevant if the value of the case needs to be increased later especially where you need to make an application.

Drafting the Pleadings

It is essential to take care in drafting the pleadings because these set out the nature and extent of each side's case as it will appear at trial. If a cause of action is not made in the particulars of claim, it may not be advanced at trial. In *Portland Stone v Barclays (infra), Stuart-Smith J (para. 30)* said:

> *"It should not need repeating that Particulars of Claim must include a concise statement of the facts on which the Claimant relies: CPR 16.4(1)(a). The "facts on which the Claimant relies" should be no less and no more than the facts which the Claimant must prove in order to succeed in her or his claim. … A statement of case exceeding 25 pages is regarded as exceptional: experience shows that most cases can be accommodated in well under 25 pages even where the most serious allegations are made. Experience also shows that prolix pleadings normally tend to obfuscate rather than to serve their proper purpose of identifying the material facts and issues that the parties have to address and the Court has to decide"*

Although permission could be sought at a later date, the court may refuse this or allow it on disadvantageous costs terms. If the defence fails to properly contest an issue or fact, it is usually taken to admit it and this can be difficult to resile from later in the case.

Before drafting the pleadings, you will need to have a very clear idea of the central issues in the case as well as evidence from the records, any other documents; the available witnesses; and the expert evidence. If any gaps in your client's case are apparent, then it is best practice to try to clarify them before the pleadings are prepared. A conference at this stage is often desirable but the clarification can be dealt with by correspondence.

As the pleadings show the extent of the dispute between the parties, the evidence to be adduced (and permitted) must also relate to what has been pleaded. In this light, proportionality focuses litigants' minds on serving evidence which relates only to the issues in dispute.

Thinking this point through, it remains the case that a well drafted pleading can lead to an earlier settlement of the case. This tends to arise in practice either where one party misinterprets the case it faces and realises too late in the day that it has been backed into a corner or where a proper narrowing of the issues has occurred which can be efficiently dealt with once the core evidence has been exchanged.

Broadly speaking, you are likely to encounter two styles of pleading in practice; the 'traditional' and 'modern' approaches. Neither is right nor wrong, but failing to appreciate their coexistence tends to result in costs being unnecessarily incurred in *inter partes* correspondence and court applications. The 'traditional' approach tends towards brevity whereas the modern approach tends towards including far greater detail. Brevity risks missing a material fact or allegation but benefits from conciseness. Providing greater detail risks elevating facts which cannot ultimately be proved to the status of material facts (see below) but benefits from being a 'cards on the table' approach.

English common law is a jurisdiction of 'ultimate fact' evidence and not 'ultimate issue' evidence (as one might find in America, for example). Accordingly, the core facts relevant to establishing the constituent elements of the cause of action (usually negligence of breach of contract) must be pleaded rather than a more generic pleading (such as an assertion that breach has occurred). Although the pleading should set the story out, it is not necessary to include everything that has happened (as might have been done in the medical chronology or expert reports).

The ambiguity lies in what amounts to the 'material facts' on a case-by-case basis. The material facts are the facts which the trial judge would rely upon in reaching his decision (i.e. the *ratio decidendi* of the case). Thus, they are the core facts which establish that a breach of duty has occurred; that an identifiable and avoidable injury has resulted from this; and the extent and value of that injury.

When drafting proceedings, it is advisable to both fully understand the evidence already presented and how this might develop to trial. It is not open to the trial judge to decide a case on an unpleaded basis as this crosses the line between an adversarial and inquisitorial system (*Al-Medenni v Mars UK Ltd [2005] EWCA Civ 1041, per Dyson LJ @ para 21*). Sometimes the way the case has been pleaded may be interpreted as achieving the same result in a more roundabout way (see *Chen v Ng (British Virgin Islands) [2017] UKPC 27, paras.39-44*). The issue in that case was that the particulars of claim stated that the breach of duty was committed by a particular person. At trial, the judge found that another, unknown employee must have committed the breach and found for the claimant. The Court of Appeal overturned this decision because the pleading had not included this possibility. Alternatively, the pleaded case may not spell out a specific point even after re-amendment. As long as the trial *"judge's conclusions are composed entirely of the acceptance of rejection of the factual assertions which were pleaded"* (*Ali v Dinc & Another [2022] EWCA Civ 34 per Birss LJ at para. 30*), then this line will not be crossed.

Accordingly, whether drafting or checking a statement of case, the aim is to ensure that all matters which you intend to rely. *CPR 1998, Rule 16.4* does set out requirements for the particulars of claim but is not especially helpful in this regard (because they are the procedural and not substantive requirements). It says only that a concise statement of facts being relied upon by the claimant is required without guiding the reader further. Additional matters set out in this rule are the claim for interest, whether aggravated or exemplary damages are being sought (extremely unlikely in a clinical negligence case) and then the matters set out in the accompanying practice direction (see further below). None of this tells you what amounts to a material fact or how much detail is reasonable which are the essential details needed in practice.

Almost since time immemorial, the substantive purpose of the pleadings is to set out the legal and factual issues which the court needs to determine at trial. This means that the claimant needs to set out:

(a) His or her right to bring the case (i.e. who they are, their relationship to the defendant and the reasons why the defendant owed them a duty of care);

(b) A description of the wrongful acts or omissions which have been committed by the defendant; and

(c) A description of the consequential damage which has resulted from this.

In order to achieve this purpose, the material facts should be set out in the order in which they happened so the court can see how the events in question unfurled and that the damage complained of did indeed occur after the breach. It is then necessary to particularise each allegation of breach separately. Itemising these is desirable because it allows you to break the central allegation(s) identified previously into their constituent parts and so precisely identify the case you want to present. It is often prudent to include a final 'catch all' allegation at the end of the list of breaches along the lines of the defendant having failed in all the circumstances to have exercised reasonable skill and care. Whilst this is arguably duplicative, it does avoid you being caught out by an unforeseen development in the evidence at trial.

Once that has been done, it should be expressly asserted that these events caused the claimant avoidable injury loss and damage before particularising these. Again, the core elements of the chain of causation should be itemised for the benefit of the court and a catch-all allegation should be included at the end.

It is then necessary to set out the particulars of injury. This is often done by reference to the accompanying condition and prognosis report. The name of the expert and date of the report should also be given. Interestingly, *CPR 1998, Practice Direction 16, Para. 4.3* does not require a report in all circumstances. Specifically, it requires a report to be served where the evidence of a medical practitioner is to be relied upon. What is desirable is a condition and prognosis report (*"a report from a medical practitioner about the personal injuries which he alleges in his claim"*) but this is not always practical.

Firstly, a report is not required to be served in a fatal case for the fairly obvious reason that the deceased's condition and prognosis is known with certainty. Secondly, where the claimant has recovered at the time of the drafting the particulars, then it may well be that a C&P report serves no practical purpose. Thirdly, if, unusually, a C&P report is desirable but not available (perhaps as a result of uncertainty as to prognosis, financial limitations and/or unavoidable limitation issues or genuinely insurmountable difficulties in obtaining one) then the wording of the practice direction is wide enough to justify a clinical letter which describes the present position being served and referred to. Fourthly, in *Mark v Universal Coatings & Services Ltd [2018] EWHC 3206 (QB)*, no medical evidence at all was served with the particulars of claim. At *para. 49 Martin Spencer J* said:

> *"It seems to me that 16 PD.4 (sic) sets a benchmark because it is a practice direction which covers all personal injury claims from the most simple to the most complicated, but which, in many of the more complicated cases, is honoured more in the breach than in the observance where the parties sensibly recognise the limitations of what can be achieved at the early stage of service of the Particulars of Claim. Thus, a defendant's advisors will often agree that service of a medical report and schedule of loss at that stage is pointless. However, as I have stated, the defendant always has the option of recourse to the court. The point is that most practitioners would strongly suspect, be surprised at the suggestion in Mitchell/Denton regime for relief from sanction applies to the obligation to serve a medical report and schedule of loss with the Particulars of Claim, with all the hurdles which need to be surmounted within those principles."*

Following this, it is desirable but not essential to set out details of any special damages being claimed. This is usually done by referring to the accompanying schedule of special damages (even if the figures are 'to be confirmed' as more evidence comes to light). At the end of the particulars comes the prayer for relief stating that the claimant seeks damages, interest thereon (pursuant to statute) and costs.

Practice Direction 16 also sets out some additional procedural matters which should be included. Some of these are unusual in the context of clinical negligence and so reference should always be made to the *PD* especially if the case is also being brought in contract. In all personal injury actions, the claimant's date of birth must be included. In fatal cases, *PD16 para 5* sets out several specific additional requirements. Taken together, the particulars must state that the claim on behalf of the deceased (e.g. for pre-death injury and the bereavement award) is made under the *Fatal Accidents Act 1976* and should state that the claim on behalf of the estate is made under the *Law Reform (Miscellaneous Provisions) Act 1934*. The identity, date of birth and details of the claim made by each dependent must also be included.

Where provisional damages are thought to be needed, then *CPR 1998, PD16 para. 4.4* requires that the statutory provision be pleaded (either under the *Senior Courts Act 1981, s32A* or *County Courts Act 1984, s51*). Both the chance (not likelihood) of there being a future deterioration in the claimant's health and the disease of type of anticipated deterioration must also be pleaded.

More generally, if the infringed legal right arises from statute, then the specific provision should be pleaded. The law does not need to be pleaded to any extent greater than this. However, if it is, then it will need a response.

Whilst evidence should not be pleaded, it can be rather difficult to distinguish between material facts and evidence. Evidence is the means by which you intend to prove the material facts constituting the cause of action. Naturally, you should avoid pleading that this witness or that expert says that a particular fact is true – this would be pleading circumstances which do no more than simply prove the truth of other facts already alleged (see *Schweiger v Vineborg (1905) 2 WLR 266 (KB)*). Instead, you simply assert that the fact occurred (based on the evidence you have in front of you). There is therefore a process of distillation involved.

However, it may well be the case that a particular piece of evidence is so close to the paraphrased distillate derived from it that it is simply more effective to plead the piece of evidence directly. An example of this is where a clinical letter from a hospital doctor to a GP advises the GP of the condition and of the need to keep it under review (or otherwise). If the GP fails to heed that advice (or if the advice was negligently unclear) then it is acceptable to quote directly from the letter. The question as to whether it is then better to plead medical records more generally is linked to a certain extent to the pleading style being adopted (traditional or modern). When considering this, bear in mind that the more evidence that is pleaded increases the risk that your client finds themselves in a straitjacket at trial (if that piece of evidence is not accepted).

Each practitioner needs to develop a style which they have confidence in. Tactical considerations may influence whether you prefer a more traditional or modern approach in each case. It does not necessarily follow that brevity indicates that the case has been poorly thought out or that a considerable amount of detail is required to avoid being caught out at trial. In *Williams v Wilcox [1835-42] All ER Rep 25 (QB), Lord Denman, CJ* stated that: *"…when a state of facts is relied on, it is enough to allege it simply without setting out the sub-ordinate facts which are the means of proving it or the evidence sustaining the allegation."* This has a clear resonance in the post-Jackson era of proportionality. *Al-Medenni* and *Ali [supra]*, in contrast, serve to remind us that proportionality does not supervene the need to be clear and precise in drafting pleadings. If you are confident that the detail you have provided is sufficiently clear and precise to tell the court what your client's cause of action or defence is, then it is likely to stand up to scrutiny. It is perfectly sensible to have a system in place where the draft pleadings are checked by one or two colleagues as long as they understand that different styles exist. Such a collegiate system is likely to be proportionate due to the importance to the court and parties of ensuring that the pleadings deal properly with the issues in dispute and does not involve duplication of effort because what is being tested is the clarity, precision and effectiveness of the central court document. Ideally, you should think ahead to the points the other side may take on any ambiguity or gaps and how this will look before procedural and trial judges if these points are taken.

Using precedents of past pleadings is useful in clinical negligence cases. They will highlight contrasting styles, the basic structure and, potentially, areas where the evidence needs clarification. Caution is required because each individual pleading ought to have been crafted to the facts of that particular case and so slavishly following a precedent will eventually cause serious problems. Even in the current era of downwards costs pressures, this needs to be a bespoke process undertaken by someone with (at the very least) a sound grasp of the central issues and facts of the case.

The statement of truth needs to be signed in order to verify that the facts contained within it. Clinical negligence pleadings are proportionately more complex than in many other types of personal injury litigation and the material facts and central allegations are not always well understood by lay clients. In most cases, it is anticipated that the lawyer with conduct of the case signs off the pleadings for this reason. It is, however, prudent to ask the lay client to approve them and to have evidence that they did so. Although a signed pleading counts as evidence, evidence should not really be pleaded (see above). Accordingly, there is little real practical merit in asking your lay client to sign the statement of truth for this reason, particularly if they are not also providing a witness statement. It is really for the lawyers to ensure that the pleadings are accurate rather than to expect the lay client to understand the legal arguments contained within them. As with the schedule of special damages, a signed copy of the particulars shows that they agree the facts being pleaded.

It is, therefore, crucial that the lay client agrees with the factual matrix being advanced on their behalf because this needs to be consistent with their evidence. It is also advisable that they understand any weak spots in the evidence. It is entirely reasonable to ask your client, the other lay witnesses and the experts difficult questions especially if you are concerned about their credibility, independence or if there is a bottleneck in the chain of evidence which they are likely to be cross-examined on (see further Chapter 6, *infra*).

The value of the case is also an important consideration. The valuation given in the claim form should be reconsidered especially if further evidence has come to light since the issue of proceedings. Furthermore, the value of the case may well show that the amount of money in issue is likely to be less than the costs of proceeding to trial. In such cases, alternatives to litigation need to be revisited and a plan put in place.

Service of Proceedings & Acknowledgement

This is a relatively straightforward step which has generated a considerable amount of case law. The reason for this is because it is left to the last minute when a mistake in procedure can lead to the entire case failing. The procedural rules are found in *CPR 1998 Part 6*.

Under *Collier v Williams & Other Appeals [2006] EWCA Civ 20*, where a defendant or their insurer has confirmed in writing that they nominate solicitors to accept service of proceedings or where the solicitors confirm that they are instructed to accept service, then service must be effected on them. This does not apply to personal service because that does not require a means of determining the correct address for service (*para. 14*). The defendant's solicitors are not obliged to confirm their client's address for service if they are not instructed to accept it (*para. 99*). It is for the claimant's solicitors to leave themselves sufficient time to make the enquiries necessary to establish the correct address for service; to understand the required formalities; and to make the appropriate court applications (including time extensions or substituted service or service by an alternate method/at an alternative address; *paras. 100-2*). If a mistake is made as to the defendant's 'last known address', then it is necessary to consider all of the facts before the court can conclude that the error was reasonable but it is necessary that the defendant has lived there at some point (e.g. *paras. 70, 99, & 101-2*). *"[T]he present case shows how dangerous it can be to make assumptions"* (*para. 103*).

Smith v Probyn & European Tour Ltd [2000] EWHC QB 136, requires that express confirmation is needed before service occurs; this specific confirmation is required even where the solicitors have been instructed on the case generally.

Where the nomination has been made, proceedings cannot be served on the defendant, only on their nominated solicitor (*Nanglegan v Royal Free Hampstead NHS Trust [2001] EWCA Civ 127* where proceedings were served on the chief executive of the defendant Trust).

In *Phoenix Healthcare Distribution Ltd v Woodward & Another [2019] EWCA Civ 985*, it was confirmed that a defendant does not owe a duty to inform a claimant that service was technically deficient before the service limitation date had passed (as long as it has not misled them). The error in this case was not obtaining written confirmation from the solicitors that they were instructed to accept service. This is congruent with a well-established principle that litigants are not under a duty to point out opponent's mistakes (e.g. *Barton v Wright Hassall LLP [2018] UKSC 12*). This needs to be borne in mind when acting collaboratively with opponents.

An exception exists for limited companies as service can also take place at the registered office under the *Companies Act 2006, s1139(1)* (see *Woodward & Another v Phoenix Healthcare Distribution Ltd [2018] EWHC 334 (Ch), para 5* and *Murphy v Staples UK Ltd [2003] EWCA Civ 656 para. 83* (one of the cases in *Cranfield & Another v Bridgegrove Ltd and Other Appeals*)).

Where service out of the jurisdiction is required, additional rules apply which are outside of the scope of this book (but see the brief discussion below and, for example, *CPR 1998 Rule 6 Part IV* and *PD 6B* and cases such as *Weston v Bates & Leeds United Football Club Ltd [2012] 590 (QB)*).

Accordingly, you should leave plenty of time to serve proceedings and, when you do it, check that all of the necessary documents are enclosed, and ask a colleague to recheck and do a brief attendance note. It is prudent to plan for the service of proceedings in the pre-issue period to maximise your chances of avoiding last minute problems arising.

CPR 1998 Part 6 contains the requirements. In essence, a claim form must be served within 4 calendar months of issue and it is the step necessary to effect service (such as placing it in the DX) which is what matters. The particulars of claim and other documents can be served up to two weeks later but only if this does not take you beyond the 4-month period. If you do serve them separately, then the relevant step is when they were received (allowing for the timescales set out in the practice direction. Additional time is allowed for foreign defendants but remember that additional procedural steps are required for service to be validly achieved. If necessary, an application for an extension of time can be made. However, extreme caution should be exercised with doing this for the claim form in case this is set aside later. It is best reserved for the particulars of claim.

More occasionally in clinical negligence, an alternate method of service might be required and justified under *CPR 1998 Rule 6.15*.

In *M v N [2021] EWHC 360 (Comm) (paras. 8 & 9) Foxton J* set out the principles for allowing alternative service outside of the jurisdiction. In essence, good reason must be shown for why '*the Hague Service Convention*' (the *Convention on the Service Abroad of Judicial and Extrajudicial Documents in Civil or Commercial Matters 1969*) cannot be used. This is most likely to be relevant when trying to serve against a foreign surgeon who has flown in to provide treatment in England and Wales but has returned to their home country. In *Gorbachev v Guriev and Others [2022] EWCA Civ 1270* it was confirmed that these rules apply to applications for third party disclosure.

In *D'Aloia v Persons Unknown & Others [2022] EWHC 1723 (Ch)*, permission was granted to serve by an alternative method and at an alternative place by both email and by non-fungible token ('NFT') by airdropping the court documents into a crypto wallet known to be accessible by the proposed defendant. Most likely, the NFT would have been a short text 'receipt' containing a link to the documents because the documents themselves would be too large to store on the blockchain. This is an embryonic area and so strict constraints exist. However, it may be a developing area. In *Jones v Persons Unknown [2022] EWHC 2543 (Comm)*, service of the order granting summary judgement was permitted by NFT airdrop. In *Osbourne v Persons Unknown Category A & Others [2023] EWHC 39 (KB)* service of the claim form and order by email to the relevant online NFT marketplace as well as to specific crypto wallets was permitted. *At paras. 49-50, Lavender J* held:

> *"One feature of service by NFT in the present case, since the NFT was to be "on the blockchain", was that the NFTs used to effect service would be open to the public and the hyperlinks contained in them could be used by anyone to view the documents served. In those circumstances, I was asked to sanction the redaction of the documents to be served in order to prevent access to personal data. I did so, but only on condition that:*
>
> *(1) the Defendants would be offered access to unredacted versions of the documents; and*
>
> *(2) the only redactions which would be made were those which were approved by the court.*
>
> *To this end, I directed that the Claimant must file a full set of the documents to be served, showing all proposed redactions, and I determined which of those proposed redactions were, and were not approved."*

Further details of how this form service is effected in practice are set out in the further judgment of *Osbourne v Persons Unknown Category A & Others [2023] EWHC 340 (KB)*. Alternate service methods are most likely to be relevant when trying to serve against a foreign surgeon who has flown in to provide treatment in England and Wales but has returned to their home country. With this in mind, whilst factual allegations should be left to the trial judge (e.g. *Tulip Trading Ltd v van der Laan & Others [2023] EWCA Civ 83, para. 91*), each cause of action does need to have a real (as opposed to fanciful) prospect of success for permission to serve out of the jurisdiction to be granted (e.g. *Wright & Others v BTC Core & Others [2023] EWHC 222 (Ch), para. 4*). Whilst this is presently unlikely to be available in clinical negligence cases, this is a rapidly developing area of technology and may become available more widely.

Following service, the certificate of service can be filed up to seven days after service, it is desirable to prepare and file it at the same time as serving proceedings (to avoid neglecting to do so within the next week). Copies of the documents served must be set out in the certificate and annexed to it. The date of deemed service is usually later than the date when the step was taken to effect service.

The defendant then has 14 days to file the acknowledgement of service. This serves three main functions. Firstly, it confirms that correct name of the defendant. Secondly, and importantly, it confirms whether the defendant wishes to make a jurisdictional challenge. This covers a challenge to the issuing court's ability to hear the case and is not necessarily limited to whether proceedings have been issued in the wrong country. Two important subsidiary points arise from this: (a) if the defendant does not challenge the court's jurisdiction, it cannot do so later; and (b) if it does do so, then this challenge is heard before anything else happens. If it wins the challenge, the case fails but, if it loses, then it must file a second acknowledgement indicating whether to wishes to defend all or part of the case. Thirdly, a failure to promptly file an acknowledgement of service which indicates whether the case is to be defended fully or partially entitles the claimant to request a default judgement.

Default judgements are procedural in nature and so are less secure than a trial judgement (similarly, summary judgements fall somewhere in between). As such, they are relatively easily set aside on an application by the defendant and so the claimant risks having an adverse costs order made against them for unreasonably refusing to agree to such an application. The relative complexity of the case is usually cited as the reason for this at the hearing. However, such reliance on 'complexity' assists the claimant in respect of proportionality and, in any event, it is often reasonable to agree to the judgement being set aside on the basis that all or part of the standard order for directions is made at the same time. Accordingly, seeking a default judgement has the benefit of using the court's case management powers at an earlier stage than would otherwise be the case.

The difficulties in holding onto a default judgement are illustrated by *Symes v St George's Healthcare NHS Trust [2014] EWHC 2505 (QB)* A specialist clinical negligence Master entered judgement in default of defence and made an order covering the initial pre-trial steps. The defendant did not seek to set this aside initially and followed the directions. However, it elected to serve a counter-schedule including a case on causation in breach of the order and inconsistent with the judgment in default. At the subsequent CMC, the Master rejected the defendant's submissions and held that the defendant was under a duty to respond to all relevant parts of the particulars of claim and had failed to do so by allowing a default judgement to be entered. It was disproportionate and contrary to the overriding objective to allow them permission to appeal. They had also not sought the court's permission to rely on the specific expert evidence in support of their position. Permission to appeal was initially refused on paper but allowed after an oral hearing. The Court of Appeal allowed the appeal in light of the *inter partes* correspondence and attendance notes showing that the pre-issue admission made it clear that the causation issues was raising in the counter-schedule would be raised. Accordingly, the default judgement reflected the limited pre-action admission and nothing more.

Judgement can reasonably be entered where a pre-action admission has been made. If the acknowledgement of service confirms that the case will not be defended, then a default judgement usually follows. If the defendant has made an admission and not withdrawn it but the acknowledgement states that the claim will be defended then clarification is required. It may be that the intention is simply to contest quantum and, if so, then judgement should be entered. Where the defendant does intend to withdraw the admission, then the reasonableness of this needs to be assessed based on all of the circumstances. In *Somoye v North West Anglia NHS Foundation Trust [2023] EWHC 191 (QB)*, this was considered in the context of complaints investigations and inquest verdicts. To summarise, the defendant made and confirmed an admission of liability based on its serious incidence investigation (which also included an expert report). The confirmation was sent before the inquest resumed and the verdict went in the defendant's favour. Although the defendant did have an arguable defence, the prejudice to the claimant and the defendant's conduct outweighed this and summary judgement was entered (*paras. 60-1*). *Master Sullivan* stated that (*para. 36*): *"[i]n my judgment, it is right to criticise the defendant's conduct. A defendant is expected to take independent legal and medical advice at an early stage and before making an admission. That is especially so where an expert not instructed by the defendant raises issues which show there may be an argument on causation which would provide a defence to the claim."* The defendant delayed in notifying the claimant of this potential defence and of its intention to withdraw the admission (*para. 38*). This case is also considered further in Chapter 8.

Summary judgements are usually appropriate where one side's statement of case discloses no reasonable prospects of success. So, in *Doorway Capital Ltd v American International Group UK Ltd [2022] EWHC 182 (Comm)*, summary judgement was granted as an alternative to striking out the claim on the basis that there was no reasonable prospect of success and no other reason to hold a trial. *Global Asset Capital Inc & Another v Aabar Block SARL & Others [2017] EWCA Civ 37, Hamblin LJ* helpfully summarised the principles relevant to granting both summary judgement and strike out applications at *para. 27*:

1. The respondent must have *"a realistic claim"* which *"carries some degree of conviction and is more than "merely arguable""*;

2. The court should avoid conducting mini-trials or determining matters of fact;

3. Short matters of law can be determined where the judge believes he has all of the relevant information available to do so.

Accordingly, in clinical negligence cases, this means clearly showing that either the impugned clinician has or has not been negligent and so the application ought to be supported and countered with evidence. In *Hewes v West Hertfordshire Hospitals NHS Trust and Others [2018] EWHC 1345 (QB)*, the third defendant supported its application with logical expert evidence to the effect that there had been no breach of duty. This required the claimant to adduce expert evidence supporting his case. Although the claimant had served a letter from his expert confirming that he remained supportive, he had not covered his reasons why the third defendant's expert's opinion was unreasonable or illogical. The Master decided (after being initially sceptical, *paras. 46 and 64*) that there had been sufficient time for this to occur following receipt of the third defendant's report and entered judgement in its favour. However, he did not grant the application based on a second argument that factual causation would not be proved because there was evidence supporting a factual dispute (*para. 69*). *Tangle Inc v One For Fun Ltd [2023] EWHC 217 (Ch), para. 30* is a useful reminder that the court also has a discretion to order a stay of proceedings or repleading the case as alternatives to a strike out.

Subject to what is said below, receipt of the defence should then close the pleadings and trigger the court serving a notice of allocation and setting the date by which the case management conference is to be held and the parties' costs budgets to be filed.

Clarifying Each Side's Case

Ideally, the pleadings should be a more precise version of the respective cases already set out pre-action. However, it may be that evidence changes after the case has been pleaded or (reasonably or otherwise) that one party believes that the case they face remains unclear in one or more aspects.

There are several procedural tools available to litigants. The most important are amendments to the pleadings (*CPR 1998 Parts 17 & 19*) and requests for further information (*Part 18*). Amendments are used to formally change the case your opponent must meet whereas requests for further information are used to fill in the gaps in the pleaded case.

Under *Part 17*, any amendment can be made before the service of the claim form (and particulars if they were issued with the claim form). If proceedings have been served, then permission from the court is required. In such cases, amendments can be made as late as trial (e.g. *XM v Leicestershire Partnership NHS Trust (supra), paras. 16 & 17*). However, if a party is being added or substituted, then the change must comply with *Part 19*. Generally speaking, the court will need to be satisfied that the relevant limitation period has not expired against the proposed new defendant. In *Mark (supra), Martin Spencer J* confirmed that permission is not required to add defendants if the claim form has not been served within the initial 4-month period (at *para. 15*).

The amendments must be clearly shown and distinguished from the original text. This can either be done by showing them in red, using a numbering system or by producing a new document (where the changes are extensive). The rules allow more than one amendment to be made. Re-amendments are in green and subsequent amendments purple (for re-re-amendments) then yellow (for re-re-re-amendments) followed by brown (for re-re-re-re-amendments) before the process is repeated. However, such extensive amendments probably indicate a fairly troublesome issue with the case and each one requires the court's permission if service has occurred. The extent to which such a series of re-amendments would be allowed would depend on the significance of each one. As a rule of thumb, the more minor the amendment and the earlier they are made, the more likely that they are to be permitted.

Realistically though, amendments should be saved for matters which genuinely go to the nature of the case to be made at trial and it should never be assumed that they will be allowed. Even where they are, they often result in your opponent being given the option to amend their case consequentially, delays and the party seeking the amendment bearing the costs arising from it. Amendments can, in suitable cases, be made at any point before the trial judge hands down judgment. Amending the case in the absence of a genuine change in the factual position tends to undermine that party's case because it demonstrates a fault in the pre-action investigations or case preparation. However, this has to be balanced against the view the trial judge is likely to take of the pleaded case if it is not amended. Just because a case can be amended does not mean that it should be: carefully weighing up the advantages and disadvantages of each of the proposed amendments and consequential amendments on each party's case should be done as part of the advice to your client. If your case will be stronger as a result, then the risk of adverse costs consequences may well be worth taking. That said, it may be that there are no genuine costs consequences if your opponents are well aware of the alternate case and have already investigated it. Everything else being equal, downwards costs pressures risk reducing the preparation that goes into pleading a case and so increases the risks of amendments being needed. Whilst QOCS protection appears to prevent the defendant from claiming its costs of the whole case following an amendment which causes it to lose, the court's wide discretion as to costs could well be exercised so as to require the claimant to bear its own costs up to the point the amendment was allowed. There is certainly a school of thought that prefers not to amend a case once it has been pleaded for this reason.

Requests for further information have similar considerations. *Part 18* comprises of two sections and these can be usefully understood by referring back to their pre-CPR names: 'requests for further & better particulars' and 'interrogatories'. Both use the same procedure now – you should try to agree them and allow a reasonable time for them to be answered before applying to the court for an order.

'Requests for further & better particulars' are used to clarify the pleaded case and 'Interrogatories' are used to try to pin down the evidence being relied upon. Care is needed, because the perceived lack of clarity in your opponent's statement of case may simply be down to the traditional style used. The party making the request needs to have a clear idea of what it is they believe is unclear and how it prevents them from understanding the case they face in terms of understanding the material facts and cause of action. 'Interrogatories' essentially seek to ascertain what evidence supports which of the pleaded facts. Whilst they can play a useful role in showing that the other party has a weak case on one or more links in the chain of causation, making the request too early risks giving your opponent a clear idea of your intended approach to the evidence at a time when they still have the opportunity to serve evidence dealing with these issues. They are, perhaps, best saved until after the factual evidence has been exchanged.

Another cautionary note is to try to avoid confusing matters which genuinely form part of the clarity of the case your client must meet with matters more properly dealt with by evidence (documentary, lay or expert evidence). The 'interrogatory' element of *Part 18* questions is there to allow you to interrogate your opponent before trial. A resourceful litigant or advocate can successfully use this to elicit details of the evidence to be served in due course or to fill in gaps of evidence so served. However, it should be borne in mind that where the evidence itself is to be served subsequently, the *Part 18* questions risk being superfluous if asked too soon. Questions going to expert evidence are best asked under *CPR 1998 Part 35* whilst *Part 36* allows suitable admissions to made (if the offer is properly worded). Notices to admit facts are available to pin your opponent down on key disputed facts; and all of these issues can be dealt with via correspondence or negotiation in any event. Accordingly, *Part 18* should really be seen as one part of a set of tools available to litigants to narrow the issues. Each tool is best used for a specific purpose and none are useful in all situations.

Al Saud & Others v Gibbs & Another [2022] EWHC 706 (Comm), para. 35, confirms that the court does not have jurisdiction to make an order compelling *Part 18 Requests* be answered if they are not *"strictly confined to matters which are reasonably necessary and proportionate"* to allow that party to either prepare its case or understand the case it faces. In *Henderson & Jones Ltd v Ross & Others [2022] EWHC 2560 (Ch)*, the pleadings were considered to be clear and so this test failed because cross-examination at trial provided a reasonable and proportionate alternative (*para. 46(b)*).

A further tool available to litigants is to serve a notice to admit facts under *CPR 1998, Rule 32.18*. Conceptually, 'admit' can mean either 'adduce' (i.e. 'to admit into evidence') or 'accept' (i.e. 'to make an admission'). *CPR 1998, Rule 32.18(1)* makes it clear that it is the latter and *CPR 1998, Rule 32.18(3)* shows that any admission made is treated in the same way as admissions under *CPR 1998, Rule 14.1* in terms of being limited to being from that party within the proceedings in which the admission was made (so do not assume that they apply to any related proceedings). Similarly, *CPR 1998, Rule 32.18(4)* requires the court's permission to amend or withdraw the admission. As with *Part 36* offers, a notice to admit facts must be served at least 21 days before trial (under *CPR 1998, Rule 32.18(2)*). As the name indicates, the party serving the notice is requesting their opponent to admit facts in the case and not issues or legal points.

As a rule of thumb, the more fundamental these facts are to the case's central allegations, the more likely it is that the party receiving the notice will try to maintain their denial. This is not necessarily unreasonable. As such, it is best to use these notices as part of the wider investigation and clarification process outlined in the rest of this book. The costs consequences flow if the fact is not admitted but is then proved later. As such it falls within the wide discretion of the court under *CPR 1998, Rules 44.2-44.4* (*viz.* the factors affecting the discretion; the assessment basis; and the amount of costs). Accordingly, it is prudent to keep a clear paper trail of the amount of costs incurred as a result of the failure to make a timely admission so this is not lost in the weeds when costs come to be determined and to understand what the court is likely to view as reasonable conduct in serving the notice.

The underlying purposes of notices to admit facts were helpfully summarised in *Ceperkovic v MacDonald & MacDonald and Patriquin v Macdonald & Others 2016 BCSC 939* (a Canadian personal injury case). At *para. 30, Dillon J* explained:

> *"The purposes of the notice to admit are multiple: The primary purpose is to "save both the Court and litigants the time and expense involved in proving the authenticity of documents or in proving facts" (Clarke v Minister of National Revenue 2000 CanLII 15090 (FC) ... at para. 43... The rule is intended to eliminate issues altogether from a case or to facilitate proof of issues that cannot be eliminated... Thus, the notice to admit can isolate important factors from a strategic and cost efficient perspective... It enables the parties to "prepare for an efficient trial focused on what is disputed" (Orlan Karigan & Associate Ltd v Hoffman 2000 CanLII 22725 (ON SC)... The notice to admit obviates the necessity and expense of calling evidence at trial... Ultimately, it is a means to foster the timely adjudication of a claim on its merits..."*

Similarly, it is useful to bear in mind what *Dillon J* said about what amounts to a reasonable justification for not making the admissions. To summarise *paras. 32-37*:

1. The truth or authenticity of the fact remains to be proven;

2. The fact is irrelevant and does not serve to save time and expense;

3. Rarely, the fact is privileged;

4. The notice is a veiled attempt to obtain further particulars (i.e. where a *Part 18* Request should be used in our jurisdiction) or to circumvent disclosure;

5. The notice actually seeks an admission of a point of law not a fact;

6. The notice is overly broad, repetitious or in the nature of an argument;

7. The notice is vague and the party serving it has not responded to clarification requests before trial;

8. The fact must be reasonably capable of evaluation within the required timescale;

9. The fact must be reasonably within the knowledge of the party served with it (although a lack of knowledge is no excuse);

10. The party reasonably believes that it will succeed on the fact at trial (e.g. due to conflicting evidence; the need for expert opinion on the fact; or the fact is central to that party's case)

As such, notices are not universally appropriate for every disputed fact and should be properly concise to be used effectively. Basing your use of notices along these lines provides a very solid foundation. This approach was followed in *Mee Hoi Bros. Company Ltd & Others v Borving Investments (Canada) Ltd & Others 2016 BCSC 2478* and echoes of *Dillon J's* list can be found in *Glaxo Wellcome UK Ltd (T/A Allen & Hanbury's) & Another v Sandoz Ltd & Others [2018] EWHC 1626 (Ch)*. It follows that a party cannot be compelled to admit these facts (*para 17*). The drafting and timing of the notice is important because the defendants submitted that the wording used did not easily lead to binary answers (i.e. 'yes' or 'no') and that the exchange of witness evidence would provide further clarity (*paras. 18-19*). *Chief Master Marsh* considered that the intent of the claimant's solicitors in trying to narrow the basic facts of the case and to clearly identify those which were uncontroversial was laudable and adjourned the application until later in the case with the express hope that the parties would collaborate on this issue (*paras. 20-22*). As such, this case helpfully illustrates that using notices to admit facts and bringing them to the court's attention can genuinely assist in narrowing the contested facts and so assist with dealing with cases proportionately. Parties who know that the court is cognisant of their opponent's desire to act reasonably take a significant risk by ignoring the court's comments even if they are not solidified into an order.

Conclusion

The importance of issuing and serving proceedings correctly cannot be overstated from the claimant's perspective. Missing the limitation or service deadlines is likely to result in the case being debarred, or at the very least, will delay the case and increase costs whilst the court hears the application. Conversely, the defendant need only wait to see if the claimant does make such a mistake.

However, in order to maximise the opportunities that this phase of the litigation brings, both parties need to proactively assess the issues that genuinely require to be litigated and to focus their respective statement of case accordingly. If this does not occur, the case is going to be much harder to conclude proportionately because the issues and evidence will not have been properly distilled. This carries with it the risk that the court will exercise its case management powers in ways which are not entirely helpful to both litigants.

CHAPTER FIVE

CASE MANAGEMENT

Introduction

The goal of case management is to agree or obtain the court's permission for the steps needed to conclude the case. This is achieved by a timetable, directions and costs budgets which assist the respective cases without being disproportionate to the case as a whole.

However, it remains relatively common for one or both sides not to make the most of this opportunity. Focussing the directions on the central issues set out in the pleadings and then the budget on these directions makes for much better case preparation. It is important to focus on those parts of the litigation phases which progress the litigation rather than becoming bogged down in the minutiae of each stage if the costs are to be kept proportionate to value. However, there will be cases where one side's approach to the litigation means that smaller battles need to be fought and costs incurred on ancillary issues. It is therefore also important that evidence be built up on these so that you can show the court that you have attempted to maintain costs at a proportionate level at all times (even on the biggest cases).

Directions Questionnaire

The Directions Questionnaire (*Form N181*) is often overlooked as source of information about the case. However, it can provide a useful indication of the approach to be taken by both parties (e.g. *Burke v Imperial College Healthcare NHS Trust (supra)*). It is necessary to provide details about settlement; witnesses names and the issues they go to, the experts' names, disciplines and issues to which their evidence relates; an estimate of their costs; and witness availability. Where a party has not properly planned its approach to the case, the DQ will usually show this by some of the details being lacking. This does not necessarily mean that the court will admonish them, but it does indicate that their case may not be as well prepared as might be expected. Where one party intends to make an application, details should also be provided so that it can be held at the CMC (if possible). The draft directions (agreed if possible) should also be attached.

Standard Directions

The standard directions order is available from the Ministry of Justice's website. This originated in the Royal Courts of Justice as a way of ensuring that clinical negligence cases are dealt with efficiently. Although some variations are used in the District Registries and County Court, the standard directions should be used unless the court indicates otherwise. Unfortunately, it is not always clear why some judges do depart from them. If your firm has saved the standard directions as an in-house template, care should be taken to ensure that it is kept up to date.

The introduction to the standard template makes the following points:

- The directions allow the court and the parties to be flexible. The timetable or the requirements can be adapted to fit the particular circumstances of each case as long as it is reasonable to do so.

- The dates in the timetable should be in bold type for clarity.

- The parties should be fully and accurately described in the title of the order. It is best practice to use the title of the action as shown in the claim form (or amended version if this has occurred) rather than from some other document (where it may have been abbreviated or misspelt).

- The order should make it clear that it is made pursuant to a case management conference, an application or both. This is best done in the preamble to the order.

- The parties are requested to specifically consider the role the experts play in the preparation of the agendas for their joint meetings.

- In the RCJ, a draft order in Word format, should be sent by e-mail to the Assigned Master at least two days before the hearing. In other courts, the notice or order listing the CMC should stipulate when the draft orders or agreed order must be submitted.

The standard directions timetable is then set out in the following manner:

1. Allocation. The notice of allocation will usually have allocated the case to the multi-track. As this is the normal track for clinical negligence cases, this part of the order usually simply confirms that the case will remain in the multi-track. However rarely, if developments have occurred which justify the case being reallocated to a lower track, then this would be the appropriate point to do so. Clinical negligence cases are very rarely suitable for the fast track or small track but an unusually simple one (perhaps involving very modest damages and either a single joint expert witness or one expert per side) might qualify.

2. Preservation of evidence. This requires that the defendant preserves the claimant's original records and allows the claimant to inspect them on seven days' written notice. This is not superseded by copies already having been provided in the pre-action period. As this is a standard order made in every case, the defendant should have ensured that they will be able to comply with it as soon as they become aware of the case if the claimant remains under their care. If the patient has died or changed practices, then GP records will have been sent for central storage or to the new practice. However, a copy of the computerised records may still be in a defendant GP's possession and an audit-trailed copy often provides useful evidence and the standard wording provides for this situation.

3. Maintenance of evidence. This direction relates to standardising the core bundle in order to improve case management. The claimant is required to create and maintain a paginated bundle of the relevant records as soon as is possible. References to these records in expert reports should be to this bundle only. All relevant electronic documents must also be safely retained. Again, as this direction is so common, preparing and maintaining such a bundle should form part of the early pre-action work and not left to after this order is made.

4. Amendments. If amendments to the pleadings are permitted, then it is usual for the judge to approve the draft before them and initial it. Alternatively, reference may be made to an agreed version already served (serving does not mean that permission will be granted, of course). Less usually, permission can be given for the amended statement of case to be served by a set date (although this is usually only permitted where the amendment is not contentious). Consequential permission may be needed to allow the other party to serve an amended statement of case and the normal costs order is for the party making the first amendment to bear the costs of, and occasioned by, that amendment.

5. Judgement. If liability has been admitted, then this should be recorded in the directions order. This can include liability being entered for a set percentage of the damages payable on a full liability basis. If liability is to be admitted, then it is usually prudent for the claimant to make an application for an interim payment and payment on account of costs and the defendant should put itself in a position to deal with this at the CMC.

   Split trial. If a split trial is needed, the court will need to be persuaded that it is proportionate and reasonable to determine liability issues before the quantum issues. This will often only be allowed where the likely value of the case is very substantial or prognosis issues will remain uncertain for a significant period of time. It is inappropriate simply to prove that there will be a split trial. Instead, it should be specifically stated that the preliminary issues of breach of duty, causation of damage and the effects of the avoidable injury (i.e. causation of consequential losses) be tried separately from quantum issues.

Mather v Ministry of Defence [2021] EWHC 811 (QB) is an example of the competing arguments for and against holding a split trial on the central causation issue in the case after the CMC had been held. The application was rejected but the issue could be revisited nearer to the trial. In *AXX v Zajac (supra)*, the court accepted that the claimant's vulnerability was a factor which was relevant to deciding whether a split trial should be held and that this would assist him in engaging with the quantum experts. This was supported by a letter from the relevant expert. In both cases, the party resisting the application submitted that the costs of a split trial exceeded that of a single trial.

6. Disclosure. The usual provision is for standard disclosure to occur by exchanging lists of documents. Where there is to be a split trial, then disclosure can be limited to the liability issues (in the first directions order) and then to quantum issues (at the CMC after the preliminary issue has been tried). The second part of this direction usually requires that requests for inspection of the documents or for copies of the disclosed documents be made one or two weeks afterwards. It is desirable to include a further, set date to provide for the provision of those documents (leaving enough time for them to be considered and witness statements to be updated in light of them). Depending on the amount of documents needing to be disclosed and the extent of disclosure during the pre-action period, it may well be reasonable for this to take place about 1 month after the CMC. Alternatively, the court may already have made an order requiring disclosure to occur before the CMC.

7. Witness statements. The usual provision is for each side's witness statements to be exchanged simultaneously. In the event that it is already known that a witness will not be able to give evidence at

trial (if they have died since providing the statement, for example), then the *Civil Evidence Act 1995, s2* notice of proposal to adduce hearsay evidence ('hearsay notice') must also be served with the statement. The reason for this is because the other side is entitled to be put on notice that this witness' evidence will be hearsay and that the proper procedure has been followed for this to be validly admitted. The option is available to serve C&P and quantum statements later (perhaps at the same time as the schedule and counter-schedules). Whether this is reasonable in any given case depends on the complexity of the issues and whether there is a split trial; there is no presumption that these will be served separately and serving one set of statements will often be more desirable in terms of proportionality. An alternate view is that having permission to serve quantum statements later makes it easier to serve additional liability evidence if something unexpected arises (because the other side is already expecting a further statement). If the provision is not there, then a separate application would be needed which itself increases costs and needs to be budgeted for.

8. Expert reports. The directions covering expert reports comprise the majority of the standard order. Due to the importance of these provisions, experts must be provided with a copy of the directions order within seven days of it being sealed (which may be considerably later than when it was made & became effective at the hearing) or when the expert is instructed (if later). The other provisions can be summarised as follows:

    (a) Single Joint Experts. There is some flexibility over what aspects of the case a single expert is to report on. This is not a mandatory paragraph. Consideration should be given as to whether a single joint expert is appropriate at all. In many cases, it will not be because there is a genuine dispute over the underlying facts on this part of the case which each side is entitled to test out at trial with the help of expert evidence. Examples of where single joint experts are useful are where the remaining issues are very narrow; for supporting quantum reports (where the central issues are dealt with by separate reports from experts in other disciplines); or where co-defendants are seeking to instruct separate causation experts. In the latter case, some degree of caution must be exercised to ensure that each co-defendant is not disadvantaged where they have differing (and mutually exclusive) causation arguments. Where single joint experts are contemplated or imposed, care must always be taken to ensure that the joint instructions are fair to all parties involved because questions and additional evidence must be shown to the other instructing parties. It is extremely unusual to use joint experts for contested liability issues between claimants and defendants.

The standard wording allows for the instruction to be limited to stated disciplines and issues. You will need to be able to argue persuasively for the scope of what best suits your client. It also provides for the date by which the instructions must be sent and so sufficient time must be factored in to allow for any negotiations over the preparation and wording of the letter of instruction and bundle to proceed effectively and for your client to be advised of these. The wording also provides for the date by which the report must be served and that this must be sent to both parties.

In light of the above comments, it will not always be possible to agree on either the choice of expert or the joint instructions. In these circumstances, the parties must restore the hearing for the judge to decide on the disputed issues. Permission for this is included in the standard wording of this paragraph. However, it is specifically stated in the guidance notes that *"At such hearing the parties are to provide details of the CVs, availability and the estimated fee of the expert they propose and reasoned objections to any other proposed."* Failing to reach agreement is therefore likely to delay the progress of the case and unreasonable behaviour is likely to lead to avoidable costs penalties. Whether this risk is worth taking must be weighed up against what needs to be proved at trial and whether this can be achieved by a less adversarial approach to this part of the case.

Where the report is uncontentious, then it may well be appropriate to release the expert from attending trial in person. Accordingly, the standard wording of the order does not permit the expert to attend trial; it only permits the parties to rely on the evidence.

(b) Separate experts will be permitted where (i) significant issues remain between the parties; and (ii) where the trial judge is likely to benefit from hearing oral evidence from experts. This is the normal position.

The standard wording divides the expert reports between breach and causation experts and then condition & prognosis and quantum reports. The requirements are, however, the same. Permission is given to rely on the evidence of named experts in defined disciplines and to call them to give live evidence at trial. Although the template states that the experts' names should be given 'where known', the assumption is that the names will be included in the majority of cases because of the need to frontload cases and plan them out proportionately.

The specific matters which each expert is permitted to address is increasingly being included by judges and is generally very helpful. Care is needed to ensure you do not paint yourself into a corner.

Whilst the breach and causation reports are usually disclosed simultaneously, the C&P and quantum reports are usually disclosed sequentially in order to allow the defendant time to consider the valuation evidence being presented by the claimant. It may be that this evidence can be agreed before the defendant incurs the costs of instructing its expert to conduct a condition and prognosis examination. This approach pre-dates *LASPO 2012* but has fairly clear costs advantages where QOCS protection applies (*q.v.*). However, the defendant ought not to assume that the court will allow it a protracted time to arrange a C&P examination and so ought to have details of its proposed experts' reporting times available at the CMC. Conversely, the claimant should not assume that they will be given permission to update the C&P report(s) served with proceedings as this depends on the nature of the claimant's prognosis.

In respect of timing, the liability reports are often ordered to be exchanged approximately two months after exchange of witness statements in order to allow time for the reports to be finalised in light of the opponent's documentary and lay witness evidence. However, it is important that the expert has provided an indication of their availability before the directions order is made in order to ensure that there is sufficient time to finalise each expert's report before the final version is served.

(c) Supporting literature. The next part of the experts' evidence directions covers the materials they believe support their medical opinion. This is not evidence which is specific to the case; it is more generic in nature.

Supporting literature which has been published already must be listed in the disclosed report. It is not necessary to disclose it (although it is good practice to do so). Unpublished literature, however, must be served with the report. The issue being addressed in this part of the standard order is that unpublished literature may not be known or readily available to the opposing expert.

An interesting additional point is that supplementary literature is allowed to be served up to one month before trial. Accordingly, it is entirely possible that this can validly be served after the experts have held their joint meeting without breaching the order made. An expert seeking to rely on additional undisclosed supporting literature within one month of trial is not automatically debarred from doing so. However, the trial judge's permission is required and the standard wording leaves the costs of this to the trial judge's discretion. This discretion will be wide and will largely depend on the view the judge takes of the evidence as a whole.

The other document referred to is the expert's cv. This need only be 'produced' at the time the report is prepared – it does not need to be served. The purpose is to ensure that there is no conflict of interests which would undermine the expert's independence. However, it is best practice to raise the possibility of conflict in the initial instructions before the costs of the report are incurred.

(d) Experts' Discussions. The standard directions contain detailed provisions on the case management for this step, perhaps reflecting the problems that have been encountered since 1999. These can be summarised as follows:

(i) The meeting is not mandatory – the parties' solicitors and their experts can agree that they are not needed. This is underused even where there are no real issues between the experts following the exchange of their respective reports. The purpose of the joint meeting is to identify the extent of the experts' agreement and disagreement; to establish what further steps can be taken to further narrow the issues and to highlight any additional issues which may assist the trial judge (and the extent to which the experts agree on these).

(ii) The discussion is on a wholly without prejudice basis and is conducted in the absence of the lawyers. Accordingly, the discussion itself cannot be referred to later in the case. In certain situations, it may be reasonable for the lawyers to attend but this must be done with the agreement of all parties and the experts. Such attendance can be terminated by the experts (i.e. they can still hold the discussion in private) and the lawyer's input should be limited to advising on any questions or legal issues which arise.

(iii) The suggested time for the joint meeting is 8 weeks after the exchange of reports. Again, the experts' availability ought to be confirmed before the order is agreed.

(iv) Experts of the same discipline meet so it is likely that several separate meetings will be needed where there are separate experts dealing with different parts of the case.

(v) Preparing an agenda is also not mandatory; as with the meeting itself, the solicitors and experts can agree to dispense with them. Again, this option is very underused. Where agendas are used, the claimant's solicitor should send the first draft the to the defendant's solicitor 35 days before the date for the meeting. This draft should be prepared in conjunction with the claimant's expert and must be reasonable in its scope (i.e. not too long or short and proportionate). It should genuinely assist the experts and should not include leading questions. It must include a list of the outstanding issues between the experts in the preamble to the agenda. The applicable legal standards should be set out and the experts should be reminded that their role is not to determine the factual issues or to stray outside of their areas of expertise. Where appropriate, a list of the relevant evidence can be provided along with an agreed bundle for use at the joint meeting.

(vi) The agreed date may be earlier than the last date for the meeting set out in the order. The defendant then has 21 days in which to consider the draft agenda (including taking instructions and discussing it with its expert) and propose amendments if it cannot be agreed. The parties then have a further seven days to agree the agenda (i.e. this date is seven days before the agreed date for the joint meeting which is the same date the standard wording says that the agreed agenda must be sent to the experts by).

(vii) If the agenda cannot be agreed then the accompanying guidance notes state that any areas of disagreement should be genuine and not semantic or matters on which the experts themselves can agree. Sadly, disagreements remain common. If the disagreement cannot be resolved, the order allows for two options: either apply to the court (which, at the very least, will delay the timetable) or agree to include additional questions. These additional questions should follow on sequentially in a single agenda. In practice, this is usually the better option as it minimises the delay to the case. Separate agendas should be avoided.

(viii) The experts should agree and produce their signed, joint statement within seven days of their meeting.

Although the order does not precisely specify this, the parties should not try to influence the wording of the joint statement during this time. Surprisingly, the neither the rules nor the standard directions order expressly or categorically prohibit discussions between an expert and their instructing lawyers occurring between the meeting and the joint statement to discuss what happened. As such, a judge hearing an application after the problem has arisen may not sanction the offending party. Accordingly, it is prudent to include an express provision in the directions order and press for this to be included to prevent this occurring by making it clear that such conduct amounts to a breach of the court order. There is usually a standard direction requiring the directions order to be sent to the experts following the CMC but they should also be made aware of it in any event.

If such specific wording is not included in the directions order, reference can be made to the editorial note at *para. 35.12.2* of the *White Book* which references *BDW (infra)* and the *Technology & Construction Court Guide 2022*: *"Whilst this guidance concerned the application of the approach in the Technology and Construction Court Guide, it is of general utility and applicability."* The *TCC Guide, para. 13.6.3* states:

> *"Whilst the parties' legal advisers may assist in identifying issues which the statement should address, those legal advisers must not be involved in either negotiating or drafting the experts' joint statement. Legal advisers should only invite the experts to consider amending any draft joint statement in exceptional circumstances where there are serious concerns*

> *that the court may misunderstand or may be misled by the terms of that joint statement. Any such concern should be raised with all experts involved in the joint statement."*

The *Chancery Guide 2022* contains similar provisions at paras. *9.27.9.33 (pp67-8)* but the *King's Bench Guide (2022) (p75)* does not contain a comparable provision. In *BDW Trading Ltd v Integral Geotechnique (Wales) Ltd [2018] EWHC 1915 (TCC)* one of the experts sent the draft of his joint statement to his instructing solicitors for comment and made changes after receiving their feedback (*para. 16*). This was held to be *"a serious transgression"* (*para. 18*) albeit the expert *"was genuinely unaware that his conduct on this respect was inappropriate"* (*para. 19*) and his *"evidence seemed to me in the main to be balanced and realistic"* and was accepted at trial (*para. 20*).

In *Pickett v Balkind [2022] EWHC 2226 (TCC)*, the issue arose incidentally when the claimant's solicitor inadvertently disclosed an unredacted letter from their expert in support of their application for a trial adjournment due to the expert's pending surgery. This letter referred to a discussion between the expert and solicitor (and requests from the solicitor) between the joint meeting and joint statement (e.g. *para. 17*). Attempts to claim privilege and filing a 'replacement' application with a redacted copy of the letter failed to resolve the issue as did an application for an injunction. Ultimately, the claimant's solicitor was ordered to provide supplementary disclosure on the issue and the defendant was permitted to cross-examine the expert on these issues at trial (e.g. *para. 119*).

- The risk is that your client loses the ability to call its own expert evidence. The severity of the sanction depends on the egregiousness of the contact and its impact when judged against all of the available evidence. In *Andrews & Others v Kronospan Ltd [2022] EWHC 479 (QB)*, permission to rely on an expert was revoked pre-trial after evidence came to light that there had been lengthy communications (spanning approximately 6 months) with his instructing solicitors between the joint meeting and the signing of the joint statement. The claimant was, however, permitted to consider obtaining evidence from another expert despite the delay this would cause to the case.

In *Dana UK Axle Ltd v Freudenberg FST GmbH [2021] EWHC 1413 (TCC)*, the defendant breached a court direction requiring disclosure of what documents had been sent to its experts; sent documents direct to their experts with little or no supervision from their instructed solicitors; failed to send them to the claimant's experts; and appear to not have fully instructed trial counsel in this respect of this. This did not become known until day 7 of the trial after the claimant's experts had given oral evidence but before the defendant's experts had done so. Permission to rely on these experts was refused as a result of these breaches of *CPR 1998 Part 35, PD 35* and the *TCC Guide (including para. 13.3.2)* leaving the defendant with no expert evidence.

The standard wording does make it clear that the experts do not need their instructing solicitor's authority to sign the joint statement – their duty to the court covers this. However, should an expert radically depart from their previous, written opinion, then the joint statement should contain an explanation of why this has occurred. The guidance notes also remind us that *CPR 1998, Rule 35.12* provides that the instructing party is not bound by such a concession unless they have agreed to be bound. However, the expert's credibility may be fatally undermined.

(e) Schedules. The basic provisions relating to the schedules of special damages/losses go towards the service dates. Service will almost always be sequential and is usually tied to the date for serving the expert evidence on condition and prognosis. Sufficient time is usually required between the two dates to allow the defendant to consider, and to take instructions on, the claimant's schedule. Usually, this will require the input of its experts and so this needs to be carefully planned out.

The guidance to the standard wording asks that the parties use a format which enables the counter-schedule to be based on the schedule. The reason for this is to make it easier for the trial judge to compare the competing valuations of the case being put forward by each party. Accordingly, the schedule should enable the defendant to insert its figures and be sent electronically to them.

The standard wording also requires the parties to set out its position on whether periodical payments are or are not appropriate for each case. The accompanying guidance also explains that the parties should be prepared to give reasons for their provisional decision at the first CMC.

(f) Trial Directions. The first of the usual directions is the date by which the claimant's solicitor applies to the Clerk of the Lists for a listing appointment. To do this, a copy of the sealed directions order must be sent to the Clerk of the Lists (Room WG15 at the RCJ) so they can see that the request is officially sanctioned. The Clerk's office will then send an appointment notice to both parties with a date where they must attend in person. This is usually no later than six weeks after the CMC which means that the trial date is likely to be listed quite early in the case.

It is usual for both sides to send counsel's clerk along with a copy of the sealed order and the dates of availability for trial counsel, the lay witnesses and the experts. It can prove difficult to find a date which suits everyone. Once the trial period has been set, then it becomes much more difficult to change it and so it pays to have a clear and accurate system in place to cross-reference all of your side's dates to avoid and availability. In terms of proportionality, it is essential that the calls, e-mails and letters sent to get these dates are fully recorded because the amount of work involved will often seem surprising at the end of the case.

Where the dates of availability prove impossible to reconcile at the Listing Appointment, the Clerk has the option to ask the parties to return for another appointment having reconsidered matters, impose a date or to refer the matter back to the Assigned Master for further directions. Where one party fails to attend, the Clerk may list the trial in their absence or set another appointment date.

The system is slightly different in the County Court and District Registries. Usually, the parties are asked to send their dates of availability to the court by the set date and the court will then list without the parties attending. Thus, the dates need to be correct at the time of sending and, if there is a delay, updated before the trial date is set. Some courts will not list the trial until after formal ADR has been tried and failed.

The standard wording refers to the 'trial window' and 'trial period'. The window is the period of 3-4 months during which the trial period will be listed. The period is the date during which the trial itself will be held and will usually allow sufficient time either side of the time estimate for the trial itself. In order to give the parties (and their expert and lay witnesses) some degree of certainty, you can write to the court nearer the trial period to ask for the exact trial fixture. However, it is often the case that the trial is not finally fixed until a few days before the start of the trial period so you need to make your witnesses aware of this. This is also likely to mean that a settlement close to the trial will incur cancellation fees from the experts.

The guidance notes indicate that there should be at least two clear months between the last event in the timetable (usually the PTR or last joint statement being provided) and the start of the trial period so the trial window will not start before this. The reason for this is to allow ADR to occur in sufficient time to allow a genuine saving in avoiding trial costs. However, this is the last date by which ADR is to occur because the standard ADR provision is that the parties are to consider ADR at the earliest possible opportunity. Where one party suggests it, their opponent has 21 days to engage. Otherwise, they are expected to file a witness statement explaining why they refused. Such a statement is to be shown to the trial judge at the end of the trial. It is prudent to keep a clear record of the attempts your client has made to narrow the issues and of the reasons they have for being unable to negotiate once they have been put on notice of the other side's case. In the event that liability is admitted during the pre-trial period, the Masters usually like to be advised of this so they can give further directions if needed (and such a direction can be included in the standard order). If such an admission is made, then it should be formalised by entering judgement via a consent order so appropriate amendments to the directions timetable should be made at that point whether or not the case is proceeding at the RCJ.

The directions as to the trial bundles are straightforward: They must be agreed and filed with the skeleton arguments in accordance with *CPR 1998 Part 39, Practice Direction, para.39.3*. This must be done at least 7 days before the start of the trial. These provisions will be considered in more detail in later chapters.

(g) In the RCJ, there then follows a direction listing a further CMC on a set date (usually agreed at the first CMC). This has a time estimate of 30 minutes (which can be amended) because it is hoped that the parties will have largely complied with the order by that stage. Often, the most productive time for this second CMC is before the experts are due to hold their joint meetings so that any delays to those meetings can be brought to the judge's attention and the court's case management powers utilised to minimise the prospects of having to vacate the trial date. Where the trial date is jeopardised, the application needs to be made to the Clerk of the Lists to be heard by a judge rather than to the Masters' Support Unit (for hearing before a Master).

The standard wording provides that the further CMC can be vacated if all of the directions have been complied with, if no further directions are required and if the judge is given reasonable notice. This is relatively straightforward at the RCJ because you simply send a suitably polite e-mail to the Assigned Master. At other courts, however, it can prove rather more difficult to obtain confirmation that the hearing has been vacated.

There is then a further direction allowing either side to restore the case for further directions. Including this clause allows the parties to make the request without submitting an application notice

(h) The final three standard directions are for costs (usually costs in the case), requiring the claimant to draw the order up, file it and serve the defendant with a sealed copy by set dates. Practice from court to court varies as to who draws up and serves the order and it might well be that the court does this. Finally, the order will now deal with the approval of the costs budgets and this is considered in more detail below.

As with any order, it is important to ensure that the wording is correct before it is sealed. The 'slip rule (*CPR 1998, Rule 40.12*) only permits accidental errors or omissions to be corrected under it. Anything more substantial requires a further application which may fail (e.g. *Vuciecevic & Another v Aleksic & Others [2020] EWHC 2236 (Ch), para. 19*). *Zeb v Frimley Park NHS Trust, para. 4 (supra)* indicates that, in the absence of new developments, an interim order needs to be appealed if one is dissatisfied with it (rather than ignoring it and making a similar application later). Accordingly, it is always prudent to double-check an order both before and after it has been sealed.

Costs Budgeting

The costs budgeting rules are found in *CPR 1998, Rules 3.12-3.18* and *PD3E*:

- A cost budget will be required unless the value of the case is over £10 million or where the claimant is a child. Where the claimant has a limited or severely impaired life expectancy, then a budget will not usually be required.

- If either the value is under £50,000 or the costs are under £25,000 then only the first page of the budget must be filed. In these cases, the budget must be filed with the Directions

Questionnaire. Otherwise, it must be filed 21 days before the CMC.

- Agreed budget discussion reports must be filed seven days before the CMC
- Details of the costs claimed in each phase of the budget are to be made available to the court when costs are assessed at the end of the case.

Form H remains the precedent to be used for preparing the cost budget. *Form R* is the precedent to be used for the budget discussion report (*CPR 1998 PD3E, paras. 6* & *6A*, respectively). The guidance for the budget must be followed in all respects (*ibid. para. 6(b)*). *Form R* requires the following information to be provided for each phase (*ibid. para. 6A(a)-(c)*):

- The amounts claimed for incurred budgeted costs for each phase.
- The amounts being offered in each phase.
- Whether this is agreed or not. If it is not, then a brief summary of that party's objection is needed.
- There is a final column for the judge's comments and figures.

Accordingly, it is necessary to attempt some form of negotiation with your opponent between service of your client's budget and the date for filing *Form R*. Where the short-form budget is used, this may well be thought to be a straightforward proposition because the costs (under £25,000) are likely to be proportionate to the amount in issue (under £50,000). However, if one party takes the view that the budget is disproportionate, then sufficient time should be allowed for negotiations to occur.

A CCMC might not be listed promptly after the budgets are exchanged. There remains the risk that there will not be enough time at the combined CMC/CCMC to deal with all issues so an application to extend the hearing length may be required). Accordingly, a useful approach to adopt in practice is to (a) file an accurate budget on time; (b) resolve the case management issues; (c) narrow the costs management issues in light of the approved directions; and (d) submit a revised costs budget reflecting these in good time before the CCMC.

Preparing the Costs Budget

The tendency here is to focus on the figures rather than the reasons why the work is required. This is understandably so because there is a fixed fee for the preparation of the budget and it is the figures which need approval. However, in order to produce a budget which reasonably and proportionately reflects the case as a whole, the issues in the case need to be clearly understood and articulated to the court. Your ultimate goal is to persuade the court (not your opponent) that the figures being presented for approval are both reasonable and so this is where the focus ought to be.

Where the budget must be filed with the directions questionnaire, it makes perfect sense to interweave the preparation of these two documents. Just as the directions are not simply about timetable dates, the budget is not only about figures. The more closely the case management and costs management issues relate to the central issues in the case, the better the chances of approval being given and your client's position being effectively protected.

The fixed preparation fee (£1,000 or 2% of the value of the approved budget, *CPR 1998 PD3E, para. 7.2(a)*) does not leave much room for tactical manoeuvre. If choose the approach of trying to persuade the court that it is a simple and low value case (perhaps to limit your client's potential exposure to adverse costs if they lose), then you risk grossly undervaluing the amount of costs (and/or work) you are able to incur in representing them. If you choose the alternate approach, you risk incurring costs in excess of the fixed recoverable amount and of producing a budget which the court will find to be disproportionate and/or unreasonable. If you use costs draftsmen to prepare the budget, you may well find that they underestimate the work required or that you spend irrecoverable time explaining what is needed or in amending the draft budget. If you prepare the budget yourself, you get the fixed fee but you need to spend time calculating the incurred costs which is more efficiently done by costs draftsmen. On this last point, whilst case management systems are available to help with this, they are only as good as the information put into them – if this has not been done correctly, then the budget will be inaccurate. There is an overall costs management cap of 2% of the budgeted and assessed incurred costs (*CPR 1998 PD3E, para. 7.2(b)*).

In order to find an efficient route through these swampy issues, it is best to go back to basics. If the claimant has front loaded the case, both parties ought to have formed a clear idea of the central issues which the court need to determine. The pleadings will have probably distilled these further or have highlighted areas which need additional work. The parties are likely to have already done a substantial amount work on the evidential phases (disclosure, statements and experts) and the trial length will have been estimated in the directions questionnaire. If the case has been prepared by building the evidence around the central issues, then it is far easier to prepare a budget which is properly focussed on the areas in dispute and what costs can justifiably incurred on pursuing these to trial.

It follows from this that the fewer concessions that have been made (either by the defendant making suitable admissions or the claimant not pursuing relatively weak, ancillary aspects of their case), the higher the costs will be. This is likely to have a far greater impact on the costs than other factors and so it does not necessarily follow that incurring costs in front-loading a case means that the costs to trial will be lower.

Part of the skill you need to exercise is to accurately anticipate what work is likely to be necessary to win the case at trial and then to assess whether it is reasonable and proportionate to expect your opponent to bear these costs. The cost of the reasonable and proportionate work should go into the costs budget whilst the cost of work which is 'only' necessary should be explained to your client and they should be given the opportunity to decide whether they wish to bear the cost of this out of their damages before it is undertaken. The standard is that set out in *CPR 1998, Rules 44.3(5)* and *44.4(3)* (*Guidance Notes, para. 3*)

As we have considered above, this assessment should be mostly performed whilst the pleadings are being prepared. The directions timetable which is reasonably needed to accommodate this work forms part of the work included in the CMC phase leaving just the costs of preparing the budget to fall within the fixed costs permitted for this task.

In terms of where to place the work within each phase, the published online guidance note provides the starting point. Most of this is fairly logical so, for example, disclosing documents falls within the disclosure phase and 'preparing' the trial bundle falls within trial preparation (note that 'assembling' the bundle is excluded entirely because it is not considered to be 'fee earning' work). The extent to which work already done should fall within the pre-action phase is clearly set out

The assumptions that you have made for each phase are recorded at the bottom of the section for it. The purpose to summarise the work that has been (or will be) incurred. This is where you include the factors which you consider have a significant impact on the proportionality and reasonableness of your budgeted figures. Broadly speaking, these fall into 2 categories: the description of the work to be done (i.e. you assume that it either was or will be done) and the triggering event for it (i.e. you assume that the event will occur). The guidance notes make it clear that only probable assumptions should be included but the vicissitudes of contested litigation also need to be accounted for. This creates a practically frustrating issue: you should not adduce evidence at the CCMC to show that an assumption is likely to occur. The rules allow for the parties to apply for revised budgets to be allowed and this is often used as the reason for disallowing part of the proposed budget. However, the additional costs, delay and uncertainty that results from this is often not obviously taken into account. Once the budget has been set, it becomes harder to depart from it in the absence of a significant development in the case and the last approved budget is the relevant one if the case settles before the amended version has been approved.

Very similar considerations apply to the issue of the contingencies. As the purpose of a budget is to plan, it might be thought that contingencies would be seen as a useful means of the parties seeing what costs are likely to be incurred if the original plan needs amending. However, what one tends to find is that contingencies become fiercely argued *ab initio* in light of the requirement that they be likely to occur and the understandable unwillingness of the courts to approve disproportionate or unreasonable budgets. This tends to result in contingencies either being entirely ignored (because the case will probably proceed smoothly) or to be much reduced during the negotiations. The risk in doing so is that they are later found to be necessary and an application for an updated budget required with no guarantee that it will be successful. However, this is the prevailing view and so, if you consider that a particular contingency is justified, you will need to be prepared to persuasively argue for this at the CCMC. The guidance note state that these should be anticipated costs which do not neatly fall within the phases. Examples include third party disclosure applications; trials of preliminary issues; and applications to amend the pleadings. Costs which are not anticipated should be dealt with in an amended budget (*CPR 1998, PD3E, para. 3.6*)

The disbursements must also be included, and these include counsel's and experts' fees. Counsel's fees should be negotiated with chambers and evidence of the agreement obtained before the CCMC. The guidance notes require counsel's brief fee to go into the trial preparation phase and their refresher fees to go into the trial phase. This is because the brief fee includes their preparation time for trial.

Likewise, the experts' fees should be confirmed with the respective experts at the same time as they are asked to comment on those aspects of the proposed directions which impact on their opinions. In practice, this requires you to be proactive and organised, especially where there are a number of experts involved in order to obtain the requisite information in time to prepare an accurate budget.

It is helpful to have a working knowledge of excel spreadsheets so that you can make any amendments to the budget quickly and without risking unforeseen errors then finding their way into the served version.

Disbursement invoices should also be rechecked during the preparation to ensure that nothing is missed out.

In practice, it can be challenging to persuade your opponent and then the judge that your figures are proportionate to the remaining issues. The budgeting process has been likened to a prospective summary assessment of costs which bears no relationship with case management (per *Master Gordon-Saker* addressing the *Costs Law Reports Annual Conference (October 2022)* and we may yet see reforms which divorce budgeting and case management. The specialist clinical negligence Masters in the RCJ have seen many costs budgets and heard many submissions. District and Circuit Judges in the County Courts may have a more variable range of experience but all have been trained to enforce proportionality. Whoever is hearing the CCMC, they are unlikely to have a substantial amount of time to consider the bundle before the hearing and so you need to clearly summarise your main points at the start of the bundle and be able to back them up. You can expect to encounter very strong headwinds and choppy waters in order to secure the budget your evidence shows is required to properly deal with the remaining issues. Evidence, preparation and patience are key habits to develop and so knowing your case inside out is essential. Even then you may not get everything you believe is necessary and an outcome compromising the differences between the parties' respective positions is not uncommon.

Conclusion

The emphasis has been on effective case management for many years now. One of the main barriers to this is where one, or both parties, are not in a position to agree on the timetable or want to extend each stage of the timetable as it is reached.

The standard approach of the court is to encourage the parties to agree on initial 28-day extensions and this makes justifying a refusal harder because the application is likely to be granted as long as it is made before the expiry of the deadline. Left unchecked, this can result in the timetable being extended by months, thus defeating the purpose of the initial CMC.

Obtaining an early trial listing puts something of an end date on this because, eventually in the timetable, the point is reached where the trial listing becomes jeopardised. However, before this point is reached, having thoroughly prepared your case before the CMC and CMCC allows you to have in place a clear idea of what remains to be dealt with, a strong plan of action and good knowledge of what it will cost for a fully contested trial.

CHAPTER SIX

FACTUAL EVIDENCE

Introduction

Factual evidence comprises the documentary evidence and the lay witness evidence. It provides the underlying framework for the expert evidence, the cause of action and must withstand cross-examination at trial. If the factual evidence you rely on is ambiguous or inconsistent, then your entire case is weakened, costs are likely to increase and a less advantageous result achieved. Cutting corners in the preparation of factual evidence is likely to result in ambiguity or inconsistency but it is often asserted that the time spent is disproportionate. Striking the right balance in practice depends on your ability to recognise what evidence is required to prove your case; marshal it into an effective whole; analyse the content; and accurately assess where the remaining weak spots lie.

Documentary evidence consists of a record of what happened at the time it was *written down* (which might be different from when the event actually *happened*). The greater the amount of time which has passed between the event occurring and it being recorded *potentially* the greater the scope for inaccuracies, ambiguities and a lack of clarity. As these are all relative concepts (depending on the evidence as a whole), the effluxion of time does not always fatally undermine a particular piece of evidence. Accordingly, you should never assume that your experts, counsel or the trial judge will read the evidence in the same way as you do or recognise a flaw which you have missed. It is also true that a reasonable explanation for the apparent discrepancy or time gap may exist and this possibility always needs to be accounted for.

Therefore, do not fall into the trap of taking one fact or apparent evidence trail in isolation or of jumping to a premature conclusion when considering the facts of a case. Any set of facts is not open-ended and so proper investigation will eventually lead to either a reasonable conclusion being drawn pre-trial or a clear idea of the reasonable inferences which the trial judge is likely to feel able to draw where gaps exist. Accordingly, proportionality in this area of the case is aimed at investigating the entire set of facts efficiently and not allowing yourself to be led up the garden path in doing so. This is best achieved by always having a clear idea of the central allegations and of always looking for corroboration from other sources of evidence.

Categories of Written Evidence

Organising your thought process is an essential ingredient in consistently achieving this on a daily basis. Identifying and marshalling factual evidence involves careful sifting to precisely identify what it says and how it should be used before it can be effectively deployed. This tends to increase costs so it is important to improve your skill level through regular practice.

'Primary' evidence is contemporaneous evidence of the fact in issue either from a person who was there or an objective test result. A simple example would be of a biopsy result showing that a tissue sample was malignant and the stage of the cancer present. There is little room for ambiguity in the result.

'Secondary' evidence is indirect evidence (including the interpretation of a primary piece of evidence). It is evidence that a fact has been contemporaneously inferred from primary evidence. The fact is what was inferred at the time not that the primary fact was correct (which is likely to be hearsay evidence). A simple example would be a reference to the biopsy result in a subsequent clinical letter.

'Tertiary' evidence is another step removed from secondary evidence. It is the least useful type of evidence because it is unlikely to be given much weight by the trial judge and should not usually be relied upon to support a case alone. It can masquerade as primary or secondary evidence. It may seem to give additional weight to the case but in fact adds nothing to what is already known about the central allegations on breach (see, for example, *Pawar v JSD Haulage Ltd [2016] EWCA Civ 551, per Thirlwell*

J @ para. 8). Lines of enquiry aimed at finding tertiary evidence are the safest to exclude purely on proportionality grounds (if needed). A simple example would be a clinical opinion based on what the clinical letter said about the test result rather than on the original test result itself.

It follows that a particular piece of evidence could be 'tertiary' with respect to the central allegations on breach or causation but 'primary' evidence in relation to proving an item of loss. Accordingly, it is important to clearly identify and divide the evidence for each part of the case to avoid cross-contamination and confusion.

The main categories of written evidence are:

- The defendant's records. These should cover the index treatment relevant to the central allegations and ancillary matters such as previous treatment subsequent treatment. They are required in all cases.

- GP records. Where the defendant is not also the GP, these records will provide a much clearer picture of the claimant's entire medical history. They should be requested in all but the most limited of cases. An example would be where a discrete injury (unrelated to previous conditions) has been caused by a straightforward breach and the GP has had no involvement in the aftercare. It follows that such a case would probably be of a modest value and so the added time and expense of dealing with the GP records would not assist the resolution of the case.

- Tertiary or quaternary treatment records. These are records from a clinician other than the defendant or GP. They usually cover the claimant's previous medical history; post-negligence treatment; causation; condition and prognosis; and quantum issues. They will usually be requested in the vast majority of cases but time can be wasted in dealing with sets of records which are particularly voluminous or which deal with conditions with no clear causal link to the index incident.

- Corroborative evidence: This includes non-medical records and documents such as the complaints investigation documents; employment, benefits, local authority or educational records; receipts, invoices and bills; correspondence; photographs; plans; diaries and recordings; and evidence of treatment protocols, pro-forma and other clinical governance documents aimed at avoiding the breach of duty by adopting a reasonable approach to the treatment. Always bear in mind that the entire document is disclosable, not just the part you want to rely on so there can be real proportionality considerations inherent in investigating and deploying this type of evidence.

The start of the analytical process is therefore to identify the facts requiring proof. For each of these, consider whether it is a core fact (needed to prove the central issues in the case) or an ancillary fact (playing a supporting, but not a central, role). Then consider whether the source of this fact is primary, secondary or tertiary followed by asking yourself whether the fact proves itself or whether it requires support from other evidence. Relevant factors are whether the fact is clearly stated in the document, whether it needs to be inferred from what is clearly said or whether what is said is open to interpretation. This is then repeated for each fact you are analysing. The role of the trial judge is to draw reasonable inferences from the available factual evidence. Primary evidence is more likely to be directly helpful with this whereas tertiary evidence is more likely to be seen as circumstantial. Secondary evidence is likely to fall between these two.

Contents of Medical Records

The Claimant's records will contain evidence on:

(a) Their current condition & prognosis.

(b) Their pre-negligence medical history.

(c) Test results – blood tests, urine tests (e.g. for kidney (renal) function), liver function, brain function, respiratory function, etc.

(d) Investigations intended to identify the cause of the claimant's illness. This will often involve excluding one of more *differential* (i.e. alternative) diagnoses. As such, they will provide you with evidence of *why* one diagnosis has been preferred to others which arise from similar circumstances.

(e) The identity of the claimant's treating doctors and their specialisms (areas of expertise). This is useful when choosing your experts.

(f) Evidence of what the claimant told their doctors about the condition they were seeking treatment for. This may support or undermine their case.

(g) Evidence of the claimant's state of health both before and after their injury.

(h) Warning signals about your case.

Why Medical Evidence Needs 'Explaining' and Interpreting'

Medical evidence is often confusing. There are numerous abbreviations and medical terms which are unfamiliar to us and this makes the meaning unclear. Handwritten notes are often next to impossible to decipher unless you can recognise a word or phrase from elsewhere in the records.

It is also complicated. The frequent use of technically precise terminology, the complexity and longstanding nature of the claimant's underlying medical conditions and sometimes voluminous nature of the records all serve to give medical records an air of impenetrability.

Fortunately, adopting a structured approach can help. It is essential that someone on each side understands the records. Invariably in the current climate, that person is the fee-earner responsible for the file.

For claimants' solicitors it is helpful to send a standard questionnaire to send to clients requesting details of the hospitals, etc that they have visited. It is not always necessary to apply for all of the records straight away because they may not be relevant to the central allegations in the case.

Sorting the Records

If the records remain unsorted then there is a much greater chance that key evidence will be missed; that costs will be unreasonably increased over the lifetime of the case (by virtue of you, counsel, the experts, the judge and your opponent taking more time to find what they need); and it looks unprofessional (which risks creating the impression that you/the firm are also disorganized in other areas of your caseload).

Conversely, spending an excessive amount of time on sorting records will not be recoverable in full at the end of the case. The time spent should be reasonable and proportionate (rather than 'necessary'). This requires you to have an idea of the likely value of your case and how complex it is. This can change during the case.

Fixed fee cases are the most common cases where there seems to be no financial incentive to spend time sorting and reviewing medical records. Even so, having a clear idea of the evidence in the claimant's medical records is desirable and so you will need to have an efficient process in place when fixed recoverable costs come into clinical negligence.

Interpreting the Records

Your goal is to understand the key facts in the records well enough to:

- Know when your opponent has not read the records;
- Instruct an expert confidently and understand their report; and

- Identify any problems with your existing understanding of limitation, liability and quantum.

Medical abbreviations are complicated but the internet or reference books will assist. There will still be abbreviations which defy reasonable attempts to decipher them and these can be referred to your expert for clarification.

The best place to start is with the GP records because these are the simplest. In the vast majority of cases, there will only ever be a maximum of four sections:

- Correspondence;

- Computerised records (also called E.M.I.S. records);

- Handwritten records (also called Lloyd George records); and

- Test results.

These records are sufficiently different from each other to make their identification, sorting and deployment relatively easy. Once done, start the review with the GP correspondence. Put it into date order (earliest to most recent in order to assist with any later updates). The correspondence section is the easiest section of any set of medical records to understand. They will allow you to get to grips with your client's case much more swiftly. Once you have highlighted the important facts from the correspondence, sorting the other sections into date order will become easier because you have a reference point to work from.

The GP records should give you a general overview of the situation and when, where and why other medical practitioners have become involved. The other records will then give you more specific evidence if your case requires it. Again, start with the correspondence so that you have an overview of the content of those records and how they fit into the other records. This should also make you more conversant with the relevant evidence; medical terms being used; the relative severity of the injury; limitation; and how your client's injury fits in with their overall medical picture.

If the correspondence stretches over many years, the earliest letters may be wholly irrelevant to your case. You can reduce the risk of wasting time by starting either with the last letter or the nearest to the date of your client's injury.

Understanding the Terminology

Reviewing medical records can seem daunting because of the scientific terminology, medical abbreviations and the almost infinite variations of ailments that humans can suffer from. You can simplify this by reviewing the notes as suggested above; cross-referencing them with the claimant's and the impugned clinicians' version of events; and then apply this new evidence to the central issues in the case. Doing so will allow you to focus on the relevant parts of the records more easily.

Using internet search engines is a quick and effective way of establishing the correct meaning of the terms you come across. The correspondence should show the most relevant terms for each particular case. Any terms which remain unclear should be referred to your appointed expert to put them in the correct context.

Disclosure

Not every document containing factual evidence needs to be disclosed in every case and standard disclosure is intended to avoid this occurring. However, standard disclosure has now been the norm for so long that the practical differences between 'total' and 'standard' disclosure in a clinical negligence case risk being long forgotten. Proportionality requires that specific thought be given to whether documents serve some helpful purpose in each case. Understanding the extent to which standard disclosure already involves a degree of proportionality is a useful practical skill to develop.

The procedural requirements are set out in *CPR 1998, Part 31* and *PD31*. To summarise:

- *Rule 31.4* defines 'document' very widely as being anything which records information. 'Copy' includes both direct and indirect methods of copying. In practice, therefore, it is unlikely that something will not be considered to be a document.

- *Rule 31.6* says that standard disclosure 'only' requires the disclosure of documents which (a) that party *relies on*; (b) *adversely affects* any party's case; (c) *supports* any party's case; or (d) is required by a practice direction. If a document falls outside of this (admittedly quite wide) scope, then it is not required to be disclosed as part of standard disclosure. It may still fall within specific disclosure, however, and this is considered further below.

- *Rule 31.7* requires only that a 'reasonable' search is made not a fully comprehensive one. 'Reasonableness' here includes the number of documents involved, the nature and complexity of the case; the ease and expense of retrieving the documents and the significance of any documents likely to be found by the search. A simple example would be that a copy of the multi-disciplinary team meeting decision should be readily available and disclosable but handwritten minutes of what was said during it might not be.

- *Rule 31.8* shows that the duty to disclose is limited to documents which either *are* or *have been* in that party's control or physical possession or where they had a right to possess it or to inspect or copy it.

- *Rule 31.9* states that only one copy of the document needs to be disclosed. However, versions of ostensibly the same document which contain deletions, amendments or annotations are separate documents *if* they are within the *Rule 31.6* definition.

- *Rule 31.10* sets out the procedure for making standard disclosure using the list of documents precedent. It is acceptable to append a detailed list of the documents being disclosed to the standard form.

- *Rule 31.11* confirms that the duty to disclose is continuous. Accordingly, it is necessary to disclose documents which come to light after standard disclosure is made. Whilst updated records post-dating the set date are unlikely to cause difficulties, disclosing documents which existed before the date set but which were not searched for or found risks an application for permission to rely on them being made and/or an adverse costs order or other sanction being imposed.

- *Rule 31.12* sets out the basic requirements for specific disclosure and the inspection of documents. The differences between standard and specific disclosure are considered below.

- *Rule 31.14* permits the inspection of documents referred to in the statements of case (which is something which needs to be taken into account when drafting proceedings) and witness statements. Such disclosure is permitted without an application being made and this is in contrast to the inspection of documents referred to in experts' reports (where an application is required under *Rule 35.10(4)*).

- *Rule 31.17* deals with non-party disclosure. The rule is more stringent here because the holder of the documents is not involved in the case. The documents being sought must (a) either support the applicant's case or undermine their opponent's; and (b) assist in fairly disposing of the case or saving costs. In many respects the position is similar to applications for pre-action disclosure (considered above) except that the respondent will almost always be awarded their reasonable costs.

- *Rule 31.20* covers the situation where a privileged document is accidentally disclosed. The receiving party can only use its contents with the permission of the court. However, an additional note of caution is required as the document can be indirectly used to the receiving party's advantage without being directly referred to. It is considered right and good practice to inform your opponent if a privileged document has been disclosed before making the application as the clearer it is to the court that you ought to have realised it was privileged, the less likely it is permission will be granted. As with most applications, the application should be made as soon as is reasonably practicable; before costs have been incurred; and should genuinely assist the judge. Similar considerations apply where the document has actually been inspected or sent over by mistake but the potential damage is much harder to rectify.

- *Rule 31.21* prevents a party which fails to disclose a relevant document or refuses to allow inspection of it. In such cases, the document cannot be relied on without the permission of the court. The court will probably want to see a very good reason for the failure as this will be an application requesting relief from sanction. However, on a practical level, the document may also help the other party so it is not necessarily in their interests to object to the late disclosure of it once they know what it says. The court is unlikely, everything else being equal, to refuse permission but is likely to impose a suitable costs sanction covering the consequences of the error.

Standard Disclosure

Broadly speaking, the following documents should be considered when dealing with standard disclosure:

- Medical records. You should ask yourself whether these need to be updated well in advance of the date set for disclosure. Updated records for treatment after this date need to be disclosed as part of the continuing duty of disclosure. Whilst this can be used for records pre-dating the date, (perhaps where these are relatively short or updated records were obtained in the months before disclosure) the disclosed set should be relatively current. The cycle of updating medical records does not always coincide with the date for disclosure even in the most well-planned cases.

- Quantum evidence. Ideally, this should have been obtained and scrutinised when preparing the schedule of special damages. Any gaps should then be filled by the time that disclosure is made which means each item of loss being claimed should have a clear documentary basis to it. In this way, the costs of disclosure (and of the overall proportionality of the case more generally) are linked to solid evidence of what the case is worth.

- Complaints documents. Standard disclosure provides a long-stop date for the disclosure of documents referred to in the defendant's duty of candour investigation. It may well have not been considered proportionate to have pursued these before now but sufficient time will have elapsed for the defendant to have found them. They may no longer be relevant if suitable admissions have been made. If the issues are still live, however, then these documents (including documents referred to in the main complaints response) fall within the definition of standard disclosure.

- Witness statements & expert reports. These do not fall within the ambit of standard disclosure and so should not be included in the list of documents. However, the documents being disclosed should be double-checked to ensure that earlier drafts are not referred to inadvertently and to confirm those aspects of the statements and reports which may be affected by your opponent's anticipated disclosure.

- Other corroborating evidence. This is most likely to take the form of letters, recordings or photographs dealing with the remaining issues. It can include evidence of relevant treatment protocols and guidelines in use at the time of the treatment or documentary materials relied on by your experts as to what should have been available to the clinician in question. As these documents can be lengthy and contain generic evidence rather than evidence specific to proving the issues in a case, consideration should be given as to whether they should be disclosed at all. If they are, then attempts should be made to reach an agreement as to what parts are needed at trial. Voluminous generic material is not helpful to a trial judge but the documents may nevertheless be included in the trial bundle be default after they have been disclosed if neither party vets them or reconsiders their relevance as the issues narrow.

Specific Disclosure

Proportionality tends to place the emphasis on getting disclosure right from the start rather than on trying to use the rules to fatally undermine your opponent's case. The increased delay and expense involved in making applications is often better employed in progressing the case to the next key pre-trial stage. However, the two considerations are not completely mutually exclusive and there is no guarantee that your opponent will not try to weaken your case, especially where they feel gaps in the evidence exist.

Specific disclosure requires that a reasonable level of detail about your case has been provided and should not be used as an alternative to pre-action disclosure. In *Balfour Beatty Regional Construction Ltd v Broadway Malyan Ltd [2022] EWHC 2022 (TCC)* an application was made at the same time as the claim for was issued for early specific disclosure before the service of proceedings. The procedural basis for this was not set out in the application with the emphasis being on a contractual entitlement for the documents sought (*para. 12*). This made the application 'wide' rather than 'narrow'. It also meant that the claimant was seeking a final remedy (i.e. the determination of a contractual right) akin to summary judgement without having pleaded its case rather than an interim relief or procedural remedy (*paras. 21 & 25*). The parties agreed that early specific disclosure is permitted under *CPR 1998 Rule 3.1(2)(m)* (*para. 33*). Early specific disclosure was inappropriate where pre-action disclosure had not been sought even where proceedings needed to be started due to limitation (*para. 45*). Secondly, the disclosure sought put the defendant in an unreasonable position of searching for, finding and identifying the relevant documents without knowing the case it faced (*para. 51*).

Where the court orders standard disclosure before the first CMC (as at the RCJ, for example), any application arising from it can at least be heard at the subsequent hearing (e.g. *Symes v St George's Healthcare NHS Trust (supra)*). Otherwise, a separate application (with its own costs consequences and effect on the pre-trial timetable) will be needed.

Disclosure ought not to be seen in isolation (for example, it overlaps with *Part 18* Requests as considered in an earlier chapter). It may not be until standard disclosure occurs that it becomes apparent that key pieces of evidence are missing. Whilst that may be insufficient to defeat or win the case immediately, it may well provide a good indication of the extent to which the witness and expert evidence is reliant on assumptions of what was expected to be contained in the documentary evidence.

By way of an example, it is often assumed that the breach or causation expert has fully understood the medical records and applied their experience of treating this particular injury in the particular circumstances the impugned clinician(s) encountered in this case. It may well have been assumed that these clinicians followed national guidelines. However, if they followed local guidelines which materially differ from what the experts were expecting, then the experts need to reconsider their opinions. If no guidelines are disclosed at all, then the trial judge may find that they have insufficient evidence before them to find for the claimant. Logically, therefore, the onus is on the claimant to pursue such disclosure.

When considering disclosure issues, it is therefore desirable to consider:

(a) The extent to which standard disclosure is likely to or does differ from the pre-action disclosure.

(b) Whether any additional documents come within standard disclosure in light of the remaining pleaded issues. If so, is an application likely to resolve any dispute which arises between the parties?

(c) Whether an application for specific disclosure is likely to succeed.

In most clinical negligence cases, the medical records covering the impugned treatment will have been disclosed pre-action. If liability remains disputed, then the issue for standard or specific disclosure is whether any other documents exist which favour one party's case over the others. This is likely to require a careful analysis of each side's interpretation of the key entries because it can be reasonably anticipated that (at the time standard disclosure is made) the clinicians involved will subsequently serve witness statements commenting on those entries. Accordingly, the extent to which additional documentary evidence exists is very relevant because it may corroborate or undermine the existing evidence or the experts' interpretation of it.

However, the difficulties that the requesting party faces are (a) not knowing whether that document exists; and, if it does, (b) whether it actually represents the 'smoking gun' hoped for. The medicine underpinning every clinical negligence case is sufficiently complex (vis-á-vis a civil litigation case of comparable value) that no single piece of evidence is likely to be sufficiently clear enough to provide the tipping point at trial. On the other hand, it may well assist in reaching that tipping point and trial judges are likely to be assisted by a clear evidence trail. Accordingly, there is genuine scope for disagreement over what should be disclosed in this regard and what is proportionate in the circumstances of each case.

As with pre-action disclosure, the main line of authority comes from other areas of civil litigation. The same general principle applies, i.e. that a missing, key medical record is likely to result in a successful application for its disclosure and so is less likely to ever reach a court. Other documents require very careful consideration, preparation of the application and persuasive advocacy to have a reasonable chance of success.

In such cases, what is really being requested are documents which show what was (a) actually being considered at the time of the impugned treatment; (b) whether that treatment was criticised or considered reasonable afterwards; or (c) provides objective evidence of a fact which will assist the trial judge. The more evidence there is that the document actually exists (such as a direct reference to it in another document), the better.

Broadly speaking, the party requiring this form of disclosure (whether by request, negotiation or an application) will be attempting to show that they are targeting a specific fact or issue in the case. Their opponent, in contrast, will be trying to show that the request is misguided or an irrelevant fishing expedition.

The courts have long acknowledged that every document potentially relates to the issues in dispute and may have some bearing on them. Documents only become relevant if they fairly lead a party to a 'train of enquiry' to determine whether it assists or undermines either side's case (*Compagnie Financiere du Pacifique v Peruvian Guano Co (1882) 11 QBD 55*). This test can now be found in *CPR 1998, PD31, para. 5.5. "It is correct to say that the test is broadly stated and the relevance is framed in the widest possible terms" (Frampton v Cyclone Productions Ltd [2019] NIQB 58, para. 7 per Colton J).*

In *Nichia Corpn v Argos Ltd [2007] EWCA Civ 741, Jacob J* explained that this test is much wider than that for standard disclosure. Standard disclosure (and pre-action disclosure) is intended to avoid the bulk disclosure of a morass of documents which would probably increase the costs of reviewing them and of dealing with them at trial and of missing some truly key documents.

In *Digicel (St. Lucia) Ltd v Cable & Wireless plc [2008] EWHC 2522 (Ch), Morgan J* applied this test to the reasonableness of looking for that key revealing statement which you suspect has been made. The importance of proving what the individual really thought is outweighed by proportionality: *"Thus, the rules do not require that no stone should be left unturned. This may mean that a relevant document, even a "smoking gun", is not found. This attitude is justified by considerations of proportionality."*

Additional consideration is required where the specific disclosure sought covers documents which are highly personal in nature or otherwise sensitive. In *Tosi Ltd v 99 Hippos Ltd & Another [2022] EWCH 878 (Ch), HHJ Matthews* applied a two-stage test. Firstly, us the specific disclosure necessary for the just disposal of the proceedings and (if so) reasonable and proportionate? In this case, this was relevant to whether they facilitated the mediation which was the next stage in the case (with different answers being possible for later stages as the case develops). Secondly, if disclosure is ordered, should it be unredacted, redacted by independent solicitors or redacted by the applicant's solicitors? Where the applicant is represented by independent solicitors, it was considered safe to allow then to receive the unredacted documents as long as they sent redacted copies to their client removing the sensitive information: *"... the risk of using personal and sensitive information for collateral purposes is high" (para. 30).* Interestingly, GDPR considerations were not referred to and the option of the respondent's solicitors or employees redacting the documents before sending them to the applicant's independent solicitor was considered reasonable only if the applicant could not appoint an independent solicitor for the limited purpose of redacting the documents. This leads to the question as to whether it is reasonable for clinical negligence defendants to send redacted copies of the claimant's medical records (for example).

The case law as a whole demonstrates that wide-ranging or generic requests for disclosure will fail. Given the judicial recognition that standard disclosure can lead to key documents being missed, what more is required to obtain ancillary or 'train of enquiry' documents not forming part of the claimant's medical records?

The most that can be done in any individual case is to use the existing evidence to develop your argument that specific additional documents either do or should exist (which support or undermine either side's case). It ought to be borne in mind that even where the other side is ordered to disclose the document(s), a reasonable and proportionate search may still fail to elicit them. Thus, evidence that the documents have been lost, destroyed or misplaced is very relevant.

It is also extremely prudent to think about whether your client actually benefits from either the disclosure or non-disclosure of the document. This can be a difficult question requiring you to consider how the case is likely to proceed at trial. This requires you to think through the differing possibilities to their logical conclusion. Included in this is weighing up whether the lack of evidence prevents the claimant from proving their case and the extent to which the court will be prepared to draw an adverse inference in your client's favour in respect of the missing evidence. It is best done at standard disclosure so the lay and expert evidence can be reconsidered in light of your conclusions.

Inferences from Missing Evidence

Given that the onus is on the party claiming that a disputed fact occurred to prove this, what happens when relevant evidence is lost, never brought into existence or not adduced by another party? An absence of evidence is not evidence of absence and the starting point is the null hypothesis that the fact (or issue or even the entire case) cannot be proved. However, to a limited extent, the trial judge may be willing to draw an inference that the disputed fact did occur either as an *adverse inference* against the other party or as *claimant's benevolence* in favour of the party making the request. The distinction between these is not always clear in practice.

(a) Adverse Inferences

In *Wisniewski v Central Manchester Health Authority [1998] PIQR 324 (@ 340), Brooke LJ* set out guidance on when the court can draw adverse inferences. To summarise:

1. The absence of evidence must go to a material fact which the source would be expected to cover;

2. The inference (if drawn) can either weaken the evidence adduced by that party or strengthen their opponent's evidence;

3. However, the party seeking the adverse inference must have adduced at least some evidence in respect of that fact before the court; and

4. No adverse inference can be drawn where the explanation is satisfactory and, even where it is credible but not wholly satisfactory, the inference may be such that is not especially detrimental.

Where there is evidence that the offending party or witness has had the chance to rectify the omission but has failed to do so (making their explanation is accordingly 'unsatisfactory' under *Wisniewski*), a line of authority deriving from *Armory v Delamirie (1722) 1 Strange 505, EWHC KB J94* (a 'measure of damages' case where *Pratt CJ's* jury direction was that they should weigh against the defendant his inability to produce the key piece of evidence at trial) permits the court to resolve any evidential doubts against that party or witness (e.g. at first instance in *Barons Bridging Finance 1 Ltd & Another v Barons Finance Ltd [2016] EWCA (Civ) 550*)). It *"raises an evidential (i.e. rebuttable) presumption in favour of the claimant which gives him the benefit of any relevant doubt. The practical effect of that is to give the claimant a fair wind in establishing the value of what he has lost."* In *Phillips & Co and Phillips v Whatley (Gibraltar) [2007] UKPC 28, Lord Mance* confirmed that this principle applied to the situation in a PI case where the defendant's negligence prevents a key aspect of the case being known. Accordingly, although this principle is also applicable to loss of a chance cases (e.g. *Intercity Telecom Ltd & Another v Solanki [2015] EWHC B3 (Mercantile), Fearns v Anglo-Dutch Paint & Chemical Co Ltd [2010] EWHC 1708 (Ch) or Coote v Ullstein [2022] EWHC 607 (QB)*), its principle is not limited to that type of case as adverse inferences can be drawn where a key piece of evidence is not adduced (e.g. *Mackenzie v Alcoa Manufacturing (GB) Ltd [2019] EWCA Civ 2110, para. 43*).

In *Marathon Asset Management LLP & Another v Seddon & Others [2017] EWHC 300 (Comm), Leggatt J* explained the *Armory* principle as having two aspects (a) difficulties in estimating the value of the loss suffered should not deprive a party of a remedy; and (b) the court will make presumptions in favour of a party where the other has destroyed evidence or wrongfully impeded or prevented relevant evidence being adduced (*para. 164*).

Bridging the gap between the 18th and 21st centuries, in *Wright v McCormack [2022] EWHC 2068 (QB), para. 131; Chamberlain J* held that culpability was a necessary element and this is to be judged against all of the evidence that is available. Illustrative considerations in this case included that the claimant had asked the defendant to destroy the category of electronic documents (defamatory tweets) he later sought to argue contained specific documents (analytic data) that should have been preserved; that the claimant had not referred to the analytics data nor of the need to download them from the relevant social media website; the defendant did not know that deleting the tweet meant its analytic data would be lost; the defendant had not yet received independent legal advice when he deleted the tweets; the claimant's solicitors did not promptly request the analytics data and, when they did, the request was unclear to their experienced opponents; and the defendant had provided significant disclosure of other, relevant documents. Weighing up all of the evidence, there was no culpability in deliberately deleting the tweets.

The requirement for evidence of wrongdoing makes persuading the court to draw an adverse inference difficult in practice. It is best seen as being part of a wider strategic approach to marshalling and interpreting the evidence.

In *Society of Lloyd's v Jaffray [2002] EWCA Civ 1101, @406 Waller LJ* explained that the effect of an adverse finding "*...simply means that where the evidence points in a certain direction an adverse inference can be drawn from a failure to call the witness to deal with it*"; it does not have to. *Manzi* *v Kings College Hospital NHS Foundation Trust [2018] EWCA Civ 1882 (paras. 30-31)* confirms that the obligation is discretionary (not obligatory) and this discretion was not exercised here as the witness evidence was tangential to the central allegations.

This discretion was articulated as a three-stage test in *Magdeev v Tsvetkov [2020] EWHC 887 (Comm) at para. 154(2) per Cockerill J.* The party wanting the court to exercise its discretion must:

1. Specify the witness that the other side might have called and that they had material evidence to give on the issue in question;

2. Identify the particular inference that they want the court to draw from this witness' absence; and

3. Explain why the inference is justified based on the evidence which is before the court.

In *Royal Mail Group v Etobi [2021] UKSC 33, Lord Leggatt (para. 41)* explained that: *"So far as is possible, tribunals should be free to draw, or to decline to draw, inferences from the facts of the case before them using their common sense without the need to consult law books when doing so. Whether any positive significance should be attached to the fact that a person has not given evidence depends entirely on the context and particular circumstances."* In *Thorley v Sandwell & West Birmingham Hospitals NHS Trust [2021] EWHC 2604 (QB) Soole J (para. 55)* commented that *"these observations were evidently intended to have the widest application."* No adverse inference was drawn from the decision by the defendant not to call evidence from either the doctors who wrote the relevant clinical guidelines or those who used it to justify the withdrawal of the relevant medication.

As such, the evidence of the evidential gap, the reasons for it and its adverse impact on judge's decision-making process needs to be clear, specific congruent with common sense.

As costs pressures continue to increase, it can be anticipated that fewer witnesses will be called and seemingly extraneous documents not adduced. Caution is also required when deciding not to contact potential witnesses or to call them. In *Ahuja Investments Ltd v Victorygame Ltd & Another [2021] EWHC 2382 (Ch)*, failing to call evidence from *"three highly relevant potential witnesses"* was a breach of the duty to assist the court under *CPR 1998, Rule 1.3* (at *para. 1*). In *British Railways Board v Herrington [1972] UKHL 1, Lord Diplock* (*3rd para.*) stated:

> *"The Appellants… elected to call no witnesses, thus depriving the court of any positive evidence of the [central issues]… This is a legitimate tactical move under our adversarial system of litigation. But a defendant who adopts it cannot complain if the court draws from the facts which have been disclosed all reasonable inferences as to what are the facts which the defendant has chosen to withhold."*

If the party calling the witness rectifies the error late in the proceedings, then *Rai v University Hospitals Coventry & Warwickshire NHS Trust [2019] EWHC 2488 (QB)* provides an example of a clinical negligence case where permission for the witness was allowed after the claimant specifically put the defendant on notice that it intended to invite the court to draw adverse inferences from the failure to serve a statement from this witness. At *para. 36, Judge Allen* stated that the overriding objective *"was best served"* by allowing this and that the evidence did not take the claimant by surprise. Although the corresponding medical records made by the witness was brought into issue in the particulars of claim, *"it did not entail that a witness statement would be provided by [the witness] and oral evidence sought."* The key practical point here seems to be that the witness evidence was broadly similar to the contested medical record.

In the commercial case of *National Bank Trust v Yurov & Others [2020] EWHC 100 (Comm)*, it was asserted that the failure to address certain facts of particular importance to piecing together a chronological narrative deprived the other party of the ability to effectively cross-examine this key witness on those events. At *para. 211* it was stated that it is necessary for the party seeking the adverse inference to do so in respect of specific witnesses in complex cases to avoid overburdening the court. Furthermore, at *para. 228* it was considered necessary to have exhausted the chance to call the witness yourself as evidence that the requesting party genuinely believed that the evidence was relevant.

These sentiments were echoed in *Jones v Taunton & Somerset NHS Foundation Trust [2019] EWHC 1409 (QB) paras. 82-87* where (see *footnote 38*), the claimant also sought to rely on the duty of candour before accepting that this added nothing to the common law rules.

Proportionality requires that the parties provide as much relevant disclosure as they can pre-action. Where the relevant medical records have been disclosed, it becomes much harder to use applications to gain a tactical advantage. Such applications should be reserved for situations where specific documents (or a very small class of documents) can be proved to be relevant and likely to assist the trial judge in their decision. It is prudent for your expert to have provided evidence (in the form of a side-letter) that the document being sought is likely to assist them in the discharge of their *Part 35* duty to the court.

This is not to say, however, that a contemporaneous document necessarily trumps other documents. It is the degree of consistency across the evidence as a whole which is important. Thus, the more congruent a particular piece of evidence is with the overall case, the more likely it is that it will also be persuasive and the so need for it to be adduced to explain the issue will be seen as being crucial.

(b) Claimant's ('*Keefe*') Benevolence

This is an inference that one party's (often, the claimant's) evidence should be given the 'benefit of the doubt' where evidential gaps have arisen more innocently from the defendant's contemporaneous conduct. This inference can be seen as being similar to an adverse inference but is separate (see *Mackenzie v Alcoa Manufacturing (supra)* and *Richins (supra)*). The usual pre-requisite is that a relevant breach of duty has been admitted or proved and that this has resulted in the evidence being missing.

Where the party is under a duty to record or maintain the missing evidence, assistance can be found from *Keefe v The Isle of Man Steam Packet Company Ltd [2010] EWCA Civ 683*. The evidence showed that the defendants had never taken measurements of the (allegedly excessive and injurious) noise levels on their ships and there was no engineering evidence of these either (*para. 6*). The *Armory v Delamirie (supra)* principle was held to be applicable (*para. 20*) and *BRB v Herrington (supra)* was also applied: *"If it is a defendant's duty to measure noise levels in places where his employees work and he does not do so, it hardly lies in his mouth to assert that the noise levels were not excessive. In such cases, the court should judge a claimant's evidence benevolently and the defendant's evidence critically. ... Similarly, a defendant who has, in breach of duty, made it difficult or impossible for a claimant to adduce relevant evidence must run the risk of adverse factual findings" (per Longmore LJ, para. 19)*.

As well as the need for a duty to have existed at the time of the alleged breach (see *Petrodel Resources Ltd v Prest [2013] UKSC 34*) (and that has actually been breached), there must also not be other relevant evidence. In *Mackenzie v Alcoa Manufacturing (supra)*, there was single joint expert evidence that the noise levels the claimant was exposed to were unlikely to have been excessive despite there being no factual recorded noise levels; the trial judge was entitled to accept that evidence (e.g. *para. 60*). This proves a significant hurdle in clinical negligence cases.

The court is also more likely to draw the requested inference where there is a closer proximity between the breach of duty and the missing evidence (after considering the effect of the other, available and unavailable evidence) (see *Shawe-Lincoln v Neelakandan [2012] EWHC 1150 (QB) per Lloyd Jones J, para 82*). It does not reverse the burden of proof on the claimant (*para. 80*).

In the absence of a clear duty to record the evidence, *Bannister v Freemans plc [2020] EWHC 1625 (QB), para. 15* indicates an unwillingness to draw the required inference. Ideally, therefore, your expert needs to be able to support an argument that there was a duty of care to record the missing evidence and this should probably be pleaded.

In the context of clinical negligence, the missing evidence needed is usually relevant to proving hypothetical causation. In *JAH v Burne & Others [2018] EWHC 3461 (QB), Martin Spencer J (paras. 65-66)* applied *Keefe*, *Herrington* and *Armory* (all *supra*) and drew support from *Raggett v King's College Hospital [2016] EWHC 1604 (QB) (para. 131 per Sir Alastair MacDuff)*. At, *para. 64*, *Martin Spencer J* held:

> *"In my judgment, on resolving issues of detail such as how long it would have taken for the claimant to be seen, how long it would have been taken for the investigations to be carried out and when a competent vascular surgeon would have appreciated that anticoagulation was the appropriate treatment, the court should err in favour of the claimant where it is the defendant's negligence that deprives the court of the best evidence and causes the need to delve into this hypothetical world."*

In respect of hypothetical diagnostic tests, the test results are missing because the tests were never performed following, and due to, the breach. As such, the court is also being asked to infer what those results would have been. In *ZZZ v Yeovil District Hospital NHS Foundation Trust [2019] EWHC 1642 (QB)*, the claimant asserted that the breach meant that no proper neurological examination had been carried out and this therefore made it impossible to prove that the neurological outcome was worse than it would have been. *Garnham J* refused to draw the requested inference because there was expert evidence and some evidence in the medical records which showed that the deterioration would have happened in any event. Overall, *"[t]he hard, scientific evidence … is compelling"* (*para. 142*). In practice, this is a fairly common issue to face and can usually be flagged up in the second risk assessment after reviewing the medical records before an expert is instructed.

Conversely, in *Younas v Okheahialham [2019] EWHC 2502 (QB)*, the court (after carefully weighing all of the available factual and expert evidence and recalibrating its initial conclusions) was prepared to draw the required inferences in respect of the likely diagnostic chronology and results so causation was made out. Also of note, is the defendant's submission (at *para. 37*) that inferring claimant's benevolence still required the claimant to prove that the event was likely to have occurred in the first place. Similarly, in *Richins (supra)*, it was submitted that claimant's benevolence had no application where there was no evidential gap and no hiding of documents (*para. 102*). This is another case where there was a panoply of available evidence to be considered. It was held that the principle did apply to the question of whether proteinuria would have been present (if tested for) and an inference that it would have been was somewhat (but not completely) congruent with the defendant's obstetric expert's concession that the likelihood of proteinuria was increasing as time passed (*para. 137*). However, overall, the trial judge was *"… not persuaded that the claimant can establish that it was probable that proteinuria would have been present at [the material time]. Claimant Benevolence on its own is not enough and I prefer the evidence and analysis of [the defendant's expert] on this point"* (*para. 138*).

(c) Other Options

Choosing not to, or being unable to, adduce a particular piece of evidence can come back to haunt you. In *Gibbs & Others v Rea [1998] UKPC 3, Gault J (para. 46)* stated: *"It was of course open to the defendants to elect to give no evidence and simply contend that the case against them was not proved. But that course carried with it the risk that should it transpire there was some evidence tending to establish the plaintiff Respondent's case, albeit slender evidence, their silence in circumstances in which they would be expected to answer might convert that evidence into proof."*

Even if your opponent fails to persuade the court to draw an inference of either of the types discussed above, this does not prevent it from deciding that it has no evidence on which to decide an issue or that the evidential gap undermines the credibility of that party's case (e.g. *Ahuja v Investments (supra), paras. 32-33*).

However, without careful investigation, many cases may appear to be similar to *Plant v El-Emir & Another (supra; para. 74*); where there was no suggestion that there had been any inappropriate conduct and the court found that the omissions and inaccuracies were not material to the central issues. Whatever the explanation was for the evidential gap, the court was satisfied that it was probably innocent. Alternatively, the issue can be dealt with as it was in *Middleton v Frimley Health NHS Foundation Trust [2022] EWHC 2981 (KB)* where additional medical records were requested by the trial judge on the second day of the trial during cross-examination of the experts; produced on day 3; and post-trial submissions were permitted to allow for the short period the claimant had to consider them. No mention of disclosure applications was made nor that submissions that an adverse inference were heard appear in the judgement. Such issues can be entirely avoided if earlier disclosure of the relevant evidence is carefully considered and effectively pursued.

With all of these options, it is best to identify the evidential gap early (e.g. from the complaints documents or medical records) and investigate the potential evidence and relevance with your experts, colleagues and counsel. Where a relevant gap might exist, recording the steps taken to investigate and plug and of your discussions and *inter partes* correspondence helps to build up the clearest evidential picture for the court and the existence of other evidence cannot be safely ignored.

Witness Statements

Congruency is especially important when it comes to witness evidence. This risks becoming lost in the drive to decrease costs because the time spent on preparing and analysing witness statements is often argued to be disproportionate.

Understanding the approach the trial judge takes to the factual evidence before you start preparing statements is important. In *Synclair v East Lancashire Hospitals NHS Trust [2015] EWCA Civ 1283, Tomlinson LJ* helpfully summarised the central principles. This case is a particularly helpful illustration of these because the defence was based entirely on the assertion that the contemporaneous records would be accepted as accurate and so more reliable than the oral evidence of the claimant and his wife. It therefore provides us with a benchmark for more complicated cases (where the additional assertions are made that the impugned clinicians' oral evidence and the expert evidence (when properly examined) will also be consistent) because it strips out those additional factors. The appeal was made on the basis that no reasonable trial judge would prefer oral evidence to contemporaneous documentary evidence.

It is also helpful that this case turned on a single clinical issue in order to understand the effect of proportionality on this area of practice. The case appears to be of a type so often portrayed as being simple and straightforward. It is also important for present purposes that there was a clear factual dispute covering the central issues on breach of duty. *Manzi v Kings College NHS Foundation Trust (supra; para. 25)*, it was held that there is no rebuttable presumption that a contemporaneous record is correct; rather there is a presumption that it is inherently reliable which is weighed against all of the evidence. This can work both for and against you as proving that a particular record is unreliable does not necessarily mean the fact can be proved from the other evidence (*Freeman v Pennine Acute Hospitals NHS Trust [2021] EWHC 3378 (QB)* provides a useful example of this process)

Accordingly, the broader issue is one of the credibility of witnesses when faced with contemporaneous written evidence which differs from their recollection of events. Whilst the cases considered above show that it is difficult or impossible to use credibility as a basis for obtaining disclosure, the position is very different for witnesses. It is far more likely that a trial judge will accept an argument that contemporaneous written evidence throws a much clearer light on matters than do witness statements produced sometime afterwards. This is the same reasoning that underpins the comments made in a previous chapter about the importance and relevance of the duty of candour investigation to the clinical negligence case.

In *Synclair, Tomlinson LJ* explained that the contemporaneous note was important for two reasons. Firstly, the trial judge had to assess the claimant's differing accounts (from their witness statements and oral evidence) against it. Secondly, it provided all of the impugned clinician's evidence on what he had said and observed because he could not remember what had happened. The note had been made by a more junior doctor who had not been called to give evidence. Accordingly, there was no evidence as to how the note had come to be made and so it was effectively uncorroborated.

The clinician's attempts to corroborate his note in his witness statement only served to highlight the lack of congruency in his evidence on this point. It was also asserted that the surrounding clinical notes were consistent with there being a non-negligent explanation and so provided the necessary corroboration for the disputed treatment records. However, as these did not corroborate the central facts in the disputed notes, the judge was entitled to give little weight to them.

It was also asserted that there was an inherent probability that the clinical record was accurate because clinicians are under a professional duty to make accurate notes. This was incongruent vis-á-vis the evidence as a whole. Although there was evidence of the claimant making potentially inconsistent statements, there was also evidence before the court that these had an innocent explanation which was congruent with the overall evidential picture.

All of these considerations are common to preparing witness statements in clinical negligence cases and it is likely to be the case that you will normally encounter a better degree of corroboration than there was in *Synclair*. When assessing witness evidence, trial judges are expected to follow the precepts set out in several well-known cases.

In *Onassis & Calogeropoulos v Vergottis [1968] 2 Lloyds Rep 403 @ 431*, *Lord Pearce's* dissenting judgement explained that 'credibility' requires more than just assessing the witness' demeanour at trial ('demeanour' is essentially assessing only whether they *now believe* they are telling the truth). It includes assessing whether the witness:

- Is essentially a truthful person;
- Is telling the truth on this occasion;
- Registered the event accurately and has now retained an accurate memory of it;

- Has had their memory of the event coloured by subsequent events, discussions or unconscious bias.

This led him to recommend the following set of tests aimed at ensuring the accuracy of witness testimony:

1. Checking the consistency of the witness' evidence with what is agreed, or clearly shown by other evidence, to have occurred.

2. Checking the internal consistency of the witness' evidence;

3. Checking the consistency with what the witness has said on other occasions.

4. Checking the credit of the witness in matters not germane to the litigation (this is the least relevant to a clinical negligence case but cannot be completely ignored)

5. Assessing the demeanour of the witness in court.

Similarly, in *Grace Shipping v Sharp & Co [1987] 1 Lloyds Rep 207 (Privy Council), Lord Goff* highlighted the need for witness evidence to be consistent with the contemporaneous documents in cases where a long period of time has elapsed (in this case it was 5 years). His comments echoed the point he had made previously (as *Goff J*) in *Armages Ltd v. Mundogas SA (The Ocean Frost) [1985] 1 Lloyd's Rep 1*:

> *"It is frequently very difficult to tell whether a witness is telling the truth or not; and where there is a conflict of evidence…, reference to the objective facts and documents, to the witness' motives, and to the overall probabilities, can be of very great assistance to a Judge in ascertaining the truth."*

The fallibility of human memory was emphasised *in Gestmin v SGPS SA v Credit Suisse (UK) Ltd & Another [2013] EWHC 3560 (Comm) (paras. 15-22)* by *Leggatt J*. To summarise:

1. A century of psychological research has shown that human memory is fallible. Stronger and more vivid memories are assumed to be more accurate and confidence is equated with accuracy.

2. Memories are malleable and can be influenced by subsequent events.

3. Memories of past beliefs are especially unreliable because they tend to conform with subsequent beliefs over time. This is particularly so where new information is presented.

4. The process of litigation is inherently likely to subject witnesses' memories to powerful biases. The witnesses may be partial to one side; feel allegiances that are not readily apparent; have ties of loyalty; or may simply want to create a good impression.

5. Repeatedly going over evidence with a witness whilst investigating or preparing a case risks embedding that information in place of the original memories the witness had.

6. Questions aimed at asking the witness to distinguish between 'recollection' and 'reconstruction' are misguided as is equating the strength, vividness or apparent authenticity of the memory with its accuracy.

7. Contemporaneous documentary events was therefore preferable to witness memory and should be given more weight and evidence based from a confident or honest witness is not necessarily reliable (at least in commercial cases).

These observations were held to be applicable outside of the commercial sphere in *Camarthenshire County Council v Y [2017] EWFC 35* and were directly applied in *Mills v Oxford University NHST (supra), paras. 181-2.* At *paras. 185-6* it is clear that the contemporaneous record was more likely to be reliable as to what had been said at the crucial consultation even though the claimant was honest. The effluxion of time is a relevant factor. In *Richins v Birmingham Women's & Children's NHSFT (supra),*

HHJ Kelly (para. 94) considered that *"[t]he lay witnesses in this case are faced with the Herculean task of recalling events that took place in July 2008 and being cross-examined about those events nearly 14 years later."* This case also contains a detailed review of the relevant authorities on this issue. These principles were re-emphasised in *R (on the application of Dutta) v General Medical Council [2020] EWHC 1974 (Admin), paras. 39-40* and *Mate v Mate [2023] EWHC 238 (Ch).*

Every fee earner should anticipate the court giving the clinicians considerable leeway in giving their evidence because busy medical professionals are not expected to remember the details of every consultation. For example, in *Taylor v Chesterfield Royal Hospital NHS Foundation Trust [2019] EWHC 1048 (QB)*, the trial judge had in mind another passage from *Synclair* when preferring a handwritten note from 1992:

> *"Clinical records are made pursuant to a clear clinical duty, serious failure in which could put at risk a practitioner's registration. Moreover, they are not compiled simply as a historical record, they fulfil an essential and ongoing purpose in informing the care and treatment of a patient. Contemporaneous records are these reasons are inherently likely to be accurate."*

However, in *EW v Johnson [2015] EWHC 276 (QB)*, reminded us that the contemporaneous nature of the record and the duty under which it was produced do not supervene other evidence of its accuracy. In *Welch v Waterworth [2015] EWCA Civ 11*, the court directly found that the surgeon's handwritten note of the operation and the version he had typed later that day were inaccurate having heard all of the evidence over a 5-day trial. The trial judge's evidential assessment was reasonable, with *McCombe LJ (@ para. 51)* concluding that:

> *"... the judge was entitled to fasten upon those aspects of the evidence which he found to be reliable pointers to what had actually occurred, without trawling seriatim through every issue, side-issue or speculation that arose on the evidence or in argument: see Biogen Inc v Medeva plc [1997] RPC 1 (per Lord Hoffman @ 31-45) and Henderson v*

Foxworth Investments Ltd [2014] 1 WLR 2600 (per Lord Reid @ [67]."

Understanding the interplay of the evidence and the level of detail required helps to find weak spots in time to fill them. *CNZ (supra)* and *XM (supra)* both contain a detailed analysis of the type undertaken by the trial judge. In *Gulf View Medical Centre Ltd. v Tesheira (supra), Lords Stephens and Pentland* held that the trial judge (in Trinidad & Tobago) was entitled to take the view that expert witnesses who had prepared witness statements in conjunction with the claimant's lawyers had merely elaborated on what they had already said in their reports and had not been assisted by the attorneys in preparing them and so was entitled to give this little weight (*paras. 78-9*)

Many witnesses have not learned English as a first language. In *Mordel v Royal Berkshire NHS Foundation Trust (supra), Jay J* expressly took this into account (*para. 22*) emphasising that care is needed to properly balance a witness's apparent fluency and daily use of English with their ability to understand and communicate in English whilst in court.

Cross-examination is not always possible where the witness suffers from certain medical conditions. In *Plant v El-Emir (supra)*, the claimant had sadly developed dementia. *Stacey J* took the fact that she was unable to be effectively cross-examined into account when weighing the factual evidence as a whole (*para. 12*) before deciding that there had been a lack of informed consent (*para. 82 and preceding this*).

When aiming to prepare a case where the evidence fits seamlessly together, it must be remembered that it is a counsel of perfection to expect to be able to achieve this. With reference to using *Onassis v Vergottis (supra)* in practice, *McCloskey LJ* in *Gilroy v Frylite Ltd [2020] NICA 45, para. 6* emphasised the difficulty of retrospectively fully understanding how the evidence unfolded at trial if you were not present: *"[t]he topic of the conduct, manner, bearing, behaviour, delivery and inflexion of a witness has two unifying themes in particular. First, none of these features is discernible in a transcript of what the witness actually said.*

Second, none of them is otherwise capable of replication before an appellate court."

This extends to preparing witness statements: in *Clarke v Edinburgh & District Tramways Company, Ltd [1919] UKHL 303, Lord Shaw (2nd para.)* in the context of trial transcripts emphasised the subtle 'tells' a witness can give at trial: *"Witnesses without any conscious bias towards a conclusion may have in their demeanour, in their manner, in their hesitation, in the nuance of their expressions, in even the turns of their eyelid left an impression upon the man who saw and heard them which can never be reproduced on the printed page."* What we can reasonably aim for is to assess the demeanour of our clients' witnesses as the case develops and try to predict and identify ambiguity and weak spots in the case which can be filled either with further evidence or persuasive advocacy. If we can also improve our understanding of how human beings make and retain memories and how we respond to pressure, then so much the better.

The Purpose of a Witness Statement

We know that a witness statement is the witness' trial evidence. Witnesses are no longer permitted to give their account of the evidence at trial (called 'evidence-in-chief'). They are permitted to be cross-examined, however. Since re-examination is only permitted to a very limited extent (*viz.* to clarify new matters brought up in cross-examination), evidence left out of a witness statement can fatally undermine the claimant's case.

However, 'effective' does not necessarily mean 'long' or 'detailed'. Short, pithy, witness statements can be just as effective as more verbose ones and have the advantage of containing less cross-examination material. Accordingly, less can sometimes be more.

It is important, therefore to be able to strike a balance between not spending too much time preparing the witness statements on your cases and not missing out anything important. By organising your thought process more effectively, you can improve your ability to strike the right balance.

The April 2020 update to the CPR requires that the statement contains a summary of the way it was taken and this should assist with assessing its accuracy. The very specific statement of truth (directly referring to the availability contempt of court proceedings) and the need for the witness statement to be in the witness' own language (translated into English for court use) are also likely to prove helpful in some cases.

Types of Statement

It helps to think about the use for which the statement the statement is to be put to. It will fall into one or more of the following categories:

(a) Liability Statements – i.e. dealing with issues of duty of care, breach of that duty and causation of damage.

(b) Quantum Statements – i.e. dealing with the causation of consequential losses, condition & prognosis and the valuation of the heads of damage.

(c) Supporting Statements – i.e. these are dealing with a part of the case only and back up the main statements.

(d) Application Statements – i.e. those signed by the fee earner in support of (or contesting) a court application for an order.

Facts, Facts, Facts

The facts of the case are crucial. The trial judge will apply the law to the facts of the case and clearly setting out the facts in each witness statement is an extremely effective way of persuading him that your case is better than your opponent's.

You should bear in mind:

(a) Witness Statements only contain facts. They should never contain opinion or law. They will be more persuasive if you avoid digression and maintain your focus on the issues in your case.

(b) We are in a jurisdiction of *ultimate fact evidence*. This means that a party must be able to prove his alleged *facts* at trial. We are not in a jurisdiction of *ultimate issue evidence* (such as the USA). Thus, you cannot gloss over proving the constituent facts of each issue in your case in the hope that the court will look only at the issue as a whole. The longer you leave identifying the facts, the more likely it is that you will fail to prove your case.

(c) Therefore, the requisite facts must be clearly identified as early as possible in the management of the case. Preferably, this should be done at the first interview. After the initial meeting or telephone interview, a preliminary statement should be produced setting out what facts need to be proved and how the witness intends to achieve this.

(d) Also, a party will only be allowed to adduce (and so prove) those facts which they plead. Consequently, the pleadings must contain every fact which is necessary to prove that party's case. We have seen that the statements of case should be based on the witness statements (including your witness' evidence on the disclosed documentary evidence).

(e) It helps to put yourself in your opponent's shoes. Pretend that you are cross-examining your own case. When you are cross-examining, you want to be managing the evidence, not the witness. You do this by asking a series of open and closed questions which are tailored to get the witness to say what you want them to say. For a witness statement, you first need to allow the witness to tell their own story before testing it. If an answer, objectively viewed, does not closely support the central allegations, then you need to do more work or accept that the case is risky (if the facts are genuinely ambiguous or unsupportive). If you thoroughly test the witness' evidence when preparing their statement, effective cross-examination becomes harder (although you are unlikely to ever consistently make it impossible).

(f) Asking tailored questions requires you to break the case into its smallest component parts. This is a fundamental step in any piece of litigation. If a fact is ambiguous, split it up and see if you can prove some of the smaller parts. Ultimately, the facts should be indivisible parts of the case with a 'yes' or 'no' answer to them.

(g) Regular reviews should be carried out to ask the question: 'if this case was at trial tomorrow, what would happen?' If you can say that you could prove all of your facts then your witness evidence is complete. If you are not happy to go to trial, then you need to do more work. Since proportionality and fixed fees mitigate against endlessly building a statement, the sooner you get the full statement, the better.

Sources of Information

(a) Face-to-face interviews. Taking evidence in person is always preferable as it allows you to personally assess their evidence and form a judgement regarding how they will come across at trial. You can form judgements about how they react to certain questions or evidence which it simply is not possible to do in any other way.

(b) Telephone and video interviews. Realistically, it is impractical and/or too expensive to see every potential witness. Conducting interviews remotely can still be effective at obtaining the information you need if you take the time to prepare for them properly. Open questions (i.e. those not requiring a 'yes' or 'no' answer) help to elicit the witness' account initially. It is often helpful to then move onto closed questions to finalise the witness' evidence on that point. Having a clear understanding of the issues in the case will also help you to focus effectively on the interview.

(c) Written instructions. A clear written account from the witness is often sufficient to use in drafting that witness' statement. You must not fall into the trap of assuming that a letter or other piece of documentary evidence will be accepted by the court as a *substitute* for a formal statement. It will not and you could leave your client with insufficient evidence to prove his case. That warning aside, documentary evidence (including medical, personnel, occupational health, benefits, employment and tax records, police investigations, diary entries, receipts, etc) can all help to fill in the gaps in your witness' memories and you should give serious consideration to obtaining their comments on any new evidence that comes in.

(d) Witness questionnaires are used by many practitioners to speed up the evidence-gathering process at the beginning of a case. A detailed witness questionnaire is a useful starting point. Again, a completed questionnaire will not be accepted as a substitute for a formal statement at trial. You can include a statement of truth in case the witness is unfortunate enough to pass away or change their evidence before their formal statement is signed.

(e) Other witnesses can be used to improve the quality of your other statements. This includes expert evidence. Again, you should always consider updating your statements upon receipt of other statements and include these costs in the budget. You should bear in mind, however, that each witness must be kept independent and too much similarity between statements is highly suspicious of collusion.

Using Headings

It is tempting to limit the use of headings only to the lengthier statements. The risk of doing this is that you inadvertently lose your focus on what you need to prove to win your case or application.

The following list of headings is a useful *aide memoire*. It does not need to be used in every case. However, it is illustrative of the sort of approach which is helpful to bear in mind when preparing a statement over the course of a case. For example, in an initial, preliminary statement, you will probably only need to cover the events surrounding the treatment in detail with a section dealing with the effects the client's injuries have had on them. As you progress to building up your client's case on liability and then on quantum, more detail can be added in other areas. By including evidence on the more of these areas, your client's schedule of special damage is better supported and the tendency is for the value of your settlements to improve.

(a) Background History

(b) Pre-Existing Employment History

(c) The Incident

(d) Follow up with the defendant

(e) Follow up at other hospitals (medical treatment)

(f) Further operations

(g) Psychological Impact

(h) Specific Physical Injuries

(i) Employment

(j) Average Day – Problems

(k) Care just after accident

(l) Care

(m) Special Damages

Procedural Requirements

Do not forget the procedural requirements. To summarise again:

(a) You must have a properly worded and signed statement of truth for the witness statement to be used ('admitted') in court as evidence. This must be in the correct format.

(b) The statement should contain the witness' evidence rather than yours and should be in the witness' own words and details of how it was taken.

(c) The statement should not contain *hearsay* – the witness should confine themselves to giving evidence of what they personally saw, heard, smelt and felt.

(d) Any failure to comply with these requirements will put you at risk of losing the case; a wasted costs order being made against your firm; a finding of fundamental dishonesty being made against your client; and or contempt of court proceedings being brought against the witness.

<u>Practical considerations</u>

When preparing witness statements, it is also helpful to bear in mind:

(a) It is important to understand how an incident happened in order to assess the witness' evidence. Even if you are not going to take a full statement, you will need to understand the central allegations relevant to that witness to assess their evidence accurately.

(b) You are not only assessing the treatment provided, but you are assessing the witness. If they are inconsistent in their story, or the facts simply do not correlate, make a note of it. If they seem uncertain, do put them at ease but do not avoid asking them difficult questions to see if they maintain consistency. Finding out that they were mistaken (or worse) at trial is far too late to correct matters.

(c) However, it is possible that they are nervous, inarticulate or just would not make a good witness. These are all factors in determining a case's success or failure.

(d) You do not want to end up at trial with a poor witness, or someone who is going to be too clever for their own good. They will get caught out.

(e) Witness evidence will be needed to prove facts, both pre-trial and at trial. It is important that the statements are sufficient to do this. This includes both the accident circumstances and the problems the injuries have caused and the losses too.

(f) If there is a dispute over any issue, the judge (especially in more modestly valued cases) is unlikely to not allow any significant evidence-in-chief from them. This means that your witness may not be able to clarify issues or give better evidence in the witness box unless the Defendant questions them about it.

(g) If you do not include it in their statement, there is a good chance that you will not get to raise it or rely on it.

Critical Factual Analysis

The following checklist is helpful in developing a consistent approach to critically analysing the factual evidence across your caseload. Once you have identified the central issues in the case, you can apply the following approach to the facts making up those issues:

1. Accurately state each fact contained in the piece of evidence under review.

2. Identify the 'common sense' or 'ordinary' meaning or interpretation of that fact.

3. Identify any alternative meanings or interpretation of this fact.

4. Are there other facts which make one meaning or interpretation of the fact under analysis more persuasive than the others (i.e. is it corroborated by other evidence)?

5. Is it possible to divide the fact being analysed further into smaller facts? If so, repeat the analysis for each of those facts.

6. Does the fact being analysed provide direct or indirect (i.e. circumstantial) evidence of the matter requiring proof?

7. Is it a primary, secondary or tertiary fact?

8. Is the fact contained in a document or a witness' testimony?

9. How contemporaneous is the fact being analysed?

10. Can you identify a chain of facts linking one meaning or interpretation together? Where is the weakest link in this chain? Is it possible to undermine this fact by finding an alternative explanation?

11. Is it possible to use alternative explanations to create more than one alternative chain? Is it possible to undermine all of these chains? Is it possible to disguise one chain by working upon it in the background?

12. Is further evidence necessary to prove this fact? Where will it come from? How will it be obtained?

13. Repeat these steps for each fact requiring proof. Start with the central larger, more general facts before moving on to their constituent smaller, more specialised facts.

In this context, a 'chain' of facts is very similar to the chain of causation being simply a series of linked facts in chronological order. The stronger the chain is, the more likely it is that it will withstand critical analysis and will be accepted by the court as helping to prove that the interpretation your client wants is the correct one.

Similar Fact Evidence

This is factual evidence from another case or complaint which is similar to the evidence in your case. As such, it is not automatically admissible and *CPR 1998, Rule 32.1(2)* can be used to exclude evidence and *CPR 1998, Rule 32.1(1)* to manage it. A hearsay notice should be served to admit the evidence into the proceedings and *Peter Sharp & Son (A Firm) v GEA Farm Technologies (UK) Ltd [2022] EWHC 64 (Ch)* sets out a two-stage test for allowing it: (a) is the evidence potentially relevant to one or more issues in the case; & (b) are there good grounds (such as the interests of justice, proportionality or expedition) for excluding it? *GKE (supra)* is a good example of a case where the credibility of the claimant and her solicitor's attempt to adduce similar fact evidence via the claimant's expert's report combined to undermine that expert's credibility as well.

Conclusion

The importance of factual evidence is often underestimated or overlooked in clinical negligence cases because the emphasis is on the expert evidence needed to prove the legal standards. What is often forgotten is that the expert evidence is only as good as the factual evidence the opinion is based on. If the factual evidence is either incomplete or ambiguous, then the foundations of the case are weak and the entire case is much easier to bring down.

It is therefore proportionate to spend time on investigating the facts of each case thoroughly as long as you do so efficiently. This means clearly identifying the facts necessary to prove the central issues, reassessing your allegations in light of them and reappraising them in light of the other evidence. The sooner you do this, the stronger your client's case is and the more likely that you will reduce the duration of the case. This difficult skill is worth making the effort to develop well. Ultimately, the careful preparation and analysis of the factual evidence reduces the risk of a crucial fact being missed at trial. *"[N]ot every detail of the relevant evidence need be or can be captured in the reasons given by the judge for his findings"* (*Kwok v Yao [2022] UKPC 22, para. 44 per Dame Geraldine Andrews*).

Clarity in the documentary evidence will allow the judge to better focus on the credibility of those giving evidence. As Lord Hoffman explained in *Biogen Inc. v Medeva plc (supra, para. 54)* and *Piglowska v Piglowski [1999] UKHL 27 (para. 43)*:

> *"[The judge's] expressed findings are always surrounded by a penumbra of imprecision as to emphasis, relative weight, minor qualifications and nuance (as Renan said, la verité est dans une nuance) of which time and language do not permit exact expression, but which may play an important part in the judge's overall evaluation."*

CHAPTER SEVEN

EXPERT EVIDENCE

Introduction

The fundamental practical principle which underpins expert evidence was made clear by *Cresswell J* in *The Ikarian Reefer [1993] 2 Lloyds LR 68*:

> *"Expert evidence presented to the Court should be, and should seen to be, the independent product of the expert uninfluenced as to form or content by the exigencies of litigation (Whitehouse v Jordan [& Others [1980] UKHL 12])"*

It is always worth bearing that in mind when instructing experts (there is no harm in including it in the letter of instruction in addition to specific references to *CPR 1998, Part 35*); when analysing expert evidence; and when seeking clarification of reports or asking questions to experts. The risk of not doing so carefully is that the evidence becomes biased. The full quote from *Lord Wilberforce* in *Whitehouse v Jordan & Others (supra) at pp8-9* is:

> *"Whilst some degree of consultation between the experts and the legal advisors is entirely proper, it is necessary that expert evidence presented to the Court should be, and should seen to be, the independent product of the expert uninfluenced as to form or content by the exigencies of litigation. To the extent to which it is not, the evidence is likely to be not only incorrect but self-defeating."*

Expert evidence forms the central plank in most cases but it is often only as good as the factual evidence supporting it. It is opinion evidence (i.e. evidence which not purely factual) and its primary purpose is to assist the trial judge in understanding the specialist elements of the standard of care received; the competing causes of the injuries sustained (and of the claimant's other co-morbidities); and the therapeutic aspects of the claimant's ongoing care needs and other items which would help to put them back into their pre-negligence position. Since it is opinion evidence, it will be necessarily based upon assumptions being made as to what has happened, what should have happened and what is likely to happen in the future. Accordingly, the better the factual evidence is, the more persuasive the expert's opinion is likely to be. The expert can then focus their experience and knowledge on the facts at hand leaving less scope for new facts or interpretations coming to light later which fatally undermine their opinion and, therefore, your client's case. Your experts need to be able to fully account for all of the known facts and assist in identifying unknown facts (e.g. see the criticisms of the claimant's expert and lawyers in *Arksey (supra) paras. 63-73*, including *"[i]n the end, the continual apologies of [the expert]… in the course of his evidence, as the magnitude of the deficiencies became apparent, were embarrassing" (para. 73, per Spencer J)*.

Therefore, proportionality recognises that costs will be incurred on this phase of litigation which might, at first glance, be relatively high and looking to save costs by selecting an expert from a less expensive discipline needs caution. Once again, however, the devil is in the detail and it is always likely that there will be some scope for arguing that both the estimated or incurred costs are/were disproportionate on the particular facts of the case and there is an incentive on your opponent to do so. Conversely, spending too little time on expert evidence, will probably result in missing a key piece of evidence or alternate argument which causes the case to fail.

Being able to effectively obtain, analyse and deploy your expert evidence remains as important as ever but downwards costs pressures mean that litigators have to do so ever more efficiently.

Procedural Considerations

CPR 1998 Part 35 sets out the procedural rules governing the courts' power to regulate the use of expert evidence in accordance with the overriding objective to deal with cases fairly and proportionately. These should be borne in mind from the outset of every case as you will, ultimately, need to obtain the courts permission to rely on expert evidence at trial.

To summarise, the requirements are:

- *Rule 35.1.* The court must limit expert evidence to what is *'reasonably required to resolve the proceedings'.* The most practical way to comply with this is to ensure that your expert is addressing the central allegations in the case or a supporting allegation which remains disputed.

- *Rule 35.3.* The experts' duty is to the court and not to the party instructing them. This is to ensure that the expert remains independent at all times and seeks to avoid 'guns for hire' being instructed. *Part 35.14* gives experts the right to ask the court for directions unilaterally of the parties although the must send a copy to their instructing party at least seven days before they file them and at least four days before filing to the other parties.

- *Rule 35.4.* The court's permission is required to *rely* on expert evidence. Accordingly, you do not need permission to *instruct* an expert. Whilst not ideal, if you do find yourself in the position where you are refused permission to rely on an expert who has already reported, then you can still use that expert's report to help prepare the rest of the case and doing so will help in recovering the costs of that report and the work surrounding it. In order to obtain permission, you must provide a costs estimate for that report; the field of expertise (e.g. 'midwifery', 'obstetrics & gynaecology', 'A&E', etc); the issues which the report will address (such as breach of duty); and, where practicable, the identity of the expert.

  You are likely to find that the judge allows you some leeway in respect of the costs estimate and identity of the expert, you will always need to be prepared to clearly explain why an expert in this particular discipline is justifiable. This is covered in more detail below. This rule also gives the court the power to limit the fees incurred by an expert. This is intended to prevent very high fees being incurred.

In clinical negligence cases, it is important to compare like with like rather than taking the view that a particular figure is (or is not) reasonable. This does allow the judge at the CCMC to reduce the amount budgeted for expert fees and, if this happens, the expert should be informed promptly following the hearing. The expert can still charge the fee and so evidence of attempted negotiation with the expert is useful in both showing the judge that the fee is within a reasonable range and consistent with other experts in this field and gives your expert the opportunity to explain their position and fee structure before the issue arises. Always remember that any evidence produced can be used later in the case and so you ought to try to ensure it is not prejudicial to the ultimate goal of winning your client's case.

- *Rule 35.5.* Expert evidence must be given in a written report. This rule appears straightforward and it largely is. Practical points to keep in mind are that side letters can be used in conjunction with a written report where it is more cost-effective to do so (on the basis that is the entirety of the expert's opinion which must be disclosed to the court) and that the report itself must have a compliant expert's declaration setting out that the expert understands and has complied with their duty to the court. Best practice remains to ensure that the report is complete and easy to read and understand before it is served (or its existence disclosed).

- *Rule 35.6* allows written questions to be put to your opponent's expert or to a joint expert. These questions must be proportionate; made within 28 days of service of the report; made for the clarification of the report; and can be put only once. Any of these can be circumvented by the parties agreeing or with the permission of the court. The answers given form part of the expert's report. Where the expert fails to answer the questions, the court may stop that expert giving evidence at trial and/or prevent that expert's fees being recoverable form the other party. Under *CPR 1998, Rule 35PD, para. 6.1*, the questions must send the questions to both the expert and to their instructing solicitor. Under *para. 6.2*, it is the *instructing* party which bears the costs of the expert answering the questions rather than the party asking them (as used to be the case). The instructing party can seek to recover these costs if they win in the usual way.

In some cases, it is useful to use this rule to ask questions pre-action before the report is served. This is typically in a case where either a letter of claim or response has been served providing a detailed explanation based on expert evidence. It may be apparent to the receiving party (perhaps after a discussing with their expert) that significant differences exist between the parties' respective experts on a key but discrete issue. The without prejudice exchange of expert evidence may quite reasonably be ill-advised at this stage for a number of legitimate reasons (see further below) but asking your opponent a limited number of questions approved by your expert has a reasonable chance of narrowing the issues and saving costs.

As long as your opponent has provided a detailed explanation of its case and confirmed that this reflects the expert evidence it has, why should you be required to await service of that report many months later after proceedings have commenced at considerable expense? If the questions are answered, you have a much better and earlier indication of your opponent's case. If your opponent refuses to allow its expert to answer the questions (remember that you will not know their name or address at this point), then that is evidence relevant to conduct relevant to the proportionality test and costs recovery.

- *Rule 35.7* permits the court to allow the use of single joint experts and *Rule 35.8* sets out how they should be instructed. This does not mean that single experts should be used in any one situation (see further below) and proportionality does not make their use mandatory. The key point is that the rules require that the instructing parties are on a level playing field and so must all see whatever materials, instructions and questions are put to the expert. Fees are shared equally but the liability is joint and several (*CPR 1998, Rule 35.8(5)*).

- *Rule 35.9* and *PD35 para. 4* confirms that any additional information an expert relies upon which is not reasonably available to the other parties, must be disclosed. The raw data itself does not need disclosing, what is required is a document setting out all of the facts, tests, experiments and assumptions which underpin any part of the information being referred to. Enough detail must be given to allow the other parties to properly interpret and investigate its potential significance to the case.

- *Rule 35.10* and *PD35 para. 3* seeks to provide some consistency to the contents of experts' reports and so it is helpful to summarise these:

    - The substance of all material instructions covering the report's preparation must be stated. Whilst the instructions themselves are not privileged, neither they nor any documents referred to will be ordered to be disclosed unless there are reasonable grounds to consider (not 'believe') that the instructions were either inaccurate or incomplete. The same test applies when trying to enquire or cross-examination an expert about their instructions.

    - The end of the report must contain a statement confirming that the expert understands their duty to the court and that they have complied with it as well as a statement of truth (the wording for which is set out at *PD35, para. 3.3*).

    - The expert must address their report to the court (not to the instructing party).

- The report must give details of the expert's qualifications and of any literature or material they have relied upon.
- Summarise the facts relevant to their opinion and to identify those which are within their own knowledge.
- Clearly identify any range of opinion which exists; summarise them; and give a reasoned explanation for the expert's own opinion.
- Cleary identify anyone who has carried out a test, examination or investigation which the expert has relied upon and confirm whether the expert was supervising when this was performed.
- Clearly summarise the conclusions being made in the report. Where the expert feels they can only draw qualified conclusions, this needs to be explained clearly. An important practical example of this is where the expert recognises that their opinion depends on whether the claimant's or defendant's interpretation of a key aspect of the factual evidence is accepted by the court. Such recognition is not evidence that the expert is weak; rather it is evidence that they are independent and objective and this is likely to make them more persuasive to the trial judge even though it highlights a potential problem with the case. Ideally, any such factual dichotomy will have been identified at the start of the case (during either the initial risk assessment or when the medical records were reviewed) and certainly by the time a letter of response has been received.

- *Rule 35.11* permits the other parties to the case to use any expert report which has been disclosed to it. As this does not have to be for the same purpose as the report was intended for, it is important that you clearly assess the potential consequences that disclosing reports on a 'without prejudice' basis and side-letters in support of applications or narrow side-issues. Even if the report itself cannot be referred to, the information in it can be and this can unexpectedly fatally undermine your client's case at a later stage.

- *Rule 35.12* covers experts' discussions. Apart from trial, these are the single most risky stage in clinical negligence actions and some practitioners and experts consider them to be *de facto* 'mini-trials'. As such, they are considered in more detail below. The procedural framework for them is as follows (and should be read in conjunction with the standard disclosure order considered in Chapter 6).

    - The court can direct a joint discussion at any stage and so there is no need to be constrained by the standard timetable. Although it is possible that this could be pre-action, it is probably unlikely that the court would order this before the pleadings have set out the parties' respective cases with the clarity required for litigation. That said, cases which pivot on the strength of the expert evidence on an issue would benefit in theory from an early discussion both in terms of narrowing the issues and avoiding avoidable costs being incurred. Accordingly, is worth considering this with your opponent given the proportionality issues which pervade modern litigation as is the court's power to specify the matters to be discussed.

    - The purpose of a joint discussion is to identify and discuss the expert issues in the proceedings and to reach an agreed position if possible. As the intention is to promote genuine attempts at narrowing the issues, the content of the discussion itself is wholly 'without prejudice'. Any agreement reached does not bind the instructing parties. However, as the court may direct (and, in practice, this means 'will direct') the experts to produce a joint statement setting out what they agree and disagree on, the party which is unhappy with the outcome is placed in the invidious position of being taken by surprise by their own expert and then having to decide whether there is still a reasonable prospect of winning the case at trial. This is largely why the standard directions order requires experts to fully explain any change of opinion and certainly why extreme vigilance is required with experts notwithstanding any continuing relatively harsh interpretation of proportionality by the courts.

- *Rule 35.13* stipulates that a failure to disclose an expert's report means that party is not permitted to use the evidence at trial or to call that expert to give evidence. You will note that there are no references to failing to serve the report or to being prevented from relying on it. However, it is inconceivable that one party can simply tell their opponent that it has a report on a contested issue (i.e. disclose its existence) and then fail to serve it (disclose its content) without incurring a serious sanction. The penalty for failing to comply with the date for service within the directions order could well be the same as under *Rule 35.13* especially if the application was made retrospectively. *PD35 para. 8* requires any order requiring an expert to do something to be promptly served on them even if the order itself does not make this clear (as the standard directions order does). Without expert evidence, the case at trial, winning would require your opponent's expert to capitulate under cross-examination. Whilst not impossible, the chances of success would probably not meet the requirements of your client's legal expenses insurer. The severity of this sanction does mean that the more normal situation faced is that the report is served late. If this appears likely to happen, then most practitioners will firstly try to agree a 28-day extension (which may already be allowed in the directions order) and/or lodge an application seeking additional time for service before the deadline. As long as the application is sent before the deadline passes, the court will view it as a prospective application and so will look more favourably on it everything else being equal.

- *PD35, para. 11* sets out the procedure for experts giving their evidence concurrently at trial. In such cases, the experts will both take the stand at the same time and either answer questions from an agreed agenda or will discuss the remaining areas of disagreement guided by the judge. The parties' barristers will then be allowed to ask questions after this has been completed and the judge has summarised the opinions given. Whether or not concurrent evidence should be chosen in any given case depends on the extent of the agreement between the experts, whether the trial judge is likely to be assisted by the experts giving evidence together and whether there are likely to be costs savings. From a trial management perspective, it can be advantageous to have both experts giving evidence at the same time as they will be able to react immediately to the points being made and will be in court for less time.

The Practical Objective

In every case, the goal is to obtain unbiased, watertight expert evidence which will persuade the trial judge that your client's case is correct. In *Mulholland v Medway NHS Foundation Trust [2015] EWHC 268 (QB), Green J* helpfully reiterated a series of principles for the proper assessment of expert evidence on breach of duty at trial. These principles are not new; he set them out previously in *C v North Cumbria University Hospitals NHS Trust [2014] EWHC 61 (QB)*. It is sensible for practitioners to take heed and apply them during the preparation of all of the expert evidence (not just on breach of duty) and they are increasingly referred to at trial.

Expert evidence can be complicated (both technically and factually) and it is often not enough for the experts to simply sign the *Part 35* declaration at the end of their report. *Green J* makes it fairly clear that he expects them to properly apply their minds to the issues in question and not to set the bar too high in applying the *Bolam/Bolitho* test. Extending this, it is fairly easy to see the advantages of applying similar discipline to contested questions of causation, condition and prognosis and quantum issues.

Firstly, the sooner you can get your expert evidence in hand, the less chance there is of missing a crucial piece of the puzzle. Secondly, following these principles increases your chances of persuading the trial judge that your interpretation is the correct one. Thirdly, in the current climate of costs budgeting and proportionality it is essential to do this as soon as is possible during your *Pre-Action Protocol* investigations and, later, to enable you to make it clear why you want to spend the predicted sums in the face of seemingly persuasive counter-submissions.

The principles are found at *para. 25* of *C* and *para. 81* of *Mulholland.* They are based on *Green J's* review of the previous case law (probably including *Stuart-Smith J's* judgement in *Loveday v Renton [1990] 1 Med LR 182.* These principles are:

1. A substantial amount of weight will be attached to a reasonable body of opinion which supports the impugned treatment even where a contrary body exists (*paras. 25(i) & (ii)*).

2. The court must not delegate this task to the experts – it must form its own view (*para 25(iii)*)

3. In doing so, the court should take into account a variety of factors. These include:

    (a) Whether the evidence is tendered in good faith;

    (b) Whether the expert is 'responsible', 'competent', and/or 'respectable'; and

    (c) Whether the opinion is 'reasonable & logical'.

    Other factors may also be relevant (*para 25(iv)*)

4. Although it is an obvious pre-requisite that expert evidence should be given in good faith and is therefore valid and relevant, it should not be assumed that this provides any support for the impugned treatment as showing it met with sound medical practice (*para. 25(v)*).

5. 'Responsible/competent/respectable'. These adjectives are relevant to whether an opinion is logical but are not determinative of it. They are material considerations, however.

    (a) 'Competence' equates to NHS experience giving them first-hand knowledge of the clinical considerations relevant to the impugned treatment at the date in question. The longer the experience, the broader the knowledge but the experience must still be current and not 'out of touch'.

    (b) 'Respectability' equates to mainstream opinions and not fringe or opinions at the end of the reasonable range of the spectrum.

    (c) 'Responsibility' equates to not adopting extreme positions or failing to make suitable concessions; and to adhering to the spirit and words of the *Part 35* declaration. (*para. 25(vi)*)

6. 'Logic & reasonableness'. Logic is the most important of the factors. The trial judge should not simply accept the opinion: it should be tested against both its internal consistency and the other evidence that comes out at trial:

    (a) Does it properly accord with the inferences to be drawn from the other evidence?

    (b) Has the expert properly addressed all of the considerations which applied at the time of the alleged negligence?

    (c) Has the expert properly placed the impugned conduct in the context of any official guidelines?

    (d) Has the expert's evidence been updated in light of developing evidence and the evidence at trial?

> Early reports are often based on evidential assumptions which prove to be incorrect. The opinion will lack logic if it is out of date. If an expert is summarising evidence, he should say so and append the actual records. The trial judge's role is to concentrate on the pith and substance of the opinion and then to evaluate it against the evidence as a whole to assess its logic. A judge should give considerable weight to an opinion which meets these criteria (*para 25(vii)*).

Drawing these together, it can be seen that the court wants to hear evidence from someone who is genuinely experienced in their field – i.e. someone who has been practising in this discipline for at least several years and is able to apply that knowledge to the correct legal tests. Other, more recent, judgements show that judges are setting out how experienced each expert is (in terms of the number of years they have practiced in the NHS). Judges do not want to hear evidence from experts who have not practiced for many years. This makes it necessary to carefully consider the expert's cv before going to the expense of instructing them. Most experts have long cvs if asked; shorter form ones are usually insufficient for this purpose. Caution should be exercised when instructing experts via an agency. Just because the other agency says the expert has the correct experience, does not always mean that they do. As the cv ought to be appended to the served report, it is open to scrutiny and cross-examination by your opponent so it is advisable to check it carefully yourself. Equally, you can show the same vigour in analysing the other side's experts' cvs.

A useful approach is to look at the publications (peer-reviewed and otherwise); articles, lectures; and special interests which the expert has. For example, in a case involving a missed radial fracture, an orthopaedic surgeon who does a weekly general fracture clinic in a District Hospital may seem to be an excellent choice. However, if their career focus and special interests are in spinal surgery, their opinion is unlikely to carry as much weight as an arm surgeon.

On occasion, it is necessary to delve into your expert's experience more thoroughly still; especially where the experts are diametrically opposed.

Knowing how many of this particular type of operation they have performed or how many times they have made each of the range of possible diagnoses in these specific circumstances can be crucial in making your expert's evidence more persuasive. Each expert ought to be able to provide figures for his or her relative, specific experience and, if they cannot, they ought to be able to explain why their particular opinion should be preferred. Always bear in mind that they may not have performed a certain procedure regularly if these are normally left to more junior colleagues under their supervision. It is the expert's experience of the matters in issue which is important and which should be checked carefully.

For example, claimant's experts must not just produce opinions which show why negligence occurred; caused an avoidable injury; or the likely consequences it will have. Rather, they must go further and persuade the trial judge that he or she cannot safely rely on what is being tendered as a reasonable, alternate explanation for these matters. Accordingly, if you have applied these principles to your expert evidence already, it is easier to persuade the trial judge that they have sufficient congruent evidence before them to go against the defendant's experts.

In a nutshell, the expert evidence needs to make sense when considered from several different angles. These angles will not be immediately obvious at an early stage in the case as either side may have obtained screening expert evidence based on limited evidence. The letters of claim and response often appear to be miles apart for this reason. Rather than getting diverted by these differences, it is advisable to establish that your expert has fully considered their argument from the other point(s) of view being raised. If your expert does not appear to understand what is being put by their opponent or is quick to dismiss that point of view, then this is something which needs to be explored further, preferably before the particulars of claim are finalised.

Given the expert's duty under *CPR Part 35*, it may also be thought that these opinions are always objective and given in good faith. Whilst they are in the vast majority of cases, there are occasions where it is not so. The risk is greatest in fringe disciplines or where, for whatever other reason, the expert loses their objectivity. This can arise innocuously. In *Graham v Altaf [2023] EWHC 156 (KB)*, the claimant's expert formed the view that the evidence of the condition must have been visible to the impugned clinician on examination and so did not accept her evidence that it was not seen and that she had followed up with the patient on that basis. *HHJ Sephton (para. 44) stated: "I formed the impression that* [the claimant's expert] *was acting as an advocate for the party by whom he was instructed, rather than providing the court with a disinterested, objective, opinion."* The fact that the expert had said that it was a factual matter for the court to decide was insufficient in this case because, overall, it *"does not detract from the fact that, in my view, he has sought to influence the court's decision on matters of fact" (para. 47).*

Similar considerations apply initially to ensuring that the expert is 'responsible', 'competent', and/or 'respectable'; unfortunately, this cannot be taken for granted. Properly selecting your expert goes a long way to minimising this risk and it is useful to review the law reports to see if this expert has been the subject of adverse judicial comment. Sometimes, even long-established experts slip below the standard expected of them.

Respectability often needs to be assessed in light of your opponent's response because it is possible that their expert has approached the case on a narrower but more mainstream basis. Even though expert reports will often not be disclosed upfront, it ought to be possible to form a view on the specific evidence the opposing expert is basing their opinion on. From this, you can assess the extent to which each expert is straying from this centre ground. The most likely scenario to cause problems is in very specialised cases where the expert has a particular interest in that this sub-specialism. This can, and does, lead them into seeking to prove that their view is the correct one and so losing their objectivity. However, it can also arise in more normal cases where a relatively inexperienced expert takes a too narrow view of the allegations or evidence.

Accordingly, respectability can overlap with responsibility. However, it is important to try to keep these two considerations separate in your own mind when preparing your evidence. 'Responsibility' is really the need to avoid allowing an expert becoming intransigent and refusing to accept that there is an alternate opinion which he needs to address. This can often arise where they have missed a piece of evidence in the medical records; have not kept themselves updated of developments in this particular treatment; or have not researched the available supporting literature thoroughly enough.

If these aspects of the expert evidence appear to be reasonable, then it makes it more likely that that expert's opinion will also be logical. However, as this is the core requirement, it is necessary to identify and fill as many of the lacunae in your expert's opinion as is possible and not to ignore those that cannot be filled with evidence.

Covering the inferences to be drawn from other evidence can become time-consuming and therefore arguably disproportionate to the value of the case. These will often not be obvious or easily discernible to the lawyers without the expert's assistance. Remember that proportionality also relates to the issues in the case, however. The underlying factual, documentary and clinical evidence is very likely to contain ambiguities and the alternate inferences which can be drawn need to be identified, categorised and prioritised so the trial judge can understand your case properly.

The need to address all of the relevant considerations which applied at the time of the alleged negligence goes to ensuring that the correct guidelines and standards are being applied. It is surprisingly common to miss the, sometimes subtle, changes that occur in national or local clinical guidelines over time. One way of reducing this risk is to seek disclosure of the guidelines that the defendant had in place at the time; to check the dates when they were requisitioned and updated (and not rely on what your opponent says) and to compare them with the national guidelines.

For example, it is far more difficult for an expert to place the impugned treatment into its proper context if he does not have the correct guidelines to hand. The standard clinical textbooks often cited in support of the opinion can differ as to the standard to be applied and this can have a crucial effect on proving breach of duty. One text may support the expert's opinion, whilst another may do so more equivocally when read in isolation. It is relatively common to find that an opposing expert has not been sent the guidelines when you see their report.

Another common failing is that experts do not fully read the clinical studies or supporting materials that they have referred to. This is an area where there is significant mileage in considering these 'supporting' materials yourself. Although this is a time-consuming exercise (relative to other tasks) it is surprisingly common to find that the supporting material has been taken out of context or has been misapplied by the expert.

Assessing whether the expert has updated their opinion in light of new evidence is also often overlooked. The purpose of the standard directions timetable is to allow the expert to finalise his report after the documentary evidence has been disclosed and then the witness evidence has been updated in light of this. Disclosing expert evidence before this has occurred risks hamstringing your expert. That said, it seems to be coming more and more common to see the preliminary expert report disclosed in proceedings where no attempt has been made to update it in light of the pleadings and other evidence. This not only increases costs in defended cases (because an early decision has been made to take the case to trial at a low cost), it also makes it significantly harder to cover all of the points discussed above (because the issues are not being properly narrowed).

This is particularly so where the defendant's case is based on their factual witnesses being believed at trial. In these cases, it is necessary to carefully prepare your expert to make sure he considers what that witness has written in the contemporaneous medical records, what they then say in their witness statements and to predict what additional details they will be allowed to give at trial. Treating clinicians are usually allowed a significant amount of leeway in straying into giving opinion evidence because they are not usually expected to write everything they considered at the time in their notes and the clinical issues in any given case are complex (vis-á-vis personal injury cases). As clinicians are generally overworked, they are also often allowed to give more evidence of what they would have done than the non-clinicians. All of this needs to be taken into account by the experts.

Single or Joint Experts?

Although single joint experts are allowed, their use should be limited to where there is likely to be no significant difference between opposing experts and/or where the issues being discussed are relatively ancillary. Allowing or agreeing to a joint expert in circumstances where there is likely to be a significant factual dispute or a range of opinion, then it is necessary to allow each side to obtain its own expert evidence so that these issues are properly explored and the trial judge has a full range of evidence before them. Accordingly, the court is most likely to consider joint experts on catastrophic injury cases for the subsidiary quantum reports.

That said, it is more reasonable for joint experts to be considered in cases where several defendants are being pursued. Although it is still likely to be unreasonable on breach of duty (where either different disciplines are needed or one defendant might be more culpable than the others), the same cannot be said for causation issues. The damage caused by the breaches of duty is likely to be of the same type and, at least between the co-defendants, the causation issues are likely to be the same. In such cases, the court should be invited to limit the expert evidence to separate experts for the claimant and the defendants on this basis and also to ensure equality of arms because, otherwise, the claimant will be faced with two opposing experts rather than one. It also harder to justify the additional costs of allowing each co-defendant as being proportionate in the absence of any specific evidence as to why one defendant will be prejudiced by sharing an expert on these issues.

Screening or Full Report?

Opinion differs as to whether it is preferable to obtain a brief screening opinion as part of your preliminary investigations or whether it is ultimately more proportionate to obtain a full report. The advantage of a screening report is that it is cheaper and quicker, but the disadvantage is that it is more likely to be inconsistent with the principles set out above.

Full reports are more likely to be fully compliant and reasoned but the expense and delay is often prohibitive across an entire portfolio of cases.

If a screening report is chosen, it is important to obtain it from a specialist on the issues to be covered. In this respect, defendant organisations are at an advantage because they have more ready access to clinical experts. If a screening report is obtained from a generalist, then there is a greater risk of that expert does not have sufficient knowledge of the specialist subject matter and so innocently misleads you.

Selecting & Instructing Experts

The approach to take in selecting and instructing experts is considered in Chapter 3. In addition to what is said there, a potential conflict of interest is not always apparent even where the potential expert has been specifically asked when approached. If a potential conflict does arise, then it needs to be investigated promptly and brought to the court's attention. Not every potential conflict will be significant or fatally undermine that party's case but it is a factor is likely to be taken into account by the trial judge when weighing that expert's evidence (e.g. *Gildea v States of Jersey and Social Services Committee [2004] JRC 206, para 9*).

In *Toth v Jarman [2006] EWCA Civ 1028*, evidence of a significant and very close relationship between an expert and a party led to that expert's evidence being excluded. In *EXP v Barker [2017] EWCA Civ 63*, the longstanding close personal relationship between the expert and the defendant was not disclosed. It had lasted many years from the defendant's training onwards and his cv would have shown this. Both individuals ought to have voluntarily disclosed this connection, however, and it was highly relevant to the disputed medical issues. The expert evidence was permitted but the failure to disclose the relationship factored heavily in the trial judge's decision in finding that a breach of duty had occurred.

Evidence as to expert's remuneration can also come to light late in proceedings and can create the inference of bias. This is why experts are not permitted to work under a cfa. *O'Leary v Mercy University Hospital*

Cork Ltd [2019] IESC 48 provides a good example of where very high expert fees were scrutinised and this judgement provides an excellent and detailed analysis of the issue of bias which should be kept in mind. Logically, is there a reason where disclosure of lower fee estimates in a costs budget not also call into question whether that expert is reasonably able to discharge their duty to the court? At the very least, it can form part of your case planning from that point onwards.

Getting the correct discipline of expert is not always obvious at the start of a case. In *Robinson v Liverpool University Hospitals NHS Trust & Mercier [2023] EWHC 21 (KB)*, the claimant's general dental expert conceded under cross-examination that the standard of care was that if a dental surgeon and the impugned treatment likely was not unreasonable. A third-party costs order against the expert was overturned on appeal; the expert had not acted outside of his expertise because tooth extraction was within the competence and scope of general dental practice even though the standard of care was that of a dental surgeon (*paras. 42-47, per Sweeting J*). From the claimant's perspective, however, this provided little comfort because they lost their case.

In order to avoid such issues arising, it is therefore prudent to ask better questions when selecting experts and consider due diligence as early as you can as the details of your opponent's evidence becomes available during the case.

Conferencing Experts

The number of conferences that are proportionate is likely to be contested at the CCMC. As a minimum, both sides should hold conferences (a) before finalising the statements of case; (b) before the exchange of expert evidence; and (c) before trial. If this is not done, then there is a considerable risk that the case is poorly prepared.

Although holding a conference in person allows the likely performances at trial to be better assessed, telephone or video conferences are often a reasonable and proportionate alternative to meeting in chambers. Not every conference needs to be in person or have every expert present simultaneously. It may be that only one expert needs to be conferenced in order to address issues specific to their opinion. That said, holding a conference with all of the experts simultaneously, can have the advantage of different perspectives on the case being freely discussed in front of the lay client.

What is essential is to properly understand the issues which need to be addressed and put yourself and counsel in the position to focus on these. An updated, paginated bundle should be sent in good time for counsel to read it and the instructions themselves should highlight the current central issues and where the associated evidence is. This should mirror the information the expert has been sent in order to minimise the scope for misunderstandings occurring which delay the conference proceeding efficiently.

This creates a risk of bias either overtly (e.g. through overly passionate interjections) or more subtly (e.g. from the common and natural desire to please those in your 'team'). In *Vernon v Bosley (No. 2) [1996] EWCA Civ 1217, Stuart-Smith LJ,* noted the trial judge commented that the defendant's experts had been allowed *"to become comparably 'parti pris', ... not through a lack of professionalism, but through the osmotic process which is an almost inevitable incident of litigation in this intensity."* The claimant's experts fared worse: *"... the demonstration of partisan commitment on this scale is corrosive of confidence in the value of the opinion not only then expressed but also previously and subsequently expressed."*

The contact details of all attendees should be kept to hand and the solicitor should be in a position to take a detailed, verbatim note of the conference as the experts and counsel will often need to see this. Details of the work which needs to be done should also be written in this note. Where the note has been handwritten, it should be typed as soon as is practicable.

<u>Experts' Joint Meetings</u>

These remains the riskiest stage of the case (other than trial) because experts remain prone to rowing back on the position they have adopted previously when directly discussing the issues with a peer. This risk is minimised by properly identifying the central issues, properly instructing the expert, analysing their reports and keeping them updated with new developments but the risk can never be entirely excluded.

It is prudent not to assume that an expert is well-versed in attending joint meetings. Accordingly, it is prudent to set out for the benefit of the expert the current state of the case before the joint meeting occurs so that it is clear what they have said previously, why they have said it and what their position is on the conflicting evidence provided by their opposing expert. This also assists in focussing their mind on any relative weak points in their opinion thus giving them the chance to find further supporting materials or to warn you that they may need to concede on a (hopefully minor) point in advance of the meeting.

The agendas for the meeting also remain an area of conflict. Downwards costs pressures on the defendants (in the form of fixed contractual fees from the defence organisations) appear to have resulted in more agendas being rejected even where they have been approved by the claimant's experts for reasons which do not always withstand scrutiny against the central issues or the evidence served to date. This really leaves neither side much room for manoeuvre and applying to the court for assistance is fairly impractical given the additional costs and delays involved. Accordingly, the only practical solution is to use separate agendas if agreement cannot be reached even though this tends to reflect poorly on the lawyers involved and increases the costs of the experts' meetings. *Yip J's* comments in *Saunders v Central Manchester University Hospitals NHS Foundation Trust [2018] EWHC 343 (QB), paras. 34-35* are a useful *aide memoire*:

> *"Both experts provided clear reports that were easy to read; thorough and attractively presented with useful diagrams attached. However, their joint statement was disappointing. It was 60 pages long and did not fulfil the purpose identified in CPR 35PD 9.2 "to agree and narrow issues". It seemed to me that the difficulty may have arisen not through the fault of the experts but through the way in which the agendas were drafted. I say "agendas" because, for reasons not*

> *explained to me, there had apparently been two separate agendas that the experts were required to consider. Both involved repetitive questions for the experts and far from producing a focus on the real issues, the result was a document that served only to confuse rather than assist.*
>
> *I can see no good reason why the parties were unable to agree a single agenda in this case. Perhaps greater input from Counsel may have assisted. The joint statement is an important document. It ought to be possible to read it and to understand the key issues and each expert's position on those issues. Sometimes less is more as far as the agenda is concerned. Parties should adopt a common sense and collaborative approach rather than allowing this stage of the litigation to become a battleground. Frankly, the approach to the joint statement in this case achieved nothing of value."*

The standard directions order does not entirely exclude the lawyers from the meetings, but this is not encouraged. Where genuine guidance on the law is required, this should be sought and offered in advance of the meeting. If the issue arises during the meeting itself, then it ought to be postponed with each expert telephoning their instructing solicitor for clarification. As not doing so risks a joint report being signed on a flawed basis, it is best to raise this in the instruction letter.

Due to the importance of the outcome of the meeting, it is always preferable for your expert to prepare the minutes and draft joint statement. Again, you should specifically ask them to do this to avoid problems arising. There will often be a travelling draft passing between the experts, but this is subject to the same 'without prejudice' basis as the meeting itself. If your expert asks you to comment on it, this should be explained to them (with reference to the issues considered in Chapter 5).

When the signed joint statement is received, it should be considered quickly and carefully so you can advise your client of the outcome. If neither expert has given ground, then the relative risks to each party remain unchanged unless one expert has refused to adopt a reasonable position. Where one of the experts has conceded ground that party needs to quickly ascertain why this has occurred and what (if anything) they can do about it. Although the parties are not bound by the joint statement, the prospects of successfully 'cross-examining' your own expert at trial are fairly remote in most practitioners' eyes. Whilst it is rare to be able to successfully rectify a complete *volte face* by your expert, it is not impossible. However, to stand any chance of doing so, it is necessary to act promptly and to accurately assess the extent of the damage to the expert's credibility at trial of both changing their opinion at the joint meeting and again under further questioning from their instructing solicitor. Accordingly, prevention through thorough case preparation is far better than trying to cure this afterwards.

Experts' Supporting Materials

Experts are expected to support their opinions with documentary materials. These usually take the form of sections from clinical textbooks and published clinical studies. More rarely, they come from unpublished studies and these must be treated with even more caution. Condition and prognosis reports will sometimes include test results done by or for the expert shortly before the examination occurred. The imaging or test data should always be made available so your opponent can verify the results or competing results can be directly compared for the benefit for the court.

One of the main issues with experts' supporting materials is that they are scientific and therefore confusing to most lawyers trying to analyse them proportionately. It is unsafe to assume that they provide the support the expert says they do because experts often only look at the abstracts of the report and, sometimes, misread the study itself. The materials are a form of generic evidence because they were not produced specifically for this case and so there is also a very real risk of mistakes creeping in when trying to apply the generic results or conclusions reached to the specific facts and issues of your case.

A useful starting point is to use the Oxford Handbook series (especially on breach and causation). This is a series of pocket-sized books which are designed to be easily available to clinicians and carried with them during their working hours. They cover a wide range of clinical disciplines and provide a good indication of the applicable standards of care within those. They were positively mentioned in *Crammond v Medway NHS Foundation Trust [2015] EWHC 3540 (QB) (para 36)*. Where clinical textbooks are used, it is crucial that the excerpt is understood in its proper context and provides a complete picture. They are not intended to address the legal tests and so an ambiguity needs to be explained by your expert.

Choosing not to analyse these materials puts you at risk of finding out too late that either your expert has inadvertently undermined your case or you have missed the opportunity to highlight significant errors in your opponent's case.

In order for the supporting materials to be genuinely helpful, they must actually support all or part of the expert's opinion. Fairly frequently, however, the materials cited support only small, ancillary points in the opinion rather than the central issues being contested. The first step in analysing this type of evidence proportionately is to ascertain what issues the document goes to. If it is of central importance to the case then you can justifiably spend more time understanding what it says and does not say.

The supporting materials must also be independent to be persuasive but this needs to be considered against all of the available evidence. Accordingly, an expert or clinician can justifiably reference their own published papers. In *Mills v Oxford University NHST (supra) (paras. 95-104)*, the impugned clinician's clinical paper describing how to perform the relevant procedure was introduced as evidence. On the one hand, it was submitted that it showed his expertise in this novel procedure. On the other, it was submitted that it showed that he was pushing an unsafe procedure and underplaying the inherent risks. The trial judge considered his credibility in court (*para. 101*); his experience (*para. 104*); his oral evidence (*paras. 162-6*); the errors in the paper highlighted in the experts' joint statement (*paras. 167-173*); before concluding that the *"criticism of the paper is fair; the paper does not give a fair impression of the impact of the operation in Mr Mills' case"* and this was therefore a relevant consideration in assessing breach (para. 173). The judge then found that there was a breach on this issue and was able to set out what should have been said (e.g. *para. 198*)

Since the supporting materials are scientific in nature, the second step is to use a systematic and logical approach to solving the problem. In '*Discourse de la Méthode*' (1637), René Descartes formulated four rules for scientific enquiry:

1. Never accept as true anything that cannot be clearly seen as such;
2. Divide difficulties into as many parts as possible;
3. Seek solutions for the simplest problems first and then proceed step by step to the most difficult;
4. Review all of your conclusions to make sure that there are no omissions.

These four precepts are generally applicable to all lines of enquiry, are simple to remember; easy to apply proportionately; and come from a time when one could be an expert in many different areas of science. Although science has become more advanced and sub-specialised, lawyers do not need to be the experts, we just need to understand what the evidence truly says about each case.

The third step is to understand both the content and the context of the supporting materials. Book extracts are usually less complicated than clinical papers because they do not contain as much technical data. In either case, it is sensible not to assume that the document says what you think it does if you do not fully understand it. As with other types of evidence, it is necessary to think of alternate interpretations which might be put on the wording so these can be covered in conference. For example, it is entirely open to a judge to find that a supporting material which does not expressly say that a certain approach is sub-standard does not actually provide support for your expert's opinion that it was.

National clinical guidelines are the most commonly encountered category of supporting materials because they are intended to deal with specific treatment scenarios. Local guidelines are sometimes also in place and may not necessarily be consistent with their national counterparts. Accordingly, it is important to understand the strength of the underlying evidence base for the recommended practice because this is variable (depending on the strength of the clinical study being relied on). The traditional hierarchy is to classify the Levels of Evidence as Grades I–V and the Recommendations A-C (corresponding to levels of evidence I; II; and III – V, respectively). Thus, a Grade A recommendation is stronger than a Grade C.

Failing to follow national guidelines warrants investigation. In *Snow v Royal UH Bath (supra)*, *HHJ Roberts* stated (*para. 69*): *"Whilst I bear in mind that failing to follow NICE guidance is not prima facie evidence of negligence, there would need to be an explanation for not following NICE's guidance."* This applies *Birss J*'s comment in *Price v Cwm Taf UHB (supra)*: *"I agree with the judge that this departure from these guidelines is not prima facie evidence of negligence. Nevertheless, what must be right is that a clinical decision which departs from the NICE Guidelines is likely to call for an explanation of some sort."*

Clinical *guidelines* do not in and of themselves set the appropriate standard of care; at most they provide generic evidence indicative of what a reasonable standard is across the population as a whole. The guidelines may seem to be frustratingly incomplete or ambiguous to a lawyer; to contradict themselves; or to contain opposing (but reasonable) recommendations. *Sanderson v Guy's & St Thomas' NHS Foundation Trust [2020] EWHC 20 (QB)* illustrates this; the trial judge assessed the overall position with reference to all of the available evidence (not just the expert evidence). In respect of the specific guidelines before him, they required the clinician to exercise their clinical judgement in implementing them (see *paras. 83-85*).

Darnley (supra) (at first instance and in the Court of Appeal) provides an example of where the experts agreed that the practicalities of what would be encountered in practice made it reasonable not to comply with the NICE Guidelines (see *[2017] EWCA Civ 151, para. 20*). In *Dowson v*

Lane [2020] EWHC 642 (QB), reference was made to the guidelines as containing a 'health warning' about not setting the standard of care (*paras. 101-102*) (although not stated in this judgement, such caveats usually are along the lines of being for reference only and requiring clinical interpretation to use). The experts agreed that the clinical guidelines did represent what should occur in practice but disagreed as to whether it meant that all or some of the symptoms needed to be found to trigger this. The trial judge found that not all of the symptoms were present and so there had been no breach of duty.

The guidelines can also represent established practice without establishing the standard of care in your particular case and a local guideline which is at odds with national guidelines may in fact be reasonable (e.g. *O'Brien v Guy's & St Thomas' NHS Trust (supra. paras. 11, 14 and 74-83*).

Similarly, compliance with the relevant clinical guidelines creates a prima facie presumption that the treatment or decision was reasonable. However, evidence that they are incomplete, ambiguous or unsatisfactory can rebut this (*C v North Cumbria University Hospitals NHS Trust (supra, para. 84(iii)-(v)*).

Local guidelines *per se* are less likely to represent a reasonable standard of care than national guidelines but can potentially do so (*O'Brien (supra., paras. 78-79*). *"If an in-house guideline could itself amount to a 'reasonable body of opinion' without more, a defendant trust could effectively determine their own standard of care, which would seem wrong in principle" (ibid. para. 78.1). "Of course, the relevant NICE/BNF or other national guideline may be less than complete or comprehensive… It is quite possible in those circumstances that a properly thought out and well-drafted 'in house guideline' which diverges from a limited or 'unsatisfactory' national one would carry real weight. However, it would do so insofar as it is <u>compliant</u> with a 'reasonable body of opinion or practice' assessed in the usual way with expert evidence, it would rarely constitute one" (ibid., para 79).*

Where the experts disagree over the correct interpretation of the guidelines, the court ought not to decide who is correct. Rather, it ought to decide whether the interpretation supporting the impugned treatment is unreasonable or incapable of withstanding logical analysis (*Dalton v Southend University Hospital NHS Foundation Trust [2019] EWHC 832 (QB) per Yip J at para. 62*). *"The key question... in relation to breach of duty therefore is whether* [the expert's] *evidence withstands logical analysis" (Middleton v Frimley Health (supra), para. 79 per Mr Jonathan Glasson KC).*

If you want to replicate regular success, it is safest ensure that the supporting materials clearly corroborate your case and are congruent with the rest of the evidence. Anything else is risky and makes replicating success less likely. However, building up the specific factual evidence to show whether the general evidence from the guidelines (or other supporting materials) puts too high a standard on this particular clinician. In the long run, this will improve your overall ability to successfully marshal this type of evidence and your success rate.

Clinical studies are more difficult for lawyers to confidently utilise but are usually in the same format as any other scientific paper. They are usually divided into sections and some of these are less relevant than others:

(a) The summary or abstract. This is often included by the expert with their report. It simply summarises the paper as a whole and is useful only in that context. Enclosing only the abstract itself shows that the expert has not read the paper and this materially increases the risk that they have not prepared their report as thoroughly as you might have hoped. Abstracts are usually found via an internet search of the relevant key words. They are usually the only free to view section of the study, the remainder being hidden behind a pay wall so you will not be able to access it without either paying just for this document or for a subscription. If the paper appears to go to a central issue in the case, you will need to ask your expert to obtain a copy of it. Sometimes, however, the paper can be found for free by conducting your own research.

(b) The introduction. This is usually useful to understand why the study was done and so puts the paper into context against the wider backdrop of studies in this area of medicine. It does not, by itself, provide any useful evidence except where it highlights a particular area of disagreement which the study hopes to resolve. In all cases, the context helps to show the potential relevance of the study to the facts of your case. Some studies are 'meta-analyses' which means they have analysed the data across a range of previous studies rather than looking at their own data. These studies are often considered to be the highest form of study with the most persuasive results. However, this does not mean that they necessarily fit your case very well and it should never be assumed that they do. Whatever the class of the study, it must still be relevant to your case.

(c) The methods and/or materials used. This is often a detailed explanation of the particular approach taken in the study and so relatively less time can be safely spent on it. This is because the actual method or materials used is unlikely to have much bearing on the facts of your case. One aspect where it is important to consider in more depth is the sample size and the breakdown of patients within it. Often, the sample size may be quite large but the actual number of patients which fit your client's circumstances is actually very small. Thus, what you are looking for is evidence of where your client would have fitted into this study. A small sample size makes it more likely that the results are not generally applicable whereas a large sample size may well include a broader range of patients than is relevant to the claimant's particular circumstances.

(d) The results. This is an important section and can be the hardest to understand. It is important to remember the purpose of the study. It was not to prove that the defendant was or was not negligent or that the claimant's injuries were probably caused by the breach of duty. It will be to prove or disprove the underlying theory the study's authors had in mind to get funding for the project. As such, there is the risk of over interpreting the results and so overly relying on them as being supportive or unsupportive. Proportionality really requires that we have the ability to either confidently assess these ourselves or wait until an appropriate juncture to get our experts to do so rather than going back and forth with them. The results are usually just set out and so the relevance of them may not be immediately understood.

(e) The discussion. This is the most important section of the study because it seeks to explain the importance and relevance of the results. It is this section which the expert is most likely to be relying on. However, it may be that they have based their decision that it supports their opinion on the summary in the abstract, introduction or conclusion which is not actually supported by the results or discussion. It does not necessarily follow that all of the observed results supported the starting objectives and the reasons for such discrepancies should be explained in the study.

Some of the terminology used in the results or discussion sections can be daunting, particularly when it relates to statistics. Some common examples are:

(i) 'Null hypothesis'; 'alternate hypothesis' and 'p-value'. The null hypothesis is the claim that is being tested. Accordingly, the alternate hypothesis is that the claim under review is wrong. The 'p value' is the test result telling you which of these is correct. It is essentially the probability that the result occurred randomly by mere chance. Although it has a value between 0 and 1, researchers are only interested in whether the value is above, near or below 0.05 (i.e. 5%). A p-value of less than 0.05 indicates that the evidence supports the claim; one over 0.05 means that the evidence does not support it; whilst one near 0.05 indicates marginal or uncertain support.

This is very different to the standard of proof in the clinical negligence case. Claimants must only prove that there was a 51% chance of a breach or consequential injury. Scientists like to see a 95% chance (or higher). Accordingly, a p-value of 0.07 indicates that (scientifically) the correlation arose by chance even though there was a 93% chance of it occurring. Experts will usually require some persuading that, legally, the correlation is reasonable and that the generic nature of the study needs to be taken into account as well in order to truly ascertain the usefulness of the study. The p-value is relevant to the study's results and irrelevant to another study or to proving whether breach or causation occurred in this or that case.

(ii) 'Relative risk' is a concept which continues to be troubling in practice. Following *Williams v BHB (supra),* the present position is probably that 'relative risk' can be used to prove 'material risk' but that a large relative risk which equates to a small increase in the overall risk will be insufficient. This seems illogical to many and logical to others.

The relative risk is essentially the ratio by which risk has increased or decreased. So, a relative risk of 1:2 means that risk has doubled and this may well be the entirely reasonable conclusion for the study in question. *Prima facie,* this relative risk would seem to be enough to prove causation (100% is more than 51%). However, the overall risk may only have doubled to a still very small amount (say, from 0.01% to 0.02%).

You are most likely to see it in the context of studies (particularly epidemiological studies) which seek to measure the effects on developing an injury from a given risky situation. What is being measured is the probability that an injury will result against the probability of it occurring in the wider population. Rightly or wrongly,

Williams indicates that the relative risk needs to be seen in the context of the overall or absolute risk of the injury occurring.

(iii) The 'confidence interval (CI)' is essentially the 'best guess' at where the true result lies. As with p-values, the CI researchers look for is 95%. However, here this means that there is a 5% chance that the result falls outside of the predicted range. Put another way, there is a 95% chance that the results are accurate (i.e. they fall within the predicted range of possible outcomes). As the CI relates to the population being studied, it is affected by the sample size. If the sample size was quadrupled, it would halve the CI.

The CI result will give the % figure followed by the range of values it covers (i.e. 95% 198-204). This is the 'Confidence Level' of the result. Whilst it may well not be reported in the study, the CL for 51% of results would likely be narrower (say 200-203) or wider (depending on what was being studied) and your expert may well be willing to make that clear in their report if asked to do so.

The CL is not the same as the 'confidence limit' but the distinction is usually clearly made in the study. The confidence limit gives the 'bookends' of the results so will be 2.5% at the top and bottom of the range where the CI is 95%.

To say whether a particular claimant falls within or outside of the CI for a generic study depends on what co-morbidities they had and other factors such as age which should all be set out in the method section of the paper being relied upon. Where this is not possible, this itself may provide sufficient ground to distinguish the claimant from the patients in the study.

(f) The references. This section lists all of the studies and papers which the authors have relied on as sources of information. They may have no relevance to your case at all but should not be entirely ignored. If there is a source cited for a key point of the study (which is also relevant to a central issue in your case), then it can be worthwhile to also read that study to confirm that it says what it has been cited as saying and is not too out of date. Some areas of medicine do not change much over time but the rigour applied to clinical studies has changed.

(g) Acknowledgements. Again, this section usually does not require a detailed analysis. However, it is sometimes possible to ascertain that the authors were not truly independent and may have links to organisations which had a vested interest in the outcome of the study. Such relationships tend to undermine the study and so caution is required.

Experts do not have to slavishly rely on the results of generic clinical studies under their *Part 35* duty to the court. In the ordinary course of things, experts are expected to rely on their own clinical experience of seeing numerous patients as well. They are entitled to use that experience of patients in the claimant's position to assess his or her prospects. They are also entitled to look at published papers and comment upon the age of these; the composition of the studies; the small sample sizes; and the degree of statistical averaging, amongst other things. They are entitled to say that their own experience outweighs a flawed paper and this clinical experience trumps the published material. Where clinical studies are cited, they should always be checked carefully in order to confirm they do what the expert thinks they do.

AB v East Lancashire NHS Trust [2019] EWHC 3542 (QB) contains further helpful judicial comment on the use of experts' supporting materials. Ambiguous references are not enough. The national guidelines being relied upon by the claimant did not precisely support their allegations. On closer examination, there were actually no national or local guidelines which did so and no other supporting materials were cited. In contrast, the defendant's expert was able to quote a contemporaneous clinical textbook supporting the impugned treatment. Accordingly, ensuring that your experts provide solid support for their opinions is essential and should be done as soon as is possible after you get their first report. Whilst analysing these materials can be difficult, leaving it until later rarely works out well. The importance of doing this fully even in a complex case is well illustrated by *NKX v Barts Health NHS Trust (supra).*

Statistical evidence continues to cause problems in practice, often being asserted to provide 'better' evidence than specific primary or secondary facts. In *Gregg v Scott (supra.)* it was said by *Lord Nicholls (para. 27)* that *"[b]ut at times, perhaps often, statistical evidence will be the main evidential aid"* in determining hypothetical causation. However, he added at *para. 28*:

> *"Statistical evidence, however, is not strictly a guide to what would have happened in one particular case. Statistics record retrospectively what happened to other patients in more or less comparable situations. They reveal trends of outcome. They are general in nature. The different way other patients responded in a similar position says nothing about how the claimant would have responded. Statistics do not show whether the claimant patient would have conformed to the trend or been an exception from it. They are an imperfect means of assessing outcomes even of groups of patients undergoing treatment, let alone a means of providing an accurate assessment of the position of one individual patient."*

Care must be taken not to misapply the generic nature of some statistical evidence. In *Wardlaw v Farrar (supra) Brook LJ (para. 35)* stated: *"While judges are of course entitled to place such weight on statistical evidence as is appropriate, they must not blind themselves to the effect of other evidence which might put a particular patient in a particular category, regardless of the particular probabilities." Schembri v Marshall [2020] EWCA Civ 358* and *King v South Tees NHS Hospital Foundation Trust [2020] EWHC 416 (QB)* both emphasise the importance of interweaving the statistical evidence appropriately with the other evidence being heard and that trial judges are entitled to prefer that other evidence. *Davies v Frimley Health*

NHS Foundation Trust [2021] EWHC 169 (QB) is a good example of where the trial judge did this and so rejected submissions that he should view the statistical evidence with caution and reject the evidence of an expert based on their approach to analysing it.

Physical Examination

Physical examination of the claimant is essential to deal with condition and prognosis and provides experts with a prime opportunity to judge the claimant's demeanour for themselves in the absence of lawyers. Accordingly, there is some degree of risk in acceding to requests and those which seem unusual in their timing, purpose or scope need to be considered with the claimant and interrogated further if appropriate.

As a practice point, the case runs more smoothly and proportionately with them and this is a relevant factor to bear in mind. If experts are instructed who are as close as possible to the claimant (where C&P examinations or home visits are likely to be required) then that can be helpful. However, the major consideration is to get the best expert you can and the defendant is often not in a position nor under an obligation to do so unless. If the issue is raised well in advance (e.g. in the letter of claim and then persuasively followed up), then suitable arrangements might be agreed. Evidence of the claimant's genuine, specific requirements are therefore relevant. In *Murphy v Ford Motor Co (Unreported) CA, Lord Denning MR* said *"[i]t is now clearly established that, if the defendants in a personal injury case make a reasonable request for the plaintiff to be medically examined by a doctor whom the defendants have chosen, then the plaintiff should accede to such a request unless he has reasonable ground for objecting to that particular doctor."*

Refusing to attend an appointment is therefore risky and careful advice is required. In *Paling v Sherwood Forest Hospitals NHS Foundation Trust [2021] EWHC 3266 (QB)*, the issue arose in the context of whether the claimant can be compelled to undergo genetic testing (which requires an 'invasive' blood test) in order to allow the defendant (via their expert) to investigate whether there was a genetic cause for the claimant's injuries. This was refused because the evidence overall showed that this was not in the claimant's best interests. Similarly, in *Read v Dorset County Hospital NHS Trust & Another [2023] EWHC 367 (KB),* the defendant's application that the claimant be examined by its causation/C&P expert earlier than is provided for by the standard directions (*q.v.*) was similarly refused.

In both of these cases, the defendants contended that the examinations were necessary in order for them to properly plead their defences (rather than being later in the case when a C&P examination would be normal). The correct test is the two-stage test in *Laycock v Lagoe [1997] EWCA Civ 2144, [1997] PIQR p518 CA* (where a PI claim stay until the claimant underwent an MRI scan was overturned because the Court of Appeal found his reticence reasonable):

1. Is the test in the interests of justice; and

2. If so, is the claimant's reason 'substantial' rather than 'imaginary' or 'illusory' taking into account factors such as the interests of justice in obtaining the test result; how it progresses the litigation; the weight of the objection raised to undergoing the test; and any assertion that the litigation will only be slightly advanced by the test. Evidence that the claimant's objection is real is likely to tip the balance in their favour.

These cases ought to be read in detail if you encounter this issue in practice. In *Paling*, the submission that the test from *Nield-Moir v Freeman (Re Birtles Deceased) [2018] EWHC 299 (Ch)* (where a DNA test was ordered) was rejected.

A distinction was drawn between where the examination refused *at that point* in the case and where it refused *at any point* or *outright*. In *Starr v National Coal Board [1977] 1 WLR 63,* the Court of Appeal considered this in the context of a party who was refusing to see a particular expert (but was not refusing the examination itself outright). In these circumstances, a fair balance needed to be struck between two fundamental rights: that individual claimant's right to personal liberty and the defendant's right to defend himself as advised by his lawyers (which includes the right to call the evidence they deem necessary). If the defendant's request was reasonable, then it needed to be determined whether the claimant's refusal was reasonable. In the limited sense of the defendant needing to justify their course of action first, personal autonomy not to undergo invasive testing has a marginal preference but this should not be overplayed. So, in *London Borough of Croydon v Y [2016] EWCA Civ 398*, the examination was ordered where there was no evidence that it would cause harm and this was held to be determinative where the party was refusing to be seen by any of the authority's proposed clinicians. That said, in *Paling*, this case did not add anything to the *Laycock* test.

Caution should also be exercised over whether such an examination can be recorded (perhaps as a pre-requisite to agreeing to it). In *Longbottom v Nulis Nominees (Australia) Limited [2020] WASC 21*, (under a procedural rule which allows one party to give the other formal notice of a medical examination (*viz. Rules of the Supreme Court 1971 (WA), Order 28, Rule 1)*, it was held that whilst it was not in the interests of justice in that particular case, it may be permissible. *Pickett v Bristol Aeroplane Co Ltd (CA unreported)* and *Edmeades v Thames Board Mills Ltd [1969] 2 QB 67, CA* (which approved *Pickett*) were relied on and held to be reflective of Order 28.

It is interesting that *Longbottom* did not completely reject this argument because *Starr* held that *Pickett* was wrongly decided and *Murphy* should be followed. All of these are Court of Appeal decisions. In *Pickett* itself, *Willmer and Donovan LLJ "decided that a plaintiff was entitled to refuse to be medically examined by a particular doctor without having to give reasons for refusing"* (*Haywood v Ritchie & Others [2005] NIQB 42, para. 14*). In *Edmeades, Lord Denning MR* (at *71*) stated that *"the Court can order a stay if the conduct of the plaintiff in refusing a reasonable request is such as to prevent the just determination of the cause"* in reaching the more general conclusion *"that the test to determine if to stay proceedings is whether in the circumstances of the particular case it is reasonable that a stay should be ordered so that justice shall be done between the parties"* (*John v Mootilal (2017) Unreported, CV 2016-03569 Trinidad & Tobago High Court*).

On balance, a lack of caution runs the risk of having proceedings stayed pending the claimant attending the medical appointment (if its purpose is justified). If good reason can be shown for the refusal, then the appointment can be resisted and a safeguard such as recording the appointment may also be imposed.

Conclusion

Expert evidence will continue to account for a significant amount of the costs incurred in most cases. The fact that *Green J* feels the need to remind practitioners of how expert evidence is being assessed 25 years after *Stuart-Smith J* shows that we do not always get this right. Expert evidence necessarily remains the backbone of any clinical negligence case and the legal burden of proof is such as to put the onus on claimants to prove their case.

The increasing costs pressures are likely to make it harder to recover the costs of considering and reconsidering expert evidence and we are already seeing judges at CCMCs limiting the costs in this phase of the budget. Unless the burden of proof changes, it essential to adopt a clear plan to ensure that your experts are providing persuasive opinions at the outset which will stand up to close scrutiny at trial whether they be on breach, causation or quantum issues.

CHAPTER EIGHT

TRIAL & SETTLEMENT

Introduction

The pre-trial period is usually the period between the final experts' joint meeting and the start of the trial. Sometimes, however, directions remain outstanding which require the original pre-trial period to be moved (if the trial needs vacating) or truncated (to allow the remaining matters to be dealt with). If you have a split trial or (less commonly) a part-heard trial, then there will be two pre-trial periods. Similar considerations apply to all pre-trial periods. Although settlement can occur (and should be considered) at any stage, it is convenient to consider it at the stage when the evidence is most likely to have coalesced into its final form.

General Considerations

During the pre-trial period, the focus is inevitably on the trial itself. It can very easily become a stressful time if matters are not planned out well, especially given the demands of a case load. This can lead to missed opportunities to tip the balance in your client's favour. The main points in the pre-trial period and at trial where costs are most likely to be proportionately incurred are:

- Holding a pre-trial conference;

- Preparation of the trial bundle & organising the witnesses' attendance; and

- Identifying late opportunities for settlement.

Counsel needs to be placed in a position where they can be most effective; i.e. allowing them enough time to prepare their arguments to maximise their persuasiveness and to prepare and lodge their skeleton. The Pre-

Trial Review can often be vacated as long as the timetable has been complied with and the court gives permission. If a PTR is required, then this will create an additional opportunity to tip the balance of the case in your client's favour and should be prepared for in the same way as for the CMC. The costs of this ought to have been included in the approved costs budget.

Pre-Trial Conferences

This is a crucial stage in the proper (and proportionate) trial preparation. It affords the parties an excellent opportunity to carefully reconsider their respective cases following the experts' joint meetings and to identify and understand any changes that have occurred.

By the time the trial is approaching, it is usually too late to make substantial changes to the case. However, it is still possible to do so and so proportionality *per se* should not be the sole consideration. Examples of late applications to break and relist the trial, adduce new evidence, strike out all or part of the case, to redact parts of the expert evidence, amend cases, regarding disclosure or to even add parties can all be found in the law reports.

Proportionality does now influence these applications as does the extent to which they should have been made more promptly. There is also a vast difference between an application which has been well planned out or where clear attempts have been to avoid it becoming necessary and applications being required because an important issue has been missed and needs to be urgently rectified.

Realistically, the majority of the case preparation and analysis should already have been done well before the pre-trial period is reached. However, it should never be assumed that nothing more can (or should) be done. The benefits of both sides leaving enough time to fully reconsider each sides' cases and their respective positions on any alternative positions or possibilities is helpfully illustrated by *Wright (A Child) v Cambridge Medical Group [2011] (supra.)*

The claimant issued proceedings only against the GP (but had notified the hospital of the claim previously). The GP's defence asserted that the hospital was also negligent and was responsible for most of the injury but did not join it to the proceedings. At some point, either at the joint meeting or at trial, the agreed expert evidence became that the hospital treatment was negligent and to blame for the permanent injury sustained. Accordingly, the trial judge found for the GP. Although the Court of Appeal overturned this (partly because the hospital treatment had probably not been grossly negligent, see Chapter 2), *Lord Neuberger MR* made the following comments:

> *"I cannot leave this case without expressing regret and surprise that neither party saw fit to join the Hospital in these proceedings. ... It was little short of absurd to have a long hearing ... without the Hospital being a party."* (*Paragraph 86*)

> *"As a general proposition, it is certainly right to keep the number of parties to a minimum, for reasons of costs and time. However, in some cases it can be more expensive in terms of costs and time to omit joining a relevant party. This, as I see it, was plainly such a case. ... Each party took an unwarranted risk in not joining the Hospital. It also seems to me that there may well have been a better chance of a negotiated settlement if the Hospital had been a party."* (*Paragraph 87*)

Dame Janet Smith made similar comments at *para. 120* and the relevance to proportionality is fairly clear. If we assume that the claimant's experts initially advised that the hospital treatment was reasonable, then they had changed their minds by trial. If the defendant's experts felt that the GP's error had no causative impact, then this evidence or the attempted legal application of it was not accepted by the Court of Appeal. The claimant had to go to an appeal to win. The defendant most likely ended up paying the claimant's costs of the trial and appeal as well as then having to potentially bring contribution proceedings against the hospital. It can be seen that this approach (however reasonable it appeared as the issue developed) is likely to be more expensive than one which has clearly identified and planned for the likely risk and consequences of this issue arising earlier in the case.

Proportionality and fixed costs tend to increase the risks of similar issues going unidentified until trial. Accordingly, the pre-trial conference represents the last best chance to thoroughly review the case whilst there is still time to apply to the court for assistance and further directions. As with other applications, evidence is key and prevention is always better than cure. However, no one is omniscient and unforeseen issues can arise late in the day through neither party's fault.

Pre-trial Review

This hearing represents the last chance for the court to exercise its case management powers before trial. It will often be vacated at the parties' request as long as all of the existing directions have been complied with. If the outstanding matters are relatively minor, then it may be possible to deal with them by consent or via a telephone hearing in order to avoid the costs of attending in person.

For more substantial issues, personal attendance by the fee earner responsible for the daily running of the file and trial counsel is often required. Whilst it is not always possible to accommodate this fully (and more than one person may legitimately work on the file), every effort should be made to assist the court at the PTR.

Trial Bundles

The proper preparation of the trial bundle is of pivotal importance to the smooth running of the trial. A well-prepared bundle shows the judge that your case has also been well prepared and so improves the prospects of them understanding the complex points in the case. Conversely, a poorly prepared bundle is most likely to frustrate them before the trial even starts and undermine their perception of your case.

Although the parties must cooperate, it is the claimant's responsibility to prepare the trial bundle. Where some or all of it is left to a junior member of the team, the conducting fee earner must check those parts carefully before the bundle is lodged and served. Whilst it is often asserted that such work is duplicative or administrative, it is not and a well-worded attendance note explaining what was done by each fee earner will greatly assist with the recovery of these costs. Accordingly, this should not be a reason for a poorly prepared trial bundle.

The most useful information on trial bundle preparation is found in the *Chancery Guide 2022, paras. 21.34-21.72.* This is available as a free download from the Courts Service website. The *King's Bench Guide 2022* contains similar guidance at paras. 14.3-14.14. The relevance of this guide was confirmed in *Portland Stone Firms Ltd & Others v Barclays Bank plc & Others [2018] EWHC 2341 (QB), para. 30 per Stuart-Smith J: "The Queen's Bench Guide provides guidelines which should be followed: they reflect good and proper practice that has been universally known by competent practitioners for decades."* They are supplementary to the provisions in *CPR 1998 Rule 39.5 and PD32, para. 27.*

To summarise, a proper trial bundle should comply with the following matters:

1. Avoid duplication. It wastes the court's time and antagonises the judge, experts and lay witnesses. It is only necessary to include one copy of each document. Where several versions of the same document exist but have different annotations or stamps on them, the parties should try to reach agreement as to which should be used. Where documents also appear as exhibits to witness statements, you should either insert a page in place of the exhibit giving the page reference in the bundle to where the documents appear or annotate the referring paragraph in the statement with it.

2. Documents should be in chronological order within each section, with the earliest coming first. Ideally, the standard direction to maintain a bundle of medical records will mean that the majority of the bundle will already have been sorted into date order at an early stage in the case. Standard disclosure should likewise mean that the other documentary evidence has also been pre-sorted. Witness statements, expert reports, pleadings and court orders will also, ideally, have been kept in date order in separate sections

on the solicitor's file. Most firms will have a trial bundle index saved as a precedent from previous cases but it is always advisable not to assume that it is accurate as it may have been prepared for a case with differing issues.

3. The bundle must be clearly and accurately paginated. Usually, the page numbering should appear in the bottom right-hand corner of the page so it can be easily found at trial. If other page numbers appear on a page, then the bundle's page number should be clear for what it is. If that means covering up part of the bottom corner of the page with a white sticker, then a copy of the document should be kept before this is done in case it needs to be referred to later. Where this part of the page is black or darkly copied, a white label can also be used to create a space so the page number can be clearly seen. The bundle should be carefully checked before pagination to make sure that it in the correct order. This order should have been agreed with the other parties first if at all possible. Where pages need to be inserted after pagination, then they should be added in between the existing pages (i.e. p1045, p1045a, p1045b, etc). If there are too many to do this, then an extra section should be added at the end of the bundle.

   Although the pagination is usually continuously sequential throughout the bundle, some practitioners prefer to restart at p1 for each lever arch file. In such a system, each page number needs to be prefixed with the file number in case the page is taken out of the bundle and for ease of reference during the trial when moving between files.

4. The number of pages in each lever arch file or section (for digital bundles) should be limited so that no one file or section is overloaded or cumbersome. It is sometimes tempting to have a paper file end at a full section. However, if the file is overloaded, the pages are likely to fall out when it is opened. Typically, a normal lever arch file comfortably holds 500 A4 pages but the *Chancery Guide 2022* requests that no more than 300 pages be

put in a file. Certain medical records are larger than A4 with continuous CTG traces and A3 observation charts are common examples. A3 records can be folded into A4 size so that it opens up without needing to take it out of the bundle. To do this, place the record face up, fold it over in half and then fold that half page back over in half again. This leaves a ¼ of the copied page visible to take the page number. For continuous CTG traces, special arrangements will need to be made if the entire trace is required in evidence. These should be agreed as far as is possible in advance. The value of cases requiring this evidence is likely to be high enough to justify the additional expense.

5. All copies of the bundle should be identical. However, it remains the case that bundles are produced with different versions of documents, different documents, different ordering, missing documents and different page numbering. The most proportionate method of avoiding this happening to you is for a core bundle to be prepared, checked and paginated. Once you are completely satisfied that it is accurate and correctly and legibly copied, then this bundle should be copied the requisite number of times. Do not prepare the different sets individually from the original documents or have different people preparing them. One person should do one bundle and then copy that after it is correct.

6. The trial bundle must be filed on time. The agreed trial bundle must usually be lodged at court three to five clear days before the trial starts. This will usually before you have been told of the exact start date so it is the first day the trial could start. Once it has been lodged, the court staff will need to get it to the judge in time for pre-reading and this means that each file should be very clearly labelled in case it becomes separated from the rest of the bundle. Ideally, each lever arch file should have identical labels on its spine and the inside front cover so that it can be easily identified when opened. It is no longer strictly necessary to put the full title of the action on the index in order to save space. The

index should clearly identify each section, document and page numbers within that file only.

7. For paper bundles, each document should be loose leaf. Staples and clips should be removed. If a particular document is illegible or difficult to read (a handwritten clinical note, for example), then an agreed transcription of it should be included for everyone's ease of reference. If this can only come from the clinician who wrote it, then this needs to be obtained well before the bundle starts to be prepared.

8. There needs to be sufficient copies of the trial bundle for use at trial. This usually means preparing one set for the judge, one for the witnesses to use when giving their evidence, one for each party's counsel and one spare copy (which is most commonly needed for the solicitor to use to help the lay client follow the evidence as the case progresses). The claimant's solicitor has to have these copies ready in time for lodging at court and must also put arrangements in place to take all of the copies with them at the end of the trial.

Whilst these considerations may appear pedantic, experience shows that they are very useful in avoiding unnecessary problems during the trial. Getting it wrong can led to direct and detrimental consequences. In *Agouman v Leigh Day (A Firm) [2016] EWHC 1324 (QB), Andrew Smith J* said:

> *"The documents were presented in agreed bundles, but their arrangement made them difficult to follow. Some were in French and many of these had no translation. Where translations were provided, they had not been agreed between the parties. At the start of the trial, I ruled … that (i) I would ignore any French document of which there was no translation; and (ii) I would assume that the translations provided were accurate unless there was evidence to the contrary…"*

Putting these considerations into a checklist for use by the fee earners preparing and checking the bundles is the most proportionate method of preparing the bundles efficiently. This is not an administrative task because it is no excuse at trial to say that an ill-prepared bundle was prepared quickly or by someone who was unfamiliar with the issues in the case or the procedural requirements.

Failing to get this right can undermine your client's case. In *ST v ZY (supra), Master Gordon-Saker* said (*paras. 18-19*): *"It was therefore unfortunate that on the day [of the hearing] [counsel] told me that he had not been provided with the full set of [his instructing solicitor's] papers in advance of the hearing, although the court had been provided with them electronically. On the previous two occasions when I have listed [this firm's] bills for detailed assessment…, counsel had not been provided with a full set of papers. … once would have been a misfortune. Thrice looks like a policy. / … I would have continued with the detailed assessment despite counsel's lack of instructions."* Adjournments to hearings caused by poorly prepared bundles run the risk of adverse costs orders being made.

Witnesses

Problems can also arise with clients, witnesses and even experts not attending at all, arriving late, double-booking themselves, or being ill-prepared.

Where a witness or client needs special measures to use the court's facilities, then the court should be advised of this as soon as is possible during the pre-trial period. These arrangements should be confirmed in writing and the name and telephone number of the court employee who is to assist on each day of the trial obtained. It is prudent to keep this person updated of any changes and to check with them that nothing has been changed before the trial starts.

In terms of avoiding non-attendance or double-booking, the witnesses' dates of availability should be obtained before the directions order is made. They should be rechecked when the listing appointment is required and all witnesses should be advised of the trial date promptly after it is set.

The same process should be followed if it becomes necessary to change the trial date. As trial approaches, you should write to all of the witnesses about two months before the start date to remind them of the coming trial and when they will be expected to attend. Although witness summonses can antagonise witnesses, they are the only way to ensure that a witness attends and so there is a legitimate reason to consider issuing them in all cases. The costs of doing so (including the issue fee and the conduct money) should be included in the first costs budget. However, there has long been a counter argument as to whether these costs could be recoverable from the losing party where there was no real prospect of the witness failing to attend. Ultimately, the only method of preventing a witness summons issued on another case taking precedence is if you have already issued and served your own witness summons for the same date. Although the costs of a vacated trial vastly outweigh the costs of a witness summons, forcing a lay or expert witness to attend may adversely affect how their evidence comes across. Avoiding the problem by keeping them updated is the best option, with witness summonses best being reserved for cases where problems are likely to occur.

Providing witnesses with clear information on where and when they need to attend and having accurate and current contact telephone numbers for them minimises the risk of them arriving late, getting lost or otherwise finding themselves in last minute difficulties in attending the trial. The fee earner attending the trial should make sure that they have these contact numbers with them as well as copies of the letters sent to them in case the trial judge needs persuading that every effort was made to prevent the problem occurring.

Preparing witnesses for trial presents a more difficult issue. On the one hand, the witness evidence is likely to have a significant bearing on the outcome of the case and how each witness comes across under cross-examination is pivotal. On the other, it is unethical and contrary to justice to unduly influence a witness which means that witness coaching is strictly prohibited. It is permissible to check that a witness understands the process, what is required of them and to review their evidence with them as long as you do not attempt to tell them what they should or should not say. It is prudent to put this advice in writing in case it is asserted in court that they are repeating what you have told them to say.

Trial

At the trial itself, the major emphasis is on the trial advocacy and this is outside the scope of this book.

The supporting role played by the solicitor (of whatever grade) is important in the context of making the advocate's job easier. This includes making sure that you have sufficient copies of all documents (courts do not always have readily accessible photocopiers), ensuring that all of the parties' and witnesses' contact details are to hand and checking in during the breaks if you have remained in the office. Unlikely or unpredictable events do occur even in the best prepared cases and being in a position to deal with these quickly and effectively is crucial. If you are unavailable, make sure that someone who has a thorough knowledge of the file is either in court and/or back in the office. Winning cases is very much a team effort and the trial is no exception.

It is always preferable to have a verbatim note of the trial and judgement so that counsel or the court can refer to it and in case an appeal is needed or a careful explanation is needed to be given to your client at the end of the case. Paying for daily transcripts during a multi-day trial is another option. Confidentiality is key and so you should always try to secure a private meeting room for infra-trial conferences but, if not, make sure that all own-client discussions are out of ear shot of the defendant's representatives and witnesses as significant damage can be done to your carefully prepared case.

There is no absolute rule prohibiting witnesses sitting through each other's testimony. This creates a potential imbalance at trial if the defendant's clinical lay and/or expert witnesses are able to sit through the claimant's witnesses' evidence but the claimant's cannot do likewise. This can arise relatively easily due to changing work commitments in busy NHS practice (one of the desirable factors influencing expert selection and credibility, *q.q.v*); other trial commitments; or via proportionality considerations (e.g. experts' fees for attending trial tend to be significant and may not have been allowed in the costs budget). Hot-tubbing experts (*q.v.*) provides a potential way around this but is not especially popular and using a witness summons for the entire period can irk experts and is expensive. Ideally, one should advise and plan for this possibility and reach an accord with the witnesses and your client before the CMC/CCMC.

Para. 32.1.4.3 of the *White Book* indicates that it is within the court's discretion to exclude witnesses from a civil trial and that it is appropriate to do so where there is a risk that their own testimony could be influenced by hearing another witness. In *Luckwell v Limata [2014] EWHC 536 (Family), Holman J (para. 21)* held that there must be good reason for believing this. *Tomlinson v Tomlinson [1980] 1 WLR 322* indicates that this discretion cannot be used to exclude a witness who is also a party to the action (e.g. a private doctor) whereas *De Costa & Another v Sargaco & Another [2016] EWCA Civ 764* indicates that some degree of discretion remains. In *BGC Brokers LP & Others v Tradition (UK) Ltd & Others and Martin Brokers Group Ltd v Bell & Another [2019] EWHC 3588 (QB)*, a pre-emptive but late application (made at the PTR) to exclude witnesses and prevent them seeing the daily transcripts at trial was refused partly because the concerns raised did not go beyond the usual risks in a trial and the witnesses were likely to have already discussed matters and seen each other's served witness statements.

Where the day ends whilst a witness is still giving evidence, then the trial judge will give a direction that the witness must not discuss anything related to their evidence with anyone before they restart (a 'purdah warning/order'). This period lasts until they resume giving evidence (e.g. *Palmer & Reed v Tsai [2017] EWHC 1860 (Ch), para. 72*). This is so even where other actions are required by the legal team (such as disclosure) during the break in testimony (e.g. *Shaw v Finnimore & Another [2009] EWHC 367 (Ch), para. 92*). Witnesses are not in purdah as a result of watching another witness giving evidence (e.g. *King & Others v Stiefel & Others [2021] EWHC 1045 (Comm), para. 442(ii)*). When in purdah, witnesses must not check or disclose any part of their evidence with/to other people (including the press, e.g. *Chidzoy v British*

Broadcasting Corporation (2017) ET Case No. 3400341/2016 where the case was struck out because a fair trial was no longer possible). Even where this is innocent or accidental, it must be brought to the court's attention immediately (e.g. *Weiss Technik UK Limited & Others v Davies & Others [2022] EWHC 2773 (Ch), para. 19*). The rule was cited by counsel in *Dana UK Axle Ltd v Freudenberg FST GmbH (supra, para. 18)* to describe the period between the experts' joint meeting and their signing the joint statement (*q.v.*). This direction must be adhered to and so you cannot discuss the evidence with witnesses who are in purdah during the break in any circumstances even if further instructions are needed. It is prudent to make it abundantly clear that any contact in the intervening period must be minimal in light of this; of the very strict limitations placed upon the witness and their legal team; and of the consequences for breaching the court's direction. As with judgement embargos (*q.v.*), social media and the ease of modern communications pose a particular risk.

Where the judgement is reserved, it will be given at a later date once the judge has considered the evidence. It will usually be sent to the parties' lawyers in draft (usually) for typographical errors to be corrected. It is important to remember that the judgement is embargoed at this point because it has not yet been handed down. As such, it cannot be made public (*CPR 1998, Practice Direction 40E*).

In *O'Connell v Rollings [2014] EWCA Civ 806,* third parties were notified of the decision by one of the solicitors and their client disclosed it business associates and family members. *Kitchin LJ* stated (*para. 3*): "*… any breach of the embargo is a very serious matter. It necessarily interferes with the administration of justice and the efforts of judges to deal with them justly and at proportionate cost.*" The court accepted that this was inadvertent and so contempt proceedings were averted. However, an adverse costs order was made.

The ease of modern communication is an area of particular concern. In *Counsel General for Wales, R (On the Application of) v The Secretary of State for Business, Energy & Industrial Strategy [2022] EWCA Civ 181*, chambers breached the embargo in a press release uploaded to their website the day before the judgement was due to be handed down. *Sir*

Geoffrey Vos, MR stated (*para. 21*) that: *"I have become aware formally and informally of other breaches in other cases. It seems, anecdotally at least, that violations of the embargo on publishing either the content or the substance of the judgements are becoming more frequent. … In future, those who break embargos can expect to find themselves the subject of contempt proceedings as paragraph 2.8 of CPR PD40E envisages."*

In *The Public Institution for Social Security v Banque Pictet & Cle SA & Others [2022] EWCA Civ 368*, the breach occurred when foreign news outlets tweeted the outcome of an appeal in a high-profile jurisdictional matter whilst the embargo was in place. Despite considerable investigations, it did not prove possible to identify who had breached the embargo leading to the tweets (*para. 14*) and a senior lawyer's WhatsApp message, whilst a breach, was not to blame (*para. 17*). At *para. 18, Carr LJ* provided additional guidance. To summarise:

1. Embargos "*…are orders of the court which prohibit communication for any purpose other than the legitimate exercise of making suggestions for the correction of errors, agreeing orders on consequential matters and preparation for the publication of the judgement.*" Informing colleagues who have not been involved in the case is unlikely to meet this criterion.

2. The use of modern technology requires greater, not less, care.

3. Any embargo breach must be immediately brought to the court's attention.

In *Wright v McCormack [2022] EWHC 3343 (KB)*, such a breach occurred by the claimant by posting messages on a social media platform. Although these did not directly refer to the judgement, *Chamberlain J* stated (at *para. 24*): *"I consider that there is a real prospect that a court might find that, by posting those messages, Dr Wright was disclosing, and intending to disclose, the substance of the judgement contrary to the clear terms of the embargo, which had been explained to him"*. A summons was therefore issued (pursuant to *CPR 1998, Rule 81.6(1)*), to attend court for directions in respect of contempt of court against the claimant.

At *para, 25, Chamberlain J* explained the principles around judgement embargos as follows:

> *"The practice of issuing judgements under embargo is an unusual feature of litigation in this jurisdiction. It has many benefits, which can only be achieved if parties abide scrupulously by the terms of the embargo. The Court of Appeal has signalled that breaches are likely to result in contempt proceedings. In my judgment, it would not be appropriate to take no further action in this case, where there is evidence showing that a litigant in High Court proceedings may have acted on deliberate breach of the embargo."*

As a minimum, a detailed explanation by way of witness statements with exhibits containing the documents showing how and where the breach occurred will be required along with unreserved apologies for any inadvertent errors. It is prudent to make it abundantly clear to anyone who must be informed of the draft judgement of the very strict limitations and consequences for breaching the embargo.

The period of the embargo, and the opportunity to comment on the judgement, will usually be short and limited (as indicated above). However, in *C & Others Re (Care Proceedings: Fact-Finding) [2023] EWCA Civ 28*, the period was 18 weeks and extensive exchanges between the court and lawyers with 6 interim orders made resulting in a final order with 7 annexes. At *para. 43, Baker LJ* provided this guidance: *"[t]his degree of interrogation of the judgment seems to me to be manifestly excessive. … It is the responsibility of counsel and courts to be disciplined when making and responding to requests for clarification."*

<u>Settlement: Negotiation or Compromise?</u>

Leaving matters to the vicissitudes of the trial judge should, by itself, encourage you to negotiate. Why voluntarily risk trial when you can keep control of the outcome? If you can develop a process allowing you to negotiate effectively with confidence, then you will be much closer to achieving excellent case outcomes rather than the more average settlements achieved by simply compromising your clients' positions.

Effective, mature negotiation in clinical negligence cases is more than a battle of the *Part 36* offers. *Part 36* has its place but ought to reserved for the right point in the case for maximum effectiveness. Proportionality provides an additional incentive to protect your client's position by using all forms of Alternative Dispute Resolution (ADR). Being poised to make an effective offer or to narrow the issues at any point in the case means you need to develop the ability to fully understand both sides' cases and underlying motivations. Refusing to negotiate or misjudging the settlement parameters costs you and your client money. Settlement offers can be money- or issue-based and can cover any part of the case. There is no mandatory need to wait until your investigation into the issues or valuation is complete and negotiation planning should start immediately.

There is almost always something to be gained by opening discussions with your opponent and to start the process of building trust and rapport early in the case. Round-table meetings and formal mediation are more detailed and expensive than making an offer by letter. Letters and telephone discussions allow greater flexibility as they can more easily be interwoven into other parts of the case and used in conjunction with *Part 18* requests for information, notices to admit and the other procedural tools referred to in previous chapters.

Misunderstandings are barriers to settlement and so constructive steps should be taken to minimise them. Always consider how you can do more to minimise them. This does not mean hurrying to compromise before you know what you are dealing with. Remaining flexible in your approach, looking at the issues from different perspectives and actively listening to your client, opponent, experts & counsel often uncovers opportunities and breakthroughs which you felt were impossible earlier in the case. It is rarely advisable to wait until the evidence or a case management decision forces you to negotiate.

Naturally, it is usually better to avoid a trial and settle the case. Negotiation is best understood in the context of preparing a case for trial because the very careful preparation of the case to trial maximises the potential for settlement. This does not mean that offers should not be planned out and made well before trial; in fact doing so is an essential ingredient in running your cases proportionality; within fixed costs limits; and in planning your successes strategically.

Procedurally, written offers are the most common means of seeking to negotiate. Always bear in mind how to use the rules in *Part 36* and *Part 44* to settle all or part of the case. As a general proposition, the more congruent any offer is with the central allegations being made and the evidence disclosed at that point in the case, the more likely it is that the court is likely to hold that it was reasonable and that your client ought to get the benefit of it. A trial is usually required to get the full costs benefit of a *Part 36* offer and so they often form part of the negotiation rather than the sole approach.

If a *Part 36* offer is made, it should be carefully checked to make sure that it is fully compliant with the wording of *Part 36*. However, it is important to remember that a technically invalid *Part 36* offer only means that the offeror does not automatically get the beneficial sanctions under this section. The offer itself may still be entirely reasonable and the court may well impose sanctions under *Part 44*. Accordingly, no offer should be ignored; the pros and cons always need to be weighed up. If you have a clear idea of the allegations, evidence and risks to both sides early in the case, then offers of any type become much easier to assess proportionately.

It is also sensible to double-check that the offer is for the amount or has the effect you intended. In *O'Grady v B15 Group Ltd. [2022] EWHC 67 (QB)* the mistake was not picked up until after the defendant accepted the offer. The offeror promptly informed their opponent of the error and applied to the court for permission to withdraw or change the terms of their offer. The defendant sought to rely on the fact that *Part 36* is a self-contained code and contains no process for rectifying such errors. Conversely, the claimant submitted that this was a plain example of an obvious error when looking at the evidence as a whole and there was no rule preventing rectification of a genuine error. At *para. 25*, *Master Thornett* held: *"I am satisfied that the doctrine of common law mistake can apply to a Part 36 offer in circumstances where a clear and obvious mistake has been made and this is appreciated by the Part 36 offeree at the point of acceptance. Authority is entirely in support with the application of the doctrine."* Although it was allowed here, rectification is not guaranteed and there will be the additional time delay, expense and potential adverse costs consequences of applying to the court.

An important consequence of beating your own *Part 36* offer is that this will attract an award of indemnity costs. If fixed fees do come in, then they would be subject to this rule. Moreover, proportionality is not one of the factors to be taken into account in assessing costs on the indemnity basis and the benefit of the doubt is with the party receiving payment. The costs budget also does not limit recoverability. There are several practical points to note in respect of these issues.

Firstly, the costs consequences bite if the offer is beaten at trial but is it remains far less clear whether they apply if settlement occurs before this. In many cases, the eventual pre-trial negotiated settlement is somewhere between the respective *Part 36* offers so the issue is avoided and costs are assessed on the standard basis only.

(a) It is sufficient to beat your own offer by any amount (however small) to get the prescribed costs consequences. In *JLE v Warrington & Halton Hospitals NHS Foundation Trust [2019] EWHC 1582 (QB)*, it was made clear that the amount by which the offer is beaten by is irrelevant (even where the amount of the additional costs payable exceeds the amount the offer was beaten by). Similarly, *Telefónica UK Ltd v The Office of Communications [2020] EWCA Civ 1374*, confirmed that the penalties for late acceptance (such as enhanced interest and indemnity costs) are irrelevant under *CPR 1998 Rule 36.17(1)(b)*: *"… the rule provides for the successful claimant… to receive each of the enhancements and there is no suggestion that the award of one in any way undermines or lessens entitlement to the others. In this case, the judge regarded the award of the two more trivial enhancements as a reason why it was unjust to award the major enhancement. I do not consider that he was entitled to do so"* (*para. 46 per Phillips LJ*). This is congruent with *Cashman v Mid Essex Hospital Services NHS Trust [2015] EWHC 1312 (QB)* where *Slade J* stated: *"[t]he rule was introduced not only to provide an incentive to a claimant to make a timely realistic Part 36 offer but also to penalise a defendant for not accepting such an offer" (para. 7)*. All of these cases are appeals from first instance decisions indicating that careful preparation is required on these issues in case you succeed on the main case.

(b) *CPR 1998 Rule 36.5* now expressly provides that *Part 36* offers are assumed to include interest up to the date of acceptance (and late acceptance unless the offer expressly states otherwise). Accordingly, this appears to distinguish between the offer amount and the accrued interest but late acceptance can now (post-April 2021) result in paying more interest. *King v City of London Corporation [2019] EWCA Civ 2266* held that offers excluding interest were invalid as *Part 36* offers and recommended that the *CPR* be reviewed (and this is what the change to *Rule 36.5* did). Accordingly, specifically excluding the accrual of interest (perhaps to reduce the risk of the offer being beaten by late acceptance) invalidates the offer as a *Part 36* offer (but it may still have relevance as a reasonable settlement offer).

(c) *Pallett v MGN Ltd [2021] EWHC 76 (Ch)* is an example of a case where the defendant deliberately chose to accept the offer on day 22 in order to bring the issue of what costs it was liable for before the court and to consider conduct arguments. The defendant was entitled to take this *"odd"* approach to invoke *CPR 1998, Rule 36.13(4)* and have the costs assessed by the court (*para. 16*) following *Optical Express Ltd & Others v Associated Newspapers Ltd [2017] EWHC 2707 (QB)* and *Dutton & Others v Minards & Others [2015] EWCA Civ 984*. However, these matters would form part of the judge's discretion (*para. 17*) and, upon weighing up the evidence of the alleged poor conduct, it was held that the usual costs consequences of accepting an offer within 21 days applied (*para. 75*). Accordingly, caution needs to be exercised before deciding to wait to accept a reasonable settlement offer in the hope of persuading the court to reduce your client's costs liability.

(d) In *Essex County Council v UBB Waste (Essex) Ltd. [2020] EWHC 2387 (TCC)*, it was unsuccessfully argued that providing 20 days to accept the offer, not 21, (due to the wording of the offer which ran from the date of the letter rather than date of service). It was held that deemed service did apply here and so the offer did attract the *Part 36* consequences having been beaten at trial (*paras. 21 and 44*).

(e) Where fixed costs are payable, then *Broadhurst & Another v Tan & Another [2016] EWCA Civ 9* confirms that the benefits of beating your own *Part 36* offer are recoverable rather than the fixed cost amount. It remains to be seen whether fixed costs do come into clinical negligence cases and if such a provision is expressly excluded from them. At present, they are most likely to be encountered under the Welsh Redress Scheme (*supra*, Chapter 1).

(f) Where your own offer is beaten, your costs budget is ignored and so this enables recovery of costs which exceed each phase (*Lejonvarn v Burgess & Burgess [2020] EWCA Civ 114*).

Accordingly, there is considerable incentive for making a reasonable *Part 36* offer and for sticking with it as well as for paying parties to seek to make offers which are lower but still within a reasonable range of settlement.

The courts do not tend to look favourably on attempts to manipulate the rules, however. One example is *Pallett (supra)*. In *Cartwright v Venduct Engineering Ltd (supra)* the defendant contended that a *Tomlin* order did not amount to an order for costs. By way of general background, *Tomlin* orders are orders which annex a record of the confidential negotiated settlement terms that the parties have reached. The terms of this schedule are not enforceable as of right; an application to the court is required. In order to be directly enforceable, the body of the order should still contain (a) that one party will pay another damages (or take some other action); and (b) a costs provision. Otherwise, these provisions are not directly enforceable without an application to the court (please see the *King's*

Bench Guide 2022, paras. 15.15-15.15.23, pp 100-1). Accordingly, agreeing to a *Tomlin* order gives you no direct right to costs (or damages) and serves no real purpose if there were no additional obligations on either party agreed at settlement. So, not all consent orders are Tomlin orders and one is not required where one party has only agreed to pay the other damages and costs by a certain date. Care is required before agreeing one on behalf of your client and the principle of open justice means the schedule is not confidential as of right.

These points were confirmed in *Zenith Logistics Services (UK) Ltd & Others v Coury [2020] EWHC 774 (QB)* where stated at *para. 70* in respect of the drafted '*Tomlin*' order: *"Crucially, it goes beyond mere case management and contains immediately enforceable provisions. The enforceable provisions take the form of undertakings, rather than orders, but for present purposes their effect is not materially different."* Further, at *para. 67: "A Tomlin order, if made, does not represent endorsement or approval of those terms, or a conclusion that they are enforceable."*

In *Community Care North East (A Partnership) v Durham County Council [2010] EWHC 959 (QB), Ramsay J* stated (*paras. 26 and 28*): *"The terms of the schedule are not ordered by the court"* and *"[t]he terms of the schedule are not an order made by the court"*, respectively. At *para.25*, he also sets out that the *White Book* confirms that the terms of the settlement can either be set out in the body of an order or in a schedule to a *Tomlin* order. Indeed, in the original *Tomlin* order case, *Dashwood v Dashwood [1927] WN 276,* and his accompanying *Practice Note [1927] WN 290, Tomlin J* made it clear that terms requiring action such as an order for costs must be included in the body of the order to be enforceable. Finally, *CPR 1998, PD 40B, para. 3.5* states that orders settling proceedings must contain provisions regarding the payment of money out of court or payment and assessment of costs in the body of the order not in the schedule. A helpful and more detailed explanation of the differences between consent and *Tomlin* orders, please see the Singapore case of *HQH Capital Ltd v Chen Liping [2022] SGHC 215 paras. 24-32* which refers to the aforementioned authorities.

However, NHS Resolution often seeks to settle uncomplicated cases by using *Tomlin* orders and it can prove difficult to persuade them otherwise. They are unlikely to default and, even if they did, would most likely pay the required sums before the required application is made. A normal order, however, gives your client a direct entitlement to their compensation and costs and permits enforcement proceedings to be started without an application to remove the stay of proceedings. It is often possible to agree a hybrid order incorporating both the settlement terms in the body and additional detail in the schedule and this avoids avoidable delay. Drawing this together, *Tomlin* orders should not be seen as a panacea universally applicable to settlement – they are appropriate where the compromise reached requires parties to make promises not necessarily forming part of the main case but which would benefit from being able to reopen it if these promises are not kept.

With this in mind, in *Dance v East Kent University Hospitals NHS Foundation Trust & Others [2022] EWHC B9 (Costs)/[2022] EWHC 2198 (SCCO)* it was argued that a *Tomlin* order is not a costs order. The argument failed here because a *Part 36* offer had been accepted within the period for acceptance and this creates the enforceable costs entitlement applying *CPR 1998, Rules 36.13(1) and 44.9(1)(b) (paras. 11-15)*. At *para. 16, Costs Judge Leonard* added *"…it is an established principle that a Tomlin order may incorporate effective provision for the payment of costs, as long as it is incorporated in the body of an order rather than the attached schedule."*

In *Chappell v Mzozek (supra)* the defendant agreed the costs liability but did not agree to an order and delayed payment of the agreed damages in order to bring the matter before the court to get a set-off for their costs against the damages. QOCS protection applied (*q.v.* Chapter 1). The defendant submitted that the correct construction of "an order for damages and interest" under the set-off provisions in *CPR 1998, Rule 44.14* included *Part 36* settlements where no order had been made. These submissions were rejected because *Cartwright (supra)* and *Adelkun (supra)* prevented set-offs in QOCS cases and also prevented expanding the scope of *Rule 44.14*. At para. 52, *Master Stevens* indicated that the position might be different if the parties had not agreed liability for costs and had applied under *CPR 1998 Rule 36.13(5)* for a costs order. This would require the court to consider *"the underlying damages claim and settlement offer in some detail."*

In *MRA v The Education Fellowship Ltd (supra)* the defendant did just this following the claimant's late acceptance of its *Part 36* offer. Again, QOCS protection applied. The defendant wanted to recover its costs after the expiry of the 21-day acceptance period and by setting them off against the damages. The claimant contested this because prognosis was known to be uncertain at the date of the offer and sought their costs after the offer's expiry accordingly. It was submitted that, where the court's permission was required to approve a settlement, then there could be no prior order for damages. The claimant contended that this would put a protected party at a disadvantage to a party with capacity (*para. 40*) but this argument was not explored fully at the hearing and so no determination of it was made (*para. 65*). The set-off was permitted on the basis that the normal *Part 36* costs order was just (*para. 82*) but there is no indication that *Master McCloud* heard submissions regarding the set-off provisions and her decision was expressly not followed in *Chappell (supra)*.

It therefore appears that there is limited scope for set-offs against damages to be permitted where a *Part 36* offer has been accepted late, the court's approval of the settlement is genuinely required before an order can be made and the parties have not agreed liability for costs. However, whether this puts protected parties at an unfair disadvantage *vis-à-vis* unprotected parties remains to be seen and this may turn on the extent to which they are protected by this difference. Taking *MRA* at face value, *Master McCloud* was not persuaded that sympathy for a vulnerable claimant or the fact that they would suffer a reduction of damages was sufficient (*paras. 6 and 81*) and the defendant made strenuous submissions that these matters did not fall within the ambit of the court's wide discretion on costs (*para. 59*). The changes to set-off against costs permitted by *The Civil Procedure (Amendments) Rules 2023, Rule 24* (*supra*, Chapter 1) is likely to bring this into even sharper focus post-6th April 2023.

Done correctly, a well-timed *Part 36* offer has genuine potency in keeping costs proportionate. However, one of the main limiting factors in achieving this is that it is often believed that the offer needs to be beaten at trial (notwithstanding *Petrograde Inc v Texaco Ltd [2000] EWCA Civ 512; [2002] 1 WLR 947*) and the offer needs to be kept open until either it is accepted or the case concludes to get these automatic sanctions. Although there is a myriad of reported cases on the finer points of *Part 36* offers, these two points always need to be borne in mind. Your opponent has little practical reason to agree to adverse costs consequences because the court's permission is required. Unless you are prepared to delay the costs recovery process whilst you wait for a hearing date for a contested hearing, many consider that the receiving party's best bet is to improve cash flow by moving onto drawing and serving the bill of costs.

Accordingly, making accurate *Part 36* offers does not always work consistently. Your opponent has to believe that the settlement is better than what they will achieve at trial. There is always likely to be a range of interpretation or valuation in any given case. The vast majority of offers are likely to be at some risk of over- or under-egging the pudding. This causes something akin to a cartel mentality forming with litigators along the lines of 'if my opponent is always likely to reject my first offer, I am better off making an offer at the end of the likely settlement range rather than a clearly protective one.' This is often the view of the lay client who tends to have their own experience of negotiation from everyday life. Logic is often replaced by emotion and the best negotiators know when and how to balance both.

Consideration of differing negotiation styles or the intricacies of game theory are regrettably outside of the scope of this book. Further reading is recommended. Always have a very clear idea of what your client's true bottom line is and how risk averse they are. It is crucial that their understanding of risk is based squarely on the issues and evidence in the case rather than on an incomplete understanding of it or because they think that simply holding out will get them a better result in the end. Knowing the true bottom line is useful for accurately assessing the risks involved but does not necessarily get the best outcome because you can often get dragged towards it. Try to resist your natural instincts to avoid conflict and compromise in the middle. What are the long-term consequences for your client of the safe option? Who really benefits from this: your client or you? Are you basing your advice on actual known facts or are their still questions which need answering by your opponent? What are their underlying concerns and motivations and what can you do to uncover them?

This means that you need to fully understand this from both sides' perspectives. This is much easier to do proportionately if you fully understand the central issues, law, evidence and tactical issues early in the case. By doing so, you can put yourself in the position where you can control the progress of the litigation and choose the points when you want to make effective offers or breakthroughs. Getting this right at the right time provides very significant protection for your client and maximises the prospects of settling the case pre-trial.

It is not essential to make the absolutely perfect offer or achieve the overwhelming breakthrough in one go. Experience shows us that no opportunity to agree on part of the case should be missed and proportionality (or fixed costs) does not change this. Showing your true hand too early can prevent the best result being achieved and so negotiation can quite justifiably comprise of a series of feints, parries, ripostes and counter attacks depending on the situation you face. Taking the time to gather information (even by a series of offers and counter offers) is needed in order to get the parties to the mutually acceptable settlement. Do not assume that this is the objectively obvious mid-point in their respective positions. Although it takes two to settle, carefully planning out your client's negotiation strategy and protecting their position with an effective offer, means that your opponent faces a much greater risk than they are comfortable with. The more time you give yourself, the less pressure to settle you will feel and the more time you have to persuade your opponent to give you the information you need or to deal with their objections.

If you should start to plan negotiations from the start of the case, how early can you make an offer? The rules say that you can make an offer on any issue at any time. In general, the reasonableness of the offer is judged against the equality of the information available to each side at the time. *Part 36* offers need additional planning. For example, a claimant making a *Part 36* offer open for 21 days only when they serve the letter of claim is unlikely to be considered reasonable as the defendant has 4 months to investigate the case. Equally, a defendant making a *Part 36* offer when they know that the claimant has not yet obtained C&P evidence may well be considered reasonable if they refuse to extend the 21-day relevant period. In each, the fact that the offeror has more information available to it than the offeree tends to work against it.

The equality of information point raises an interesting issue with respect to the duty of candour clinicians are now expected to comply with and *Part 36* liability-only offers. Ideally, a duty of candour report accepting substandard care ought to result in a prompt admission of liability; but this is not always the case. A compliant investigation means that the defendant has fully and contemporaneously investigated the impugned treatment before the pressures of litigation are brought to bear. Modern clinical governance is designed to avoid adverse incidents occurring. Accordingly, a compliant investigation report (which clearly states that (a) the impugned treatment fell below the accepted clinical standards then in place and (b) caused an injury) is substantially similar to an admission of liability. In such circumstances, it is difficult to understand how it is proportionate for the claimant to incur the costs of instructing lawyers to investigate the case before giving the defendant the opportunity to admit liability in full. Nonetheless, such admissions are not always forthcoming. One approach is to use *Part 36* to explore obtaining such an admission of liability.

One counter-argument is that the basis of the complaints investigation is very different from that in a clinical negligence case (and this entitles the defendant to reinvestigate the case afresh once a full letter of claim has been sent). If correct, it significantly reduces the effectiveness of the duty of candour. This argument ignores the lessons learned from many years of contesting inquests and trials; *viz* that different tribunals hearing the same set of facts are likely to come to the same conclusion (e.g. as occurred in *GKE v Gunning (supra)*). A civil trial judge is likely to find for the claimant if the report is accurate. Accordingly, an early invitation or offer to avoid incurring significant costs on liability in return for a formal admission is a genuine attempt to progress a case proportionately by narrowing the issues.

Another argument is that 100% liability offers are not genuine settlement offers at all and so should not be made. The editorial notes in the *White Book* (to *Rule 36.17*) confirms that 100% offers "do not work" but do not otherwise define them or the types of litigation or specific circumstances this applies to. So, it could be that all offers to accept liability are invalid under *Part 36*.

In *Huck v Robson [2002] EWCA Civ 398, Tuckey LJ* stated (in respect of an offer to split liability 95%:5%) that:

> "... *if it was self-evident that that the offer made was merely a tactical step designed to secure the benefit of the incentives provided by the Rule (e.g. an offer to settle for 99.9% of the full value of the claim) I would agree ... that the judge would have a discretion to refuse indemnity costs. But that cannot be said in this case, which I think did provide the Defendant with a real opportunity for settlement even though it did not represent any possible apportionment of liability.*" (*para. 71*)

Schliemann LJ made similar comments (at *paras. 74-83*) whereas *Jonathan Parker LJ* dissented holding that the offer was one which the defendant "*would inevitably reject and, on that basis to conclude, in the exercise of his discretion, that it would in the circumstances be unjust to award indemnity costs*" (*para. 66*).

Offers which can be construed as 100% liability offers have a high hurdle to pass to be persuasively seen as a genuine settlement offer which was reasonable to make in all the circumstances of the case. Initially at least, they will often be argued to be inappropriate. For example, they should not be attempted where there is clear evidence that the defendant might succeed. This is less likely to be the case where the defendant's own pre-litigation investigations show breach and causation are accepted. It cannot be safely assumed that all of the claimant's investigation costs on liability issues will be recovered or that the pre-litigation investigation will automatically bind the defendant. A *Part 36* offer asking the defendant to admit liability in appropriate circumstances seeks to protect the claimant and balance the competing considerations but nevertheless risks being seen as an attempt to get the benefit of the costs consequences rather than as a genuine settlement attempt if care is not taken.

In *AB v CD & Others [2011] EWHC 602 (Ch), para. 22, Henderson J* explained that tactical offers in this context relate to those where the primary purpose is to obtain the costs protection from the offer so as to threaten your opponent. An offer must involve some element of concession:

> *"The concept of an "offer to settle" is nowhere defined by Part 36. I think it is clear, however, that a request to a defendant to submit to judgement for the entirety of the relief sought by the claimant cannot be an "offer to settle" within the meaning of Part 36. If it were otherwise, any claimant could obtain the favourable consequences of a successful Part 36 offer, by the simple expedient of making an "offer" which required total capitulation by the defendant. In my judgement, the offer must contain some genuine element of concession on the part of the claimant, to which a significant value can be attached in the context of the litigation. The basic policy of Part 36 is to encourage the sensible settlement of claims before trial, or even before the issue of proceedings. … The concept of settlement must, by its very nature, involve an element of give and take. A so-called "settlement" which was all take and no give would in my view be a contradiction in terms."*

Thus, it seems from this that any offer on liability only can be valid if it gives up something of real value to the claimant (*para. 23*); but the final judgement need only match the offer made (not beat it, *para. 33*). What is this 'thing of value' in clinical negligence cases? Of course, there is value in obtaining the early admission to both sides. The claimant knows they will not need to incur the costs and risks of investigating and proving breach and causation of damage in light of the duty of candour investigation and the defendant knows that it has saved these costs as a result of being open and honest. These are tangible and objectively observable 'things of value'. But what 'thing of value' is the claimant giving up? The context of the specific trademark infringement in *AB* indicates that the defendant would have been placed under commercial restrictions wider than the scope of the case it faced if it had accepted the offer and had already taken action to prevent the issue arising again against the claimant. Such considerations do not exist in any practical sense in clinical negligence cases. No clinician intends to repeat the breach and admitting liability does not affect other cases. The clinical negligence claimant does not have a 'thing of value' to give up as part of the offer. Rather, they are trying to seek an assurance that the pre-litigation admissions will be honoured. Does this prevent them making an enforceable *Part 36* offer on this issue?

Some further assistance was provided by *Foskett J*'s obiter comments in *Surrey v Barnett & Chase Farm Hospitals NHS Trust [2018] (supra.), para. 103*:

> *"The NHSLA has a difficult path to steer between defending robustly allegations of negligence that are unfounded, or at least properly defensible, and simply "giving in" to such allegations when made. … History shows where that where concessions concerning liability and causation are necessary, the NHSLA does indeed make such concessions on behalf of those it represents (where appropriate at an early stage) and suitable apologies are offered."*

However, it is tautologous to rely on this comment to prove that the defendant's decision in your case was reasonable. Unless defendants get a second bite of the cherry, we need to dig deeper. In *JMX v Norfolk & Norwich Hospitals NHS Foundation Trust [2018] EWHC 185 (QB), Foskett J* recalled his earlier comment (see *para. 13*):

> *"… the NHSR (formerly the NHSLA) admits liability commendably early in cases where it is obviously right to do so and where there is plainly no defence. All cases do carry some risk, quite frequently associated with the way in a witness, whether expert or otherwise, is likely to 'perform'. That may often be difficult to assess, but experienced practitioners can usually reach an informed view on such an issue."*

It is unclear whether *Foskett, J* only had in mind 'never events' but he acknowledges that the risk can be accurately assessed given the right information and experience. As you will know, 'barn door negligence' tends to be a matter of opinion in each case but a duty of candour investigation report often provides a reliable indication. This is shown by *Somoye v North West Anglia NHS Foundation Trust* (*q.v.* Chapter 4). At *para. 34*, *Master Sullivan* said: *"The defendant's motivation for the admission pre inquest was in part to restrict the costs the claimant would be able to recover in respect of the inquest process."* At *paras. 37 & 43*, there was evidence that the claimant had relied on the admission in not investigating liability further (*q.v.* Chapter 3). At *para. 37*: *"In this case, it led to the agreement that the factual clinician witnesses need not be called. The expectation that a defendant who has access to proper representation should be held to an admission has particular force in that context."* If the defendant is unable to point to evidence which exists and can be disclosed in response to the liability-only offer, the courts ought to be prepared to impose the costs consequences under *Part 36*. *Foskett J* also makes it clear that there is no punitive element to indemnity costs, they merely indicate that the party misjudged the position.

In *JMX, Foskett J* was prepared to find a 90% liability offer (made 22 days before trial) was valid. By this stage, each side had its full panoply of expert evidence available and it was possible to assess the offer in light of the trial decision. The defendant contended that it was necessary for claimants to explain how the reduction has been arrived at. It was not; at *para. 12*, *Foskett, J* said: *"How one side perceives the risks in a piece of litigation (whether in the clinical negligence sphere or any other sphere) will almost invariably be different from the way the other side perceives them"* before approving the comment in the editorial note in the *White Book* that judges should prefer *"to take a broad brush view largely informed by their own assessment of the strength of the case that they have just tried and therefore the extent to which the offer appeared to be a genuine attempt to settle. Of course, there is nothing inherently wrong with very high claimant offers in extremely strong cases, but it may be prudent in such cases for claimants to explain in their offer letters why such a small discount is being offered for settlement."* A liability-only offer in light of a clear duty of candour report appears to provide all the explanation needed.

The need for the offer to reflect a possible outcome in the case (from *AB v CD (supra))* was endorsed by *Edwards-Stuart, J* in *Jockey Club Racecourse Ltd v Willmott Dixon Construction Ltd. [2016] EWHC 167 (TCC), @ para.28. Edwards-Stuart J* then took time to distinguish between cases where the damages are known (such as some commercial cases) and those where the amount sought is unspecified (such as a personal injury action). At *para. 29*, he stated that:

> *"There is, ..., a difference in essence between an offer ... which, in a personal injury case, would reflect an available outcome of the litigation, and a similar offer made in, say, a claim under a guarantee, where the quantum of the claim is fixed... In a personal injury case, where there are issues of contributory negligence as well as quantum, success to the extent of only 15% may be unlikely on the facts of a particular case, but is theoretically possible. In practice, such an offer probably reflects an assessment of the risk of failure on liability and the uncertainties as to quantum, but that is a different matter. However, in the claim under the guarantee success to the extent of 15% is not an available outcome. The offer is entirely commercial, based on an assessment of the risk of failure."*

CPR 1998, Rule 36.14(1)(a) introduces the test of whether the offer is a *"genuine attempt to settle the proceedings."* At *para. 36, Edwards-Stuart J* stated that this is the very point that *Tuckey, J* made in *Huck v Robson (para 71), supra.* At *para. 40*, he went on to explain that, once the defendant knew about the offer and what the case was about, it should promptly *"put itself in a position to make an informed assessment of its position on liability"*

Furthermore, in *Petrograde (supra), Lord Woolf* stated that:

> *"If a defendant involves a claimant in proceedings after an offer has been made, and in the event the result is no more favourable to the defendant that that which would have been achieved if the claimant's*

> *offer had been accepted without the need for those proceedings, the message … is that, prima facie, it is just to make an indemnity order for costs and for interest at an enhanced rate to be awarded."*

What constitutes a genuine attempt to settle a low value case was considered in *Seabrook v Adam [2021] EWCA Civ 382*. The claimant had made two subtly different *Part 36* offers concurrently: the first was to accept 90% of damages if liability was admitted whilst the second was to agree liability on the basis that he would accept 90% of damages. He won at trial and so contended that he had beaten both offers and appealed the District Judge's decision that these were not genuine attempts to settle. Accepting the offer would have meant admitting that he had caused both of the claimant's injuries when he had only been found liable for one of them at trial. At *para. 22, Asplin LJ* provided the following guidance:

> *"Cases of this kind turn, inevitably, on the precise wording of the pleadings and the particular terms of the Part 36 offer. In order to avoid the kind of dispute which has arisen here, especially in a low value claim, it is important to make express reference in the Part 36 offer to whether the offer relates to the whole claim or part of it and/or the precise issue to which it relates, in accordance with CPR 36.5(1)(d). In particular, if the issue to be settled is "liability", it would be sensible to make clear whether the defendant is being invited only to admit breach of duty, or if the admission is intended to go further, what damage the defendant is being invited to accept by the breach of duty."*

Conversely, in *Mundy v TUI UK Ltd [2023] EWHC 385 (Ch), Collins Rice J* was not persuaded that the claimant's offer to accept a 90%:10% split on liability superseded the defendant's *Part 36* offer of £4,000 (which was not beaten). The relevant court rule being cited was *CPR 1998, Rule 36.17(1)*. The claimant had also made his offer concurrently with an offer of £20,000 and, despite contributory negligence being pleaded by the defendant, no competent legal advisor would have considered such a finding realistic (*para. 12*). As such, the 90% offer had to be seen as '90% of £20,000' rather than a concession on liability (*para. 13*) in a case where causation was entirely defended. The claimant had won but not beaten its own offer and failed to better the defendant's. Furthermore, at *para. 36*: *"A 90/10 liability offer is not straightforward to recognise as an offer to settle a whole claim on quantified or quantifiable financial terms, in a case where there is no genuine question of issues-based liability."* At *para. 40*:

> *"A simple case like this in which liability is not fought on a distinct issues basis but in its entirety cannot produce anything other than a 100% result on liability either way; the value of a win on liability 'in money terms' is difficult if not impossible to separate from the quantum of damages awarded, and that will always and axiomatically be more advantageous to a claimant than 90% of it. There is a problematic degree of artificiality in all of this."*

Drawing this together, much depends on whether the court hearing the application for indemnity costs sees the liability-only offer as an attempt to settle the issue of liability & avoid incurring costs or as an attempt to enforce total capitulation. Ultimately, the reasonableness of any *Part 36* offer is a question of fact and so you need to be prepared to test it at court. Evidence of the clarity congruent with *Seabrook (supra)* will assist as will offering a small discount. As yet, the courts have not had to determine whether a defendant ought to promptly admit liability in a case where it appears to have admitted it in the duty of candour investigation report. The costs consequences only automatically apply if the case goes to trial, so early offers suffer from having to be left open for the rest of the case. This means that you need to ask yourself whether any offer is a genuine attempt to settle or an attempt to hold the *Part 36* costs consequences over your opponent's head like the Sword of Damocles. In reality, is any *Part 36* offer really an effective method of getting the settlement if the costs consequences cause your opponent to prefer to fight at trial? Offers which can clearly be seen to be well grounded in the evidence and genuinely seeking to narrow the areas or issues in dispute stand a much better chance of being persuasive and seen as reasonable attempts to settle rather than as mechanistic, box-ticking exercises. If the changes to set-off after 6th April 2023 (*q.v.*) do result in more issue-based *Part 36* offers being made, then ensuring that these are clear in their terminology and evidential basis will be even more crucial to properly assessing the risk they pose and advising our clients.

If it is ultimately held that *Part 36* consequences do not apply or you decide to use another type of offer, the court can nonetheless exercise its discretion under *Part 44* (*q.v.* Chapter 1). This further increases uncertainty (resulting from all of the circumstances in the case being taken into account) but can nevertheless improve the chances of getting the right settlement for your client because there is more flexibility in the type of offer (e.g. using 'time bomb' offers or global offers) and your opponent will be more confident of avoiding the *Part 36* costs consequences. Accordingly, the best advice is to focus on getting the settlement that works for your client. Spending your time on gathering the right information as to your client's and opponent's underlying motivations is likely to result in better resolutions than unswerving reliance on *Part 36* offers. The ultimate goal of achieving justice between the parties does not necessarily require an award of indemnity costs even in circumstances where one party's conduct demonstrably increases costs disproportionately.

This proposition has a more general application to the entire case. QOCS protection can be overridden if the defendant's *Part 36* offer is not beaten. This appears to be equally applicable to liability and issue-based offers. The defendant's costs of dealing with such issues would then be deducted from the claimant's damages making the victory far less attractive and potentially even entirely pyrrhic. As this *Part 36* risk is usually insured, the litigation insurer would require very clear advice on the prospects of succeeding on these issues. Accordingly, there is a clear incentive to all parties to provide evidence up front and to make a reasonable attempt to agree on the likely realistic interpretation of it at trial.

Conclusion

The key to winning cases proportionately is to pick your battles carefully, plan for a trial and to look for opportunities to narrow the issues. This approach will create more opportunities for outright settlement. The early identification of the pressure points in the pre-trial and trial stages allows both sides to work towards dealing with these well before they arise and should build upon what has been done in the earlier phases of the litigation. This, in turn, is likely result in well-presented cases with clearly identified central allegations and supporting evidence. Any gaps or ambiguities in the evidence are also more likely to be identified at a time when there is still time to do something about them.

In turn, this is likely to make the risks of pursuing the case to trial clearer to everyone involved which tends to result in earlier settlements. The definition of a compromise is a result which nobody is truly happy with but nonetheless accepts. The sooner this is reached in any given case, the more likely it is that the costs will be proportionate in the sense currently understood by recent judgements. However, the careful preparation of the case is necessary to obtain this degree of clarity and so it becomes prudent to focus your efforts on those parts of the case which are likely to make the key differences when it comes to trial. These pressure points in the life of a case are therefore the most likely to result in judicial acceptance that the costs incurred in dealing with them were proportionate because the correct balance will have been struck between careful investigation and case progression.

AFTERWORD

I write this afterword at a critical point of inflection – for the NHS, which many are describing as at its worst crisis in its 75 years of existence. The progress in patient safety, fought so hard for by AvMA and many other people and bodies, is coming under increasing strain and is likely to deteriorate before it gets better. That is not a criticism of the many good people who work in the system, but rather a sad reflection of the well-reported workforce pressures they are having to carry. I hope I am wrong about all of this, but I fear I am not.

So, in that context, the law and good practice of clinical negligence remains ever and more important. But equally the climate for practicing it remains very uncertain. Not least because the Government has consulted on various possible reforms to clinical negligence costs and their recovery, principally to the Fixed Costs Recovery regime. But having consulted we are currently, at the time of writing, none the wiser as to their actual intentions.

But we do know that the public purse is under greater scrutiny than ever and there is bound to be more pressure on all spending departments to find cost savings. An obvious area to look at within the NHS budget overall, is the cost of the litigation even though, in the grand scheme of that budget, litigation costs are comparatively small.

However, I did not join a charity like AvMA to wallow in self-pity. Rather, I joined AvMA in order to create opportunities and to grasp the possibility of meaningful change including to the legal landscape. AvMA exists to fight for better patient safety and access to justice and fight we will. In the process we will look to our friends in the legal community (as well as other supporters) to help us share the vision to make these possibilities a reality. I have a favourite saying which I never tire of: In the end it will be OK. And if it is not OK then it is not the end!

Paul Whiteing
Chief Executive,Action against Medical Accidents (AvMA)
February 2023

ABRIDGED INDEX

MORE BOOKS BY LAW BRIEF PUBLISHING

A selection of our other titles available now:-

'A Practical Guide to Estate Administration and Crypto Assets' by Richard Marshall
'A Practical Guide to Managing GDPR Data Subject Access Requests – Second Edition' by Patrick O'Kane
'A Practical Guide to Parental Alienation in Private and Public Law Children Cases' by Sam King QC & Frankie Shama
'Contested Heritage – Removing Art from Land and Historic Buildings' by Richard Harwood QC, Catherine Dobson, David Sawtell
'The Limits of Separate Legal Personality: When Those Running a Company Can Be Held Personally Liable for Losses Caused to Third Parties Outside of the Company' by Dr Mike Wilkinson
'A Practical Guide to Transgender Law' by Robin Moira White & Nicola Newbegin
'Artificial Intelligence – The Practical Legal Issues (2nd Edition)' by John Buyers
'A Practical Guide to Residential Freehold Conveyancing' by Lorraine Richardson
'A Practical Guide to Pensions on Divorce for Lawyers' by Bryan Scant
'A Practical Guide to Challenging Sham Marriage Allegations in Immigration Law' by Priya Solanki
'A Practical Guide to Legal Rights in Scotland' by Sarah-Jane Macdonald
'A Practical Guide to New Build Conveyancing' by Paul Sams & Rebecca East
'A Practical Guide to Defending Barristers in Disciplinary Cases' by Marc Beaumont
'A Practical Guide to Inherited Wealth on Divorce' by Hayley Trim
'A Practical Guide to Practice Direction 12J and Domestic Abuse in Private Law Children Proceedings' by Rebecca Cross & Malvika Jaganmohan
'A Practical Guide to Confiscation and Restraint' by Narita Bahra QC, John Carl Townsend, David Winch
'A Practical Guide to the Law of Forests in Scotland' by Philip Buchan
'A Practical Guide to Health and Medical Cases in Immigration Law' by Rebecca Chapman & Miranda Butler

'A Practical Guide to Bad Character Evidence for Criminal Practitioners by Aparna Rao
'A Practical Guide to Extradition Law post-Brexit' by Myles Grandison et al
'A Practical Guide to Hoarding and Mental Health for Housing Lawyers' by Rachel Coyle
'A Practical Guide to Psychiatric Claims in Personal Injury – 2nd Edition' by Liam Ryan
'Stephens on Contractual Indemnities' by Richard Stephens
'A Practical Guide to the EU Succession Regulation' by Richard Frimston
'A Practical Guide to Solicitor and Client Costs – 2nd Edition' by Robin Dunne
'Constructive Dismissal – Practice Pointers and Principles' by Benjimin Burgher
'A Practical Guide to Religion and Belief Discrimination Claims in the Workplace' by Kashif Ali
'A Practical Guide to the Law of Medical Treatment Decisions' by Ben Troke
'Fundamental Dishonesty and QOCS in Personal Injury Proceedings: Law and Practice' by Jake Rowley
'A Practical Guide to the Law in Relation to School Exclusions' by Charlotte Hadfield & Alice de Coverley
'A Practical Guide to Divorce for the Silver Separators' by Karin Walker
'The Right to be Forgotten – The Law and Practical Issues' by Melissa Stock
'A Practical Guide to Planning Law and Rights of Way in National Parks, the Broads and AONBs' by James Maurici QC, James Neill et al
'A Practical Guide to Election Law' by Tom Tabori
'A Practical Guide to the Law in Relation to Surrogacy' by Andrew Powell
'A Practical Guide to Claims Arising from Fatal Accidents – 2nd Edition' by James Patience
'A Practical Guide to the Ownership of Employee Inventions – From Entitlement to Compensation' by James Tumbridge & Ashley Roughton
'A Practical Guide to Asbestos Claims' by Jonathan Owen & Gareth McAloon
'A Practical Guide to Stamp Duty Land Tax in England and Northern Ireland' by Suzanne O'Hara
'A Practical Guide to the Law of Farming Partnerships' by Philip Whitcomb
'Covid-19, Homeworking and the Law – The Essential Guide to Employment and GDPR Issues' by Forbes Solicitors
'Covid-19 and Criminal Law – The Essential Guide' by Ramya Nagesh

'Covid-19 and Family Law in England and Wales – The Essential Guide' by Safda Mahmood

'A Practical Guide to the Law of Unlawful Eviction and Harassment – 2nd Edition' by Stephanie Lovegrove

'Covid-19, Brexit and the Law of Commercial Leases – The Essential Guide' by Mark Shelton

'A Practical Guide to Costs in Personal Injury Claims – 2nd Edition' by Matthew Hoe

'A Practical Guide to the General Data Protection Regulation (GDPR) – 2nd Edition' by Keith Markham

'Ellis on Credit Hire – Sixth Edition' by Aidan Ellis & Tim Kevan

'A Practical Guide to Working with Litigants in Person and McKenzie Friends in Family Cases' by Stuart Barlow

'Protecting Unregistered Brands: A Practical Guide to the Law of Passing Off' by Lorna Brazell

'A Practical Guide to Secondary Liability and Joint Enterprise Post-Jogee' by Joanne Cecil & James Mehigan

'A Practical Guide to the Pre-Action RTA Claims Protocol for Personal Injury Lawyers' by Antonia Ford

'A Practical Guide to Neighbour Disputes and the Law' by Alexander Walsh

'A Practical Guide to Forfeiture of Leases' by Mark Shelton

'A Practical Guide to Coercive Control for Legal Practitioners and Victims' by Rachel Horman

'A Practical Guide to Rights Over Airspace and Subsoil' by Daniel Gatty

'Tackling Disclosure in the Criminal Courts – A Practitioner's Guide' by Narita Bahra QC & Don Ramble

'A Practical Guide to the Law of Driverless Cars – Second Edition' by Alex Glassbrook, Emma Northey & Scarlett Milligan

'A Practical Guide to TOLATA Claims' by Greg Williams

'A Practical Guide to Elderly Law – 2nd Edition' by Justin Patten

'A Practical Guide to Responding to Housing Disrepair and Unfitness Claims' by Iain Wightwick

'A Practical Guide to the Construction and Rectification of Wills and Trust Instruments' by Edward Hewitt

'A Practical Guide to the Law of Bullying and Harassment in the Workplace' by Philip Hyland

'How to Be a Freelance Solicitor: A Practical Guide to the SRA-Regulated Freelance Solicitor Model' by Paul Bennett
'A Practical Guide to Prison Injury Claims' by Malcolm Johnson
'A Practical Guide to the Small Claims Track - 2nd Edition' by Dominic Bright
'A Practical Guide to Advising Clients at the Police Station' by Colin Stephen McKeown-Beaumont
'A Practical Guide to Antisocial Behaviour Injunctions' by Iain Wightwick
'Practical Mediation: A Guide for Mediators, Advocates, Advisers, Lawyers, and Students in Civil, Commercial, Business, Property, Workplace, and Employment Cases' by Jonathan Dingle with John Sephton
'The Mini-Pupillage Workbook' by David Boyle
'A Practical Guide to Crofting Law' by Brian Inkster
'A Practical Guide to Spousal Maintenance' by Liz Cowell
'A Practical Guide to the Law of Domain Names and Cybersquatting' by Andrew Clemson
'A Practical Guide to the Law of Gender Pay Gap Reporting' by Harini Iyengar
'NHS Whistleblowing and the Law' by Joseph England
'Employment Law and the Gig Economy' by Nigel Mackay & Annie Powell
'A Practical Guide to Noise Induced Hearing Loss (NIHL) Claims' by Andrew Mckie, Ian Skeate, Gareth McAloon
'An Introduction to Beauty Negligence Claims – A Practical Guide for the Personal Injury Practitioner' by Greg Almond
'Intercompany Agreements for Transfer Pricing Compliance' by Paul Sutton
'Zen and the Art of Mediation' by Martin Plowman
'A Practical Guide to the SRA Principles, Individual and Law Firm Codes of Conduct 2019 – What Every Law Firm Needs to Know' by Paul Bennett
'A Practical Guide to Adoption for Family Lawyers' by Graham Pegg
'A Practical Guide to Industrial Disease Claims' by Andrew Mckie & Ian Skeate
'A Practical Guide to Redundancy' by Philip Hyland
'A Practical Guide to Vicarious Liability' by Mariel Irvine
'A Practical Guide to Applications for Landlord's Consent and Variation of Leases' by Mark Shelton
'A Practical Guide to Relief from Sanctions Post-Mitchell and Denton' by Peter Causton

‘A Practical Guide to Equity Release for Advisors’ by Paul Sams
‘A Practical Guide to Financial Services Claims’ by Chris Hegarty
‘The Law of Houses in Multiple Occupation: A Practical Guide to HMO Proceedings’ by Julian Hunt
‘Occupiers, Highways and Defective Premises Claims: A Practical Guide Post-Jackson 2nd Edition’ by Andrew Mckie
‘A Practical Guide to Financial Ombudsman Service Claims’ by Adam Temple & Robert Scrivenor
'A Practical Guide to Advising Schools on Employment Law' by Jonathan Holden
‘A Practical Guide to Running Housing Disrepair and Cavity Wall Claims: 2nd Edition’ by Andrew Mckie & Ian Skeate
‘A Practical Guide to Holiday Sickness Claims – 2nd Edition’ by Andrew Mckie & Ian Skeate
‘Arguments and Tactics for Personal Injury and Clinical Negligence Claims’ by Dorian Williams
‘A Practical Guide to Drone Law’ by Rufus Ballaster, Andrew Firman, Eleanor Clot
‘A Practical Guide to Compliance for Personal Injury Firms Working With Claims Management Companies’ by Paul Bennett
‘RTA Allegations of Fraud in a Post-Jackson Era: The Handbook – 2nd Edition’ by Andrew Mckie
‘RTA Personal Injury Claims: A Practical Guide Post-Jackson’ by Andrew Mckie
‘On Experts: CPR35 for Lawyers and Experts’ by David Boyle
‘An Introduction to Personal Injury Law’ by David Boyle

These books and more are available to order online direct from the publisher at www.lawbriefpublishing.com, where you can also read free sample chapters. For any queries, contact us on 0844 587 2383 or mail@lawbriefpublishing.com.

Our books are also usually in stock at www.amazon.co.uk with free next day delivery for Prime members, and at good legal bookshops such as Wildy & Sons.

We are regularly launching new books in our series of practical day-to-day practitioners' guides. Visit our website and join our free newsletter to be kept informed and to receive special offers, free chapters, etc.

You can also follow us on Twitter at www.twitter.com/lawbriefpub.

www.ingramcontent.com/pod-product-compliance
Lightning Source LLC
LaVergne TN
LVHW052223200926
848481LV00001B/193